Analyzing Educational Research

7

WADSWORTH PROGRAM IN EDUCATIONAL PSYCHOLOGY

Analyzing
Educational
Research

Evelyn J. Sowell
UNIVERSITY OF TEXAS AT TYLER

Rita J. Casey
UNIVERSITY OF TEXAS AT AUSTIN

WADSWORTH PUBLISHING COMPANY
Belmont, California • A Division of Wadsworth, Inc.

Education Editor: Marshall Aronson
Production Editor: Gary Mcdonald
Managing Designer: Lois Stanfield
Text Designer: Wendy Calmenson
Cover Designer: Lois Stanfield
Copy Editors: Carol Reitz, Pat Tompkins
Technical Illustration: Innographics

Credits

Academic Press: Excerpts from L. A. Serbin, J. M. Connor, C. J. Burchardt, and C. C. Citron, "Effects of Peer Presence on Sex-Typing of Children's Play Behavior," *Journal of Experimental Child Psychology*, 1979, 27, 303–309. Reprinted by permission. (Chs. 2, 3, 4, 5, 6, 7.)

American Educational Research Association: Excerpts from D. T. Campbell and J. C. Stanley, *Experimental and Quasi-Experimental Designs for Research*, Rand McNally, 1963. Reprinted by permission of the American Educational Research Association. (Pp. 97, 98–99.)

Journal of Negro Education: Excerpts from C. E. Babbitt and H. J. Burbach, "Perceptions of Social Control Among Black College Students," *Journal of Negro Education*, 1979, 48, 37–42. Reprinted by permission. (Chs. 2, 3, 4, 5, 6, 7.)

Printed in the United States of America

1 2 3 4 5 6 7 8 9 10---86 85 84 83 82

Library of Congress Cataloging in Publication Data

Sowell, Evelyn J.
   Analyzing educational research.

   Includes bibliographies and index.
   1. Educational research. I. Casey, Rita J.
II. Title.
LB1028.S67   370'.7'8   81-19844
   ISBN 0-534-01133-0   AACR2

Contents

Preface

Most people in educational research courses will be consumers of research throughout their professional careers. They will use their knowledge of research methods primarily to evaluate reports of research. Even those who produce research must also study the work of others. We believe, therefore, that the first goal for beginning students of educational research is to become proficient consumers of research. This text is designed to help readers reach that goal.

In *Analyzing Educational Research* students are given a simple holistic idea of what research is like. The first chapter introduces some basic concepts and purposes of research. Chapters 2 through 7 follow the typical structure of research reports, showing students how to analyze the introduction, method, results, and discussion sections of research reports. The first portions of the chapters contain essential information for understanding these sections. Specific aids for reading reports include information on content and form, suggestions for reading and analysis, and criteria for evaluating each section of a report. There are two complete research reports in Chapters 2 through 7. Exercises at the ends of each chapter lead students through the analysis of these reports. Feedback for the exercises follows immediately. Chapter 8 explains the ethics of research and some limitations of educational research.

Several features of the book help readers learn the concepts of each chapter and provide opportunities for instructors to go beyond the basic ideas according to their own and their students' interests and emphases. Every chapter begins with an outline, and all chapters except 1 and 8 contain objectives that are tied directly to the exercises at the end of the chapter. Suggested readings relating to the main topics are cited with annotations. Checkpoints within most chapters allow students to monitor their understanding as they read. Each new term is highlighted and defined when it is first introduced, and it is also included in the glossary at the end of the book for quick reference.

Appendices to the text provide resources for students and instructors. The first one contains five research reports for additional practice. Because students vary greatly in their ability to locate research reports, one appendix is devoted to the use of educational resources. Four statistical appendices provide explanations of basic terminology, correlation and prediction, analysis of variance, and statistical tables. Descriptions of some commercial instruments frequently used in research and a brief discussion of historical research are also included as appendices.

We assume no prior knowledge of statistical analysis in the text. However, students are referred frequently to the statistical appendices if they want more explanation of the terminology and procedures mentioned in the text. It is beyond the scope of this text to teach students how to compute statistical tests. Instead, the meaning and general purposes of statistical procedures are emphasized.

Analyzing Educational Research is based on the first eight chapters of our book *Research Methods in Education*, also published by Wadsworth Publishing Company. The longer text extends and treats the concepts from the viewpoint of the producer of educational research. RME contains four additional chapters on research production and two sample proposals.

Our intention has been to produce a book corresponding to the way that research serves educators as consumers of research. During the development of the text, drafts of the manuscript were used and evaluated by students. Their suggestions were invaluable to the development of the present text. We would like to incorporate feedback from other sources in subsequent revisions, and we welcome comments or suggestions from instructors or students who use the book. Please direct any feedback to Evelyn J. Sowell and Rita J. Casey, c/o Education Editor, Wadsworth Publishing Company, 10 Davis Drive, Belmont, CA 94002.

E.J.S.
R.J.C.

Acknowledgments

We are pleased to acknowledge the assistance of many people who helped make this book possible. Insightful comments and reviews of the manuscript were made by the following people: Ed Anderson, Oregon State University; Donald G. Barker, Texas A & M University; Ralph O. Blackwood, The University of Akron; E. Wayne Courtney, Oregon State University; John P. Dolly, University of Wyoming; Kenneth H. Hoover, Arizona State University; Samuel Levine, San Francisco State University; Thomas R. Oaster, Eastern Montana College; Marvin Powell, Northern Illinois University; William M. Stallings, Georgia State University; Ezra Wyeth, California State University, Northridge. The staff at Wadsworth has been supportive and helpful through the difficult process of translating an idea into reality. We particularly thank our editor, Marshall Aronson.

Also many faculty and staff people at the University of Texas at Tyler aided this project. Chip Fischer made valuable suggestions on initial drafts of Chapter 6. Steve Daniels used early drafts of the book in his classes and shared student feedback with us. Vicki Betts of the library staff assisted with Appendix D and, along with Ann Williams, tracked down hard-to-find references. Also, Dorothy Welch clearly went beyond mere typing because of her encouragement and concern with helping us meet deadlines.

We owe a special debt of thanks to all students who used the materials in various drafts over the last few years; they helped us learn a great many things. We also appreciate the cooperation of the authors and publishers who allowed us to reproduce their materials for this book.

Finally, we thank our families who lived through extended absences and the briefest of vacations. Their support helped make the hard work worthwhile.

E.J.S.
R.J.C.

To the Student

Nearly 2,500 years ago, the Greek philosopher Pythagoras and a few of his friends were involved in exploring some ideas that were to change mathematics from that time onward. The group held clandestine meetings, used special symbols, and even had secret passwords. Many of their contemporaries had no idea what the group was excited about. Unfortunately, some educators today are like those outsiders, seeing research as an area that is mysterious and clouded with mumbo jumbo. We want to demystify research for you by teaching you some of its passwords and rituals as painlessly as possible. We tell you about the nature of research and show you how to understand the research of others.

There are good reasons for understanding research beyond meeting graduate school requirements. If you are a teacher, supervisor, or administrator, many aspects of your work have been studied through research processes. If you are equipped with the skills to read and analyze this research, you are in a position to make informed judgments about your professional responsibilities. Also, results of research are frequently used to initiate and justify changes in all areas of education. Keeping informed about current research trends gives you a basis on which to evaluate these alternatives. Finally, reading research is a very good way to stimulate your thoughts and feelings about your work.

The first seven chapters focus on reading and analyzing research—the skills of the consumer. Chapter 1 introduces you to some of the basic concepts of research and the terminology that will be discussed in more detail throughout the book. Chapters 2–7 develop skills and information that you will use in analyzing and evaluating the various sections of research reports. Chapter 8 provides information about ethics and other issues important to consumers of research.

At the beginnings of Chapters 2–7, you will find a brief introduction, an outline, and a set of objectives. These objectives tell you exactly which skills you should be able to perform when you have completed the chapter. Chapters are generally divided into two parts. First, background sections present information about particular topics that are necessary for understanding research reports. The second parts show how to analyze the various sections of research reports. The content and form of each report section and suggestions for reading and analysis are discussed. Criteria are included to evaluate the actual research reports in the exercises near the ends of the chapters. Sample answers follow the exercises. Finally, additional readings are suggested for each chapter.

1

Introduction to the Study of Research

The purpose of this chapter is to start you on the road toward consuming research. We must begin with a common understanding of some of the basic processes and terminology of research. The ideas in the next few pages form the core of our communication about research. You will encounter the same ideas with increasing sophistication throughout the book.

This chapter starts by clarifying just what we mean by the word *research*. After this, four important basic concepts of research are introduced: variables, operational definitions, the goals of science, and variance. An overview of the stages of research is given next, followed by a discussion of the assumptions and limitations of research. Finally, you are introduced to the most important form in which you will encounter research as a consumer, the research report.

RESEARCH AND THE SCIENTIFIC METHOD

What thoughts cross your mind when you hear the word *research*? Do you picture scientists in white coats mixing chemicals in their laboratories? Perhaps you think of business executives squinting at graphs, or pollsters going from door to door asking people their political preferences. Do you envision a student (maybe even you) poring over mounds of books in a library? Do you think of someone tabulating information from the national census? It may come as a surprise to you that these activities may not be research.

Those scientists may simply be combining chemical compounds according to known recipes to produce other chemicals. This is not research. However, if the scientists are trying new combinations in a search for additional information to answer a problem, they may be using the research processes. The executives with their graphs are probably just looking at a visual description of their sales record. Using a graph doesn't make an activity research. In a similar way, pollsters with their surveys are using a technique available to researchers, but the survey method alone isn't research. But you're sure the student spending all that time in the library is researching. Sorry! It's research only if previously unrelated information is drawn together to shed new light on a problem or question that the student is trying to answer. Usually work in the library consists of collecting known facts. Even totaling impressive sets of figures from a census is not research. These may be little more than summaries of information describing characteristics of the country's population.

As these examples point out, the term *research* is used by different individuals in a variety of ways. Each of these meanings may be appropriate in certain situations. However, the many popular uses of the word *research* do not necessarily conform to the definition generally used by educational researchers.

CHAPTER ONE

Definition of Research

In this text we look at **research** as the application of the scientific method to the investigation of problems. You may recall that the scientific method uses steps such as the following:

Observing and becoming aware of a problem
Defining the problem
Developing possible solutions to the problem (hypotheses)
Experimenting to test hypotheses
Drawing conclusions about results of the experimentation

Research as we define it follows this same general methodology. It is the scientific investigation of the relationship between two or more variables. **Educational research,** the subject of this book, is research devoted to problems related to education. To study educational research, you must first understand some basic concepts. The first of these is the meaning of variables.

Definition of Variables

The term **variable** applies to something that can take on different values quantitatively or qualitatively in a given situation. To get a better idea of what we mean by variables, think about two classrooms of second grade students. Consider how students, teachers, and the environment, for example, differ in the two hypothetical classrooms.

Although the students are roughly the same age, they differ in many respects. They possess different personalities—some children are outgoing and effervescent, while others are shy and withdrawn. Some youngsters perform much better in music than in mathematics, while others give just the opposite performance. Although a relatively large number of second-graders in both classes would probably perform in the average range on an intelligence test, some children would be above the average and others would be below average.

In addition to the individual characteristics of the students, the learning environment is not identical in both classrooms. Teachers of each class structure time, space, and student interactions quite differently, even though essentially the same skills may be taught. Students in one class may work independently most of the time, while those in the other class perform more activities cooperatively. Also, students relate to their peers and teacher in ways unique to each setting.

Each differing characteristic represents a variable. Sometimes a variable is thought of by a general term, such as time structuring, achievement, or psychomotor development. At other times variables are stated more specifically—for example, academic time structuring, self-paced timing, or instructor-paced timing. In the description of second grade classes, some characteristics mentioned were variables stated by their general labels, such as intelligence or academic performance. Other variables were given in more specific form such as independent work or cooperative work.

The definition of *variable* indicated that quantitative or qualitative values can be assigned to a characteristic. To describe a characteristic as a variable, variations must be possible. Sometimes these variations are easily expressed in numerical form; other times variations are differences in qualities or attributes that are not so simply expressed with numbers. Quantitative values can be given to many variables such as measures of achievement, hours spent in laboratory work, or times a response is made. Variations in other variables are better described qualitatively—role-play or discussion methods of teaching social studies, high or low need to achieve, or cooperation versus competition. Either quantitative or qualitative values can be assigned depending on the nature of the variable and the setting in which it is studied.

Although the number and kind of variables that can be studied by researchers are limitless, many variables of the most general interest in educational research are evident in the second grade classrooms described. These include variables in the broad areas of achievement, intelligence, aptitude, personal-social adjustment, motivation, and psychomotor skills.

Operational Definitions

To think of all the educationally relevant variables in a particular setting is overwhelming. How can the variables in such a complicated setting as a classroom ever be studied in a manageable systematic fashion? The first step in such a task is to decide precisely what you are looking at. If particular variables are to be investigated by a researcher, they must be observable or measurable in some way. When something can't be measured, there is no tangible way to tell how it differs in quantity or quality from one situation to another. Therefore, it can't be used by researchers as a variable in a research study.

To make sure that the task of observation is manageable as well as thorough, researchers may decide on an operational definition for each variable they are concerned about. An **operational definition** is a definition that assigns meaning to a variable by stating the observable behavior or operations that will represent the variable. It tells how some abstract or general idea of a variable, such as achievement or intelligence, will be defined in a particular setting. One way of doing this is to state exactly how the concept will be measured. Here are some examples:

Achievement is evaluated by the composite grade-level scores
   on the California Achievement Test.
Intelligence is assessed by determining the Full Scale IQ scores
   obtained on the Wechsler Adult Intelligence Scale.
Time-on-task is calculated as the percentage of total class time
   individual students actually spend paying attention to in-

struction, doing assigned work, and working with instructional material.

Sometimes operational definitions describe the precise set of actions or operations used to represent one or more values of a variable. This is common with variables such as teaching method, learning environment, and cognitive style, which are not easily represented by a quantity or score. Two examples are:

Teacher expectancy is defined by a rank-ordering of students based on teacher perceptions of expected achievement.

The learning-center method of teaching is defined as the assignment of students to self-paced instructional activities and materials including a controlled reader, a cyclo-teaching machine, and "listen-and-think" tape recordings in a location outside the regular classroom for 30 minutes a day.

An operational definition permits both precise observation and meaningful communication about what is observed. Two different researchers might have such radically different ideas about a concept that they could not observe the same situations and communicate with any understanding about their observations. However, when operational definitions are used, the precise statement of what is being observed permits researchers to communicate even if they do not agree about the concept. These definitions also allow a research study to be duplicated with some degree of exactness.

Although operational definitions are very useful and essential in research, a word of caution is in order. In precisely defining a concept in terms of a set of operations, some of the meaning may be left out (Ennis, 1964). For example, suppose a person studying aggression between students in the two second grade classrooms described earlier defined aggression as "a student's use of his or her hands or feet to strike the body of another student." Certainly such actions are easy to observe and could be counted, but other marks of aggression may be overlooked because they don't fit the definition. Related to this narrowness of definitions is the problem of applying the results of this study to other situations involving aggression. If another person who is interested in aggression between school children uses a very different definition, it may be hard to draw conclusions using both studies.

Despite their imperfections, operational definitions are universally used in research. They allow rather precise measurement and enable researchers to analyze systematically the relationships between two or more variables. You may wish to check your understanding of operational definitions by doing the exercise on the next page.

Here are some definitions of variables that may or may not be operational definitions. Mark each one as operational or nonoperational.

1. Verbal production is measured by counting the average number of words (omitting duplications) spoken in a 15-minute play period.
2. Intelligence is assessed by scores on the Stanford-Binet Intelligence Scale, Form L-M.
3. An open classroom is a classroom in which there is little structure, characterized by shared decision making between students and teacher.
4. Self-concept is the individual's view of the world as a result of his or her interaction with the environment.
5. Test anxiety is measured by the Test Anxiety Questionnaire.

ANSWERS: 1. operational 2. operational 3. nonoperational 4. nonoperational 5. operational

GOALS OF SCIENCE

There are several ways to study research. One common approach is to learn how researchers collect data about the variables they investigate. With this viewpoint, you may study "survey research" or "observational research." Another way is to note the time frame of different kinds of studies and look at the methodology suited for each, such as "longitudinal research" or "cross-sectional research." A third way is to study research according to the setting in which it is done—for example, "classroom research" or "laboratory research." Although you will read about timing, settings, and methods of collecting data in this text, we have chosen *not* to use any of these as a way of discussing different kinds of research. Instead we will show you how to look at research in terms of the goals of science. This will help you focus more on the problems studied and less on the methods used to collect information.

Research as we defined it involves using the scientific method to look at relationships between two or more variables. Whenever researchers investigate a set of variables, they have a broad purpose that corresponds to one of the three goals of science: explanation, prediction, and control.

You are familiar with the general idea of explanation as a process of making something clear or understandable. As a goal of science, **explanation** has the same meaning, with the goal being the understanding of the relationship between variables. When researchers want to describe and understand the relationship between variables to see if one variable is associated with another, their investigation has explanation as a goal. It may seem that digging out information from library resources involves the explanation of variables. In a sense this is true, but explanation as a goal of science focuses on explaining relationships among variables. This is different from reporting facts about variables without seeing how they relate to each other.

Here are two examples of research questions that have explanation as their goal: Is there a relationship between height and intelligence? Can socioeconomic status (SES) in adults be related to years of schooling? In both cases, researchers would look at more than the individual variables. They would collect information to see whether certain patterns of height were found together with certain patterns of intelligence, or if variations in SES were associated with variations in years of schooling.

The goal of prediction is based on explanation. **Prediction** involves making the best guess possible about how a particular set of variables will be related, based on what you know about the past and current relationship of the variables. It is necessary to know in advance that two variables are associated before speculating that information about one variable can be used to predict the quantity or quality of the second variable. This is a question that could be tested in a prediction study: Can elementary school achievement be used to predict success in high school?

Researchers would start with a known association—that children tend to establish a certain quality of performance in the elementary grades and keep up this level of achievement throughout their schooling. The strength of this association between variables could be measured and used to predict the future success in high school of a group of elementary students, based on their current school achievement.

In many cases researchers are not content with finding associations among variables. They are curious to see whether they can control the relationships between phenomena. **Control** is the ability to direct or influence a variable to bring about change in another related variable. In these situations researchers manipulate or change the values of one variable and then look at what happens to a second related variable in the same setting. The manipulated variable in such a research study is called the **independent variable.** The second variable, called the **dependent variable,** changes in response to the manipulated variable if there is a true cause-and-effect relationship between them. Of course, if no cause-and-effect relationship exists, the dependent variable will not be changed with alterations in the independent variable. Dependency simply refers to the possibility that altering one variable may produce changes in a second variable.

Some example questions involving control as a goal of investigation are: Will democratic school-management techniques produce better faculty morale than autocratic management techniques? Does education in values produce higher levels of moral development in children than those in children who do not receive values education?

The first question calls for the alteration of management techniques to be democratic or autocratic. Faculty morale would be measured under each kind of technique and compared to see if differences in management techniques result in different levels of morale. In a similar fashion, the second question asks whether differences in moral development will result from having or not having values education.

The three goals, explanation, prediction, and control, form a kind of hierarchy. It's easy to see that the explanation of relationships between variables can be useful and allows predictions based on our knowledge of these associations. More powerful than these goals, however, is the ability to identify and demonstrate cause-and-effect relationships, because this enables us to control events.

The complexities of educational settings often make research that involves control very difficult, so it is common for educational research to focus on explanation and prediction. Actually, the three goals may function as a loop, with the identification and explanation of associations between variables leading ultimately to the exploration of cause-and-effect relationships. New questions are usually generated that may result in a search for more explanation, prediction, and so on in cycles (Rosenshine and Furst, 1973). People who are hooked on research really understand the idea: "The more you know, the more you know that you don't know."

THE RESEARCH PROCESS

An attempt to investigate relationships between variables doesn't proceed in a haphazard manner. In every situation of interest to researchers, many things can affect the variables under study. Unless the research situation is very carefully structured, the researchers' ability to explain, predict, or control may be destroyed by unaccounted-for variance.

Variance

What is **variance**? It is any aspect of the research setting that produces changes in the variables. Sometimes variance is intentionally introduced into a research study. This happens when control is the goal; an independent variable is deliberately manipulated to see whether changes will result in the dependent variable. In most cases, however, researchers try to eliminate undesirable variance or carefully contain it. Research effort is wasted unless the relationship between variables can be investigated without the strong possibility of an uncontrolled factor altering the variables in the situation and contaminating the results.

Stages of Research

In order to manage variance, researchers follow a careful sequence of actions in carrying out the scientific method. The steps in this sequence are commonly called the stages of research. These stages are:

1. observation and definition of the problem
2. formulation of hypotheses

3. formulation of a plan that includes selection of a research strategy and ways to collect evidence and select participants
4. execution of the research plan
5. examination of the results of the study

The first stage of research incorporates observation and definition of the problem in the scientific method. It is both the most important and the least specific step. Researchers observe a situation, noting particularly the things that are of special interest. Usually there is a problem to be solved that holds the interest of researchers. A set of variables is identified and defined that will be the focus of a problem statement. At the same time observation is taking place, researchers review literature related to the problem, including theory and research about the same variables. The formulation of the problem statement may require repeated observation and analysis of related research and theory. Nevertheless, when the problem is clearly defined and stated, researchers will know precisely what variables are to be studied and which goal of science they seek as the relationship is investigated.

The second step, formulation of hypotheses, grows out of observation and review of literature. By carefully observing the problem situation and relating it to theory and other research efforts, researchers can state one or more tentative solutions to the problem. These are hypotheses that researchers believe may describe the relationship between the variables in the problem situation.

The third step includes making a plan for the project. Selecting a research strategy or method, choosing ways to collect data, and locating people to use in testing the hypotheses are parts of the plan. After the research plan is made, the fourth stage consists of carrying it out. Participants are selected, variables are manipulated (if this is part of the study), and information about the variables of interest is collected and analyzed.

Finally, researchers look closely at the results of the study. At this point conclusions are reached about the relationship between the problem variables. Researchers carefully explain the results in light of their hypothesis-testing strategy; they also compare this set of results with other research and related theory. Usually the entire research effort is summarized in a report, which enables other persons to benefit from the results of the investigation.

Assumptions and Limitations of Research

So far we've told you very generally about the stages of research and the goals of science that provide general aims for research efforts. We've tried to help you see the simple but elegant structure of using the scientific method to investigate and solve problems. Naturally, we think research is interesting (otherwise we wouldn't use a word like *elegant* to describe it), but it has its limits, too. A few qualifiers should be kept in mind as you become involved in research.

Research is based on a set of assumptions. When you use research, you are in effect accepting these assumptions, which imply a certain philosophical viewpoint about the world. Among these assumptions is the idea that the world is real. Furthermore, research as we've described it assumes that this real world can be understood through means available to human beings. A third assumption is that events in this real and knowable world proceed in some orderly fashion. These assumptions may sound like what most persons believe without too much argument. But think of this: Do you really believe that everything that happens in this world is available for human knowledge and understanding? If your answer is yes, consider how little is known about brain function and human thought. You are using your thinking processes right now, but just how real and knowable are they? Do your thoughts arise in an orderly manner? Is there a way that someone else can see the reality of your thoughts and how they occur? Perhaps so, but the task is not easy and the present methods for understanding thought are primitive in comparison to the complexities of what our brains can do. As we hope you can see, these assumptions may not apply to every situation. To the extent that you cannot accept these assumptions, your use of the scientific method is limited. If there is no way to observe something, you can't define it operationally, and it will be impossible to collect direct information about it. When observations are possible, they will not be useful in drawing conclusions about explanation, prediction, or control unless you believe that they provide real information about events and that these events happen with some consistency from one occurrence to the next.

Research is limited whenever it touches on problems from other perspectives on the world, such as religion, aesthetics, and philosophy. It is not possible to decide what is beautiful or what is worthwhile through research. These are value-laden issues that must be resolved in other arenas. Frequently research can shed insight on issues that involve values, but it cannot provide solutions to problems about which people differ philosophically.

Another closely related concern is the ethics of research. Anytime researchers manipulate variables in a study using human subjects, limitations must be carefully observed. Even the process of observation can violate the rightful privacy of persons. We'll discuss this issue in greater depth in Chapter 8.

USES OF RESEARCH

What good is research anyway? Research can be cited as if it were written on stone tablets that came straight from the mountaintop. Other times it may be spoken of with a note of derision, as a useless activity completely removed from practical realities, involving only such esoterica as studies of the relationship between the body weight and eye color of vestigial-winged fruit flies. We ask you to go beyond these two caricatures to see what research can be in education. Research is useful as both a process and a product. It is both a set of actions and an outcome.

Research processes are intended to test and formulate theory for providing explanation, prediction, and control of the phenomena in the world. Finding solutions to a highly specific problem in a classroom may seem far removed in setting from the formulation and testing of theory. For example, which of two teaching methods brings about more long-term learning? The two methods under study could be based on particular theories of how learning occurs. Therefore, if a research project is conducted about these two methods and their effects, this study is a small-scale test of theory. The process is the same whether the project is a very sophisticated one that endeavors to build a new theory or simply seeks a better way to teach students.

Your first contact with research occurred long before this book was placed in your hands. We are willing to bet that you first encountered research in product form by reading or hearing about the results of a research effort. One of the primary reasons that researchers record their results is to share them with others who are concerned about similar problems and variables. Many journals of professional organizations, books, and popular magazines describe results of research to help people gain insight and understanding into various aspects of life. As an educator, this is possibly your most common contact with research.

RESEARCH REPORTS

The remaining chapters of Part One follow the standard order of topics and information in research reports. In recent years, published research reports have used a standardized format consisting of title, abstract (sometimes), introduction, method or procedures, results, discussion, and references. Each section is important because it relays specific information to readers.

Titles of reports communicate the major focus of research projects. Sometimes an *abstract* is included in research reports. When this section is present, it follows the title. As the name implies, the abstract condenses the entire report into a few well-chosen sentences.

The body of a research report begins with an *introduction*, which is not usually labeled. It is simply the first section. Here authors usually review the literature (tell the findings of similar research projects). They do this to establish a setting or context for the research problem. Near the end of most introductions is the statement of the problem that is under investigation. Sometimes, though infrequently, researchers follow the problem statement with a hypothesis (predicted outcome) that their research sought to test.

The next major section of the report is usually titled *method* or *procedures*. Here authors detail the project design, indicating who participated (subjects) and how data were gathered (kinds of instruments, conditions for collecting data, etc.).

Results follow the method section. Their main purpose is to tell what the researchers found. Findings may be recorded pictorially in figures and tables or verbally, or both ways. Beginners in research may find this section threatening because of the unfamiliar symbols and widespread use of numbers. Results are sometimes organized according to hypotheses of the study, with data given to confirm or reject hypotheses. In the *discussion* section, authors elaborate on findings, relating them to those of previous research studies in the problem area.

References to all works cited in the research report are included in a section by that name. Normally complete information regarding a source is available only in the reference list, rather than within the text of the report.

If you are unfamiliar with the appearance of research reports, look through Appendix A at the format of the reports reproduced there. Appendix D, Using Educational Resources, tells you how to locate research reports.

SUMMARY

Research is the application of the scientific method to the investigation of problems. Five stages are included in this process: becoming aware of the problem, defining the problem, developing hypotheses, testing hypotheses, and drawing conclusions about the test results.

Variables are labels for things or characteristics that can take on different values quantitatively or qualitatively within the same situation. Variables are most useful to researchers when their meaning has been described in terms of specific operations or activities. Only by defining variables in this way can researchers communicate adequately what they expect to do and what they found out after the investigation is completed.

Three goals of science are explanation, prediction, and control. Explanation simply describes the relationships among variables, while prediction makes use of known relationships to predict the strength and direction of other possible relationships. Control goes beyond both these goals to determine whether a deliberate change in one variable will effect changes in other related variables.

The research process is more accurate when it includes the appropriate control of variance. Anything that produces changes in variables is a potential source of variance. Sometimes variance is intentionally introduced into a study. More often, however, it occurs unintentionally, possibly ruining a study.

The research process itself consists of stages in which the researcher carries out the scientific method. For the process to work, researchers assume that events in a real and knowable world take place in some orderly fashion. Because these assumptions are made, some problems involving values or philosophy are very difficult to study through the research process.

Research is useful both as a process and as a product. As a process, research tests theories or parts of theories to create knowledge. As a product, reported research can provide insight and help in understanding life.

Reports of research efforts are commonly available from many sources. Similar formats are found in most reports, including these main parts: abstract, introduction, method, results, and discussion. In the following chapters you will learn how to analyze and evaluate the information in each of these report sections.

RECOMMENDED REFERENCES

Ennis, R. H. Operational definitions. *American Educational Research Journal,* 1964, *1,* 183-201. In this paper Ennis discusses various forms of operational definitions and a set of guidelines for making them. It's worth reading.

Gephart, W. J. *The most significant educational research contributions of the past ten years.* Occasional Paper 16. Phi Delta Kappa Center on Evaluation, Development and Research, n.d. The title describes the contents of this short paper.

Marx, M. H. Formal theory. In M. H. Marx & F. E. Goodson (Eds.), *Theories in contemporary psychology* (2nd ed.). New York: Macmillan, 1976. Marx defines formal theory as interpretive efforts in which hypotheses are announced. The section on the role of theory can help a reader of research understand why authors take such pains to present the background of their studies.

Rosenshine, B., & Furst, N. The use of direct observation to study teaching. In R.M.W. Travers (Ed.), *Second handbook of research on teaching.* Chicago: Rand McNally, 1973. The authors present information on instrumentation and research on teaching in natural and seminatural settings. For people interested in reading research in these areas, this is an excellent place to begin.

2

Reading
Introductory
Sections

In this chapter you will begin to analyze research reports. To do this, it is essential that you understand the research problem and the kind of study reported. Because these are such important concepts, the background section of this chapter discusses research problems and kinds of studies in detail. Then information is presented about reading and analyzing each part of the introductory sections of reports.

Chapter objective.   After you have completed this chapter, you should be able to apply criteria for identification of well-constructed *problems/hypotheses, abstracts, titles,* and *contexts for problem statements* in selected reports.

BACKGROUND FOR READING INTRODUCTORY SECTIONS

Definition of a Research Problem/Hypothesis

Research was defined in Chapter 1 as the scientific and systematic investigation of the relationship between two or more variables. This investigation begins by identifying the precise problem to be studied. Suppose, for example, a group of researchers is interested in the study of intelligence. Since intelligence is measurable (however imperfectly!) and it can vary from one person or situation to another, it qualifies as a variable. When the researchers think about the concept of intelligence, they may consider its relationship to many other variables—achievement, creativity, test anxiety, self-concept, or socioeconomic status, to name only a few possibilities. As they wonder about these relationships, the researchers are beginning to create research problems. At this point, simple but broadly stated questions may emerge similar to the following:

1.   What is the relationship between intelligence and achievement?
2.   What is the relationship between intelligence and creativity?
3.   Will lowering test anxiety result in higher intelligence scores?
4.   Will increasing socioeconomic status raise intelligence levels?

Before researchers can conclude that these are their research problems, they must decide whether answers to the statements can be determined through scientific investigation. At least two criteria must be satisfied: Can there be more than one possible answer to each question? Can objective evidence be collected that will enable investigators to decide which one of the possibilities is best? A **research problem**, then, is a question about the relationship between two or more variables. It potentially has more than one answer, with the selection of a particular answer based on the evaluation of collected observations.

Let's apply the criteria to some of the previous questions. In response to question 1, "What is the relationship between intelligence and achievement?" these possible answers could be posed:

Intelligence *is* related to achievement; more specifically:
- As intelligence increases, achievement increases.
- As intelligence increases, achievement decreases.

Intelligence *is not* related to achievement.

If you stop to think about it, you will see that this list exhausts the possible answers that imply a simple, direct relationship between intelligence and achievement. Other, more complex relationships are possible, such as achievement increasing and then decreasing as intelligence increases. For the moment, however, our discussion will be limited to the simple relationships. Since more than one possible answer can be identified, the first criterion is satisfied. Also, it is conceivable that researchers could collect objective data on intelligence and achievement from a group of people and determine which of the possible answers is best for that group.

Question 3 asked "Will lowering test anxiety result in higher intelligence scores?" These are some possible answers:

Lowering test anxiety *will* result in higher intelligence scores.
Lowering test anxiety *will not* result in higher intelligence
  scores.

Again, objective data on intelligence could be obtained from people who had undergone exercises to reduce test anxiety; these could then be compared with the intelligence scores of people who did not have the exercises. A decision about which of the possible answers is more adequate could be made based on the data.

More complicated research problems can involve several variables, yet each question should be testable in the same manner as the preceding examples. Some problems, however, are so value-laden that they are impossible to answer using research methodology. Consider these examples:

5. Should we have closed high school campuses?
6. Should tax dollars be spent to teach drug education in schools?

Questions 5 and 6 may be answered either yes or no. However, researchers run into trouble when they try to collect objective data on which to base a decision about the answers. When the questions are asked of a large group of people, there is likely to be a variety of responses. The crucial point is that those answers represent the particular value systems of the persons who responded to the question. Who will decide whether a yes is better than a no? Although researchers would get answers to the question, there is no satisfactory way of deciding which is correct because the question is a philosophical one.

Notice what happens when questions 5 and 6 are restated:

5a. Does having a closed or open high school campus result in more student participation in cocurricular activities?

6a. Are there fewer arrests for drug violations among students who take drug education courses than among those who do not take the courses?

Restating these problems permits objective data to be collected on which to base decisions about the better answers.

The possible answers given for questions 1 and 3 are called *hypotheses*. We emphasize "possible" because researchers really don't know what the answers to their problems will be until they have carried out their projects. A **hypothesis,** then, is a tentative answer to a research question.

Hypotheses take different forms depending on the function they serve. At the outset of a project, researchers usually make simple statements indicating what the expected outcomes will be. They review related theory and similar research to get an idea of what can be expected in the current study. Projected outcomes are expressed as research hypotheses. Here are some examples:

Having an open high school campus results in more student participation in cocurricular activities than having a closed high school campus.

There are fewer arrests for drug violations among students who have taken drug education courses than among those students who have not taken the courses.

More information about hypotheses will be given in Chapter 6, where they are discussed in the context of analyzing the results of research.

Research Problems in Two Kinds of Studies

You have now read a few simply stated research problems that differ somewhat in structure. Some ask what kind of relationship (if any) exists between the variables. Others inquire whether the manipulation of one variable produces differences or changes in another variable. These two ways of structuring research problems call for the two approaches to research methods that we will discuss throughout this book: association studies and difference studies.

Association studies. The phrasing in questions 1 and 2 indicates that the research project is designed to discover the nature of the relationship between intelligence and achievement or creativity. *Relationship,* as we use the term, means the degree or amount of association between the variables as well as its direction (positive or negative). Suppose the researchers proceeded to answer question 1 by measuring first the intelligence and then the achievement of several dozen people. These data would then be analyzed by correlational procedures. (See Appendix C-2 for additional information.) Results would probably show that individuals who have higher intelligence scores also tend to have higher achievement, and people with lower intelligence scores usually have lower achievement. If researchers used a similar procedure to answer question 2, the results would likely be different. People who have higher intelligence scores do not necessarily score higher in creativity. When projects are conducted primarily to assess the degree and direction of association between variables, we will call them **association studies.** They are also called **correlation studies.**

So what's the point of knowing how variables are associated? A common use of correlation studies is to make predictions. Suppose intelligence is highly associated with achievement for students at a particular college. Based on this information, the probable achievement of an incoming freshman could be predicted from an appropriate measure of his or her intelligence. These association studies are also named **prediction studies.** For the sake of clarity, however, in subsequent chapters both correlation and prediction studies will be called by the general name, association studies.

Difference studies.   Questions 3 and 4 seem to assume that the variables are associated; they ask more specifically whether or not their relationship is one of cause and effect. In both questions researchers are asking whether altering one of the variables, test anxiety or socioeconomic status, will result in changed intelligence scores.

To actually find out, question 3 needs to be restated more specifically: Will students trained in exercises to reduce test anxiety score higher on intelligence tests than students who do not receive this training? In a nutshell, the procedure is to give two groups of students an intelligence test, which would be scored and recorded. Then one group of students would participate in exercises to reduce test anxiety, while the second group participated in other activities unrelated to reducing test anxiety. At the end of the exercises, a second measurement of intelligence would be taken for both groups. Scores from both sets of tests would then be analyzed. If the group that took the exercises to reduce test anxiety does indeed score higher than the group that did not take the exercises, researchers may be able to attribute the improvement to the exercises.

The focus of this problem is on whether there is a cause-and-effect relationship between the variables test anxiety and intelligence. It is true that there is an implied association between the variables in questions 3 and 4. But look again: The intent of these questions goes beyond merely establishing the existence of an association to trying to determine the precise relationship between the variables.

In the procedures described for finding out the answer, there were two groups of students. This is a common characteristic of many studies of this kind. It is difficult to show cause-and-effect relationships because the researcher has to show that the "cause" claimed as making the "effect" is in fact the cause. The investigation is helped a great deal by using at least two groups of people, one exposed to the cause and the other not exposed. Comparisons between the groups are the primary reason we call studies of this type **difference studies.**

To see how well you're understanding problem statements and relationships between variables, take time to do Checkpoint 2.1.

Importance of the Problem

We cannot overemphasize the importance of understanding the problem of a research study. The problem is like the hub of a wheel, for around it revolve all other concerns in the study. The problem dictates the choice of methods used, and the results and conclusions are meaningful only if the problem is understood. In the next section of this chapter you will be asked to apply information about problems and kinds of studies as you learn to analyze the introductory sections of research reports.

READING AND ANALYZING INTRODUCTORY SECTIONS

Content and Form

Titles.   Most people probably read more titles of research reports than reports themselves. This is understandable when you consider that entries in tables of contents, reference lists, and indexes all use titles. The title functions much like a key to unlock the report. If the title indicates a topic of interest, you may take the time to read the report. Otherwise, you will probably keep looking for titles that have some appeal.

Titles assist in the selection of research reports by communicating both the topic and the scope of the report. A direct statement identifying the variables studied in the research project presents the topic. An example is "Values Clarification: Its Effect on Self-Concept and World Views. . . ." This title allows you to see at once if the principal concerns of the study are related to your particular purpose in searching the literature.

Mention of variables alone, however, does not tell the person scanning a list of titles about the circumstances in which the variables were studied. Therefore, titles also indicate something about the scope of the research. Perhaps the subjects of the study were teenagers, kindergarteners, or senior citizens. The research may have been done in a particular location or in a designated curriculum area. Usually one or more of the words in the title also provides a clue to the setting of the research project. Suppose you are a principal interested in the effect of values clarification on the self-concept of your faculty. Reading the partial title in the preceding paragraph may make you think that the study would shed light on your concerns. However,

CHECKPOINT 2.1

Identify the variables and determine their probable relationship. Then identify the kind of study (association or difference) that could be used for each problem.

1. Which of two approaches to teaching word recognition, multisensory or auditory-visual, enables first-graders to learn the greater number of new words?
2. What will be the effects of a perceptual-motor development program on the eye-hand coordination of kindergarten children?
3. How well do mental age and prealgebra aptitude predict success in Algebra I?
4. Do counterconditioning procedures improve the spelling performance of upper elementary grade children?
5. Is self-concept related to public-speaking abilities in high school students?

ANSWERS: 1. approaches to teaching word recognition and the number of words learned (achieved); difference 2. perceptual-motor development program and eye-hand coordination; difference 3. mental age, prealgebra aptitude, and success in algebra; association 4. counterconditioning procedures and spelling performance; difference 5. self-concept and public-speaking abilities; association.

the full title is "Values Clarification: Its Effect on Self-Concept and World Views of College Students." This tells that the study did not focus on teachers. You could then choose to skip that particular report in favor of searching for one that used teachers as participants. Or, because the variables are so similar to your interests, you could read further in the report, keeping in mind that information about values clarification and the self-concept of college students might not apply to a setting with teachers. Try your hand at identifying the variables and scope of studies by completing Checkpoint 2.2.

Both the content and form of titles are important. When a variable is mentioned at the beginning of a title, it is easy for the report to be located in a subject index. Shorter titles without unnecessary words are also preferred over longer ones. Phrases such as "a study of . . . ," "an investigation into . . . ," and "analysis of . . ." do not tell whether a report is worth reading. These phrases may also make it hard for information to be found in an alphabetical listing.

Titles are intended to tell only a minimal amount of information. If the variables and the scope of a report as presented in the title are of interest, the next step is to read the abstract.

Abstracts. An **abstract,** usually located at the beginning of a report, is a summary of the research project. In journal reports, the abstract, if there is one, appears immediately following the title and the author's name. Frequently the abstract is set in smaller type and has fairly wide margins. Journal abstracts are usually about 100 to 200 words long. In other reports such as theses and dissertations, the abstract is commonly designated by that label and is at the very beginning of the report. In these cases, the abstract is usually somewhat longer, often as much as 500 to 1,000 words. Abstracts are

Identify the variables and scope of the study in each title.

1. Academic Achievement and Self-Concept in Middle School Students
2. A Well-Balanced Physical Education Program: Effects on Kindergarten Children's Classroom Behavior
3. Small Groups as an Instructional Strategy for Increasing Interest in High School English
4. Teaching Word Recognition to First-Graders: Multisensory versus Auditory-Visual Approaches
5. Using a Learning Hierarchy for Division of Fractions to Increase Elementary Mathematics Achievement

ANSWERS: 1. academic achievement and self-concept; middle school 2. physical education program and classroom behavior; kindergarten 3. interest in English and small-group instruction; high school 4. word recognition and multisensory versus auditory-visual teaching approaches; first grade 5. learning hierarchy and math achievement; elementary school

also included in the reference works that index journals, such as *Dissertation Abstracts International, Psychological Abstracts,* and *Current Index to Journals in Education.*

Regardless of its location or length, an abstract should provide a thumbnail sketch of the research project. A typical abstract includes a general problem statement, brief information about the subjects and methods used to investigate the problem, the major findings or results of the study, and recommendations based on the study. After reading the abstract, you should have some idea of whether you need or want to read the complete report. Exhibit 2.1 is one example of an abstract.

Were you able to determine in general what the problem was, how it was investigated, and what results and conclusions were drawn from the study? Even though you may not yet understand what is meant by some of the terms used in the example, you should have an overall picture of what took place in the research effort.

Contexts for problem statements. The **context** for the problem statement in a journal report is a brief review of literature in the introduction. In longer reports the context may consist of brief references to literature in the introduction and a longer separate section with the label "Review of Literature." Specifically, the context of a research problem sets the stage for understanding the circumstances surrounding the formulation of the problem.

Recall from Chapter 1 that an initial step in conducting research is to review reports that are related to the problem being investigated. Often in the reviewing process, specific hypotheses are suggested, instruments are found or analyzed, and key terms are defined, which aid researchers in planning and executing their own effort. In the review they summarize this information to assist the understanding of the problem of the current study.

In addition, authors usually state some kind of need or **justification** for their study. Some common justifications are replications of previous studies,

Perceptions of social control among black college students in three different institutional settings were analyzed. Subjects were 60 randomly selected freshman and sophomore students from each location: a large urban university, a medium-sized urban college, and a small urban center. Three indexes were designed to measure perceptions of social control focusing on administrative control, faculty control, and peer control, respectively. Scores were obtained for each representative group on each index. Group means were compared using the t-test. In all comparisons, urban center students perceived their school's authority structure in a significantly more positive light than did college or university students. Students from the university setting were significantly more negative in their attitudes toward administrative and faculty authority than were the college students. However, perceptions of peer control were not significantly different for these two groups.

EXHIBIT 2.1   An abstract based on "Perceptions of Social Control Among Black College Students" by C. E. Babbit and H. J. Burbach, *Journal of Negro Education*, 1979, *48* (1), 37–42.

explorations in new fields, and studies involving problems of long standing. **Replication** is the repetition of the test of a hypothesis in a new study, to see if the results are the same from one situation to another. Such studies are justifiable when researchers believe that repeating an investigation in a different setting or with different subjects or slightly different methods might give additional information about the variables. To cite one example, replication studies on the topic of learned helplessness have flourished in recent years. Seligman first defined this phenomenon in animal research in 1967 (Seligman and Maier, 1967). Since that time literally scores of research projects have attempted to replicate his findings with different groups of people in various locations. (See Huesmann, 1978, for additional information.) As findings from these studies are pieced together, more and more information about learned helplessness is forthcoming, thereby justifying the expense and time of the researchers.

Exploring a new field is a justification that could be used by mathematics educators investigating the use of handheld calculators. There haven't been many studies in this area (Bell, 1977). Teachers want to know whether using the small calculators benefits or endangers student understanding of mathematics. At this time there is little hard evidence to answer this question, so teachers are forced to operate according to their individual beliefs.

When we mention problems of long standing as a possible justification, we're talking about questions such as phonics versus sight-reading methods, nature versus nurture as the determiner of personality, and others. There are die-hards on both sides of each of these questions. What's more, each side has research findings to support its position.

Although their function is the same, introductions and reviews of literature vary in form and content according to the type of report and even among reports of the same type. Reviews in journal articles, for example, differ in rigor from one journal to another. In longer reports such as theses and dissertations, the separate section titled "Review of Literature" provides an in-depth analysis of research and theory that relates to the current study. Often this review is organized into subsections corresponding to the variables. Although all researchers are obligated to investigate the related literature as carefully as possible, the space limitations of a written report usually require that the review cite only literature that is most essential to an adequate understanding of the problem of the study.

Problem statements and hypotheses. In research reports other than those in journals, problems and hypotheses should be easily located by their labels. In journals, however, a problem statement is usually found by looking in the introduction, often near the end of that section. Clues are phrases such as ". . . in the present study," "the purpose of the study was to . . . ," and "the problem of this study was. . . ." Although hypotheses are not always stated in journal research reports (Grover and Charlton, 1979), when they are, these kinds of words are used: "it was hypothesized that . . ." or "the researchers predicted. . . ."

The preferred form for research problems is usually the question, but they can be written as declarative statements and worded broadly or made specific to a particular situation. Regardless of form, the problem statement needs to specify clearly the kind of relationship between the variables.

Both problem statements and hypotheses give valuable information about what the researchers expected to do or find out. While problem statements tell what questions researchers hoped to answer, hypotheses indicate tentative answers to those questions. It's a matter of preference whether researchers report the problem statement, the hypothesis, or both. Regardless of which is reported, the remainder of the research report makes sense only when the problem of the study is well understood.

Suggestions for Reading and Analysis

There are different kinds of research reports that vary in length, format, style, and sophistication. These variations are best understood when you realize that reports are written for audiences that differ in interest, experience, and familiarity with research processes. When researchers become authors, they usually write for a specific journal audience and tailor their writing to particular publication requirements. If researchers prepare reports for a funding agency, they adhere to that agency's guidelines. Shorter reports are often published as journal articles; theses, dissertations, and reports of grants and projects are longer reports. No matter what kind of reports you read, there are basic similarities that enable you to use some general guidelines for analyzing and evaluating any report.

When you first begin to read a report, it saves time to quickly read the first sections including the title, abstract, and introduction to get an idea of their contents. Only after you have some general knowledge of what the report is about will specifics make sense.

Then reread for details. Find the problem or hypothesis of the study by reading either the abstract or the introduction. Try to get a sense of the kind of study by examining the relationship between variables. When you have these things well in mind, use the questions in the exercises at the end of this chapter as a guide for analyzing the report. As you grow more proficient in reading research reports, work out a personal sequence for reading and thinking about their parts.

In the meantime, while you are becoming skilled at reviewing research literature, try to avoid some common mistakes. Don't skip over the context or you are likely to miss the authors' statement about why their study is important. Another mistake is to read past the introductory sections without being sure that you know what the problem of the study is. If the context and problem are not well understood, it can be difficult to learn much from the rest of the report.

As you read a research report, you can use the criteria listed below in analyzing and evaluating the introductory sections. Each criterion represents a feature that is present in well-constructed introductory sections.

1. *Titles should mention the variables of the study, possibly suggesting their relationship, and the scope of the study.* Variables are key words that you look for in searching for reports. Major variables in the title make it easy for you to know the topic of the study without actually locating the report. There should be some clue to the magnitude of the study. Telling who the subjects were, giving an approximate geographic location, or mentioning the curriculum area are ways of communicating scope.

2. *In titles the most important word or phrase should be first. Unnecessary words should be eliminated.* Since titles are commonly alphabetized by the first major word, the use of a variable is important. Unnecessary phrases should be omitted especially at the beginning of titles, since they do not help persons decide whether or not to read a report, and they could prevent people from finding the report.

3. *Abstracts should summarize the research effort, mentioning the problem, methodology, results, and conclusions.* These basic parts of the study are essential. Additional information about the people in the study, the research procedures, and the nature of the results is also helpful.

4. *Abstracts should be brief, written in the past tense with complete sentences.* Journal abstracts are usually 100 to 200 words long, while abstracts for theses and dissertations may be as long as 500 to 1,000 words. The length should conform to the type of research report. Since abstracts report the entire research effort, they should be

stated in the past tense. The use of incomplete sentences is not allowed, even when there is a concern for brevity.

5. *The context should cite previous research related to the problem and may be used as justification for the current study.* Similar research efforts should be mentioned, noting particularly how they added to the formulation of the problem in the current study. The review may also show that the study will explore a previously unresearched question, provide a needed replication of previous efforts, or bring new insights to an unresolved question.

6. *Relationships between two or more variables should be evident in both problem statements and hypotheses.* These relationships focus on differences or associations that are clearly recognizable if the problem or hypothesis is read in its context.

7. *Problems or hypotheses should be stated in ways that permit the collection of data for an objective answer or test.* Questions involving value orientations are excluded as research problems unless they are constructed to permit the unbiased collection of information to support hypothetical answers.

SUMMARY

Understanding the problem or the hypothesis of a research project is critical. A problem poses a question about the relationship between two or more variables, while a hypothesis states a tentative answer to the problem. In examining the problem or hypothesis in its context, figure out whether the researchers are trying to establish the existence of a relationship between the variables or trying to see whether an existing relationship is a cause-and-effect one. Projects of the first kind are called association studies and those of the second are labeled difference studies.

The title of a research report is the first contact with a study. Titles should contain information about the variables and scope of the study to signal whether or not you should read further. Abstracts are the next section that is read if the title seems interesting. Abstracts present the study in a nutshell, giving an abbreviated version of the problem, procedures, results, and implications. Under most circumstances an abstract appears immediately following the title of a report.

The next section in most reports is an introduction. In journal reports, literature is reviewed and a justification for the study is presented. In longer reports there may be a separate review of literature, which is generally more inclusive than that in journal reports. Most researchers use the literature to support their justification for their studies. Replication of previous studies, explorations in new fields, and studies involving problems of long standing are the most frequently used justifications.

We suggest that you quickly skim the introduction to journal reports to get an idea of what the report is about. Then locate and try to understand the problem statement or the hypothesis, whichever is reported. Afterward, re-read the whole introduction, taking into account the details. Don't skip the introduction, because the rest of the report is not likely to make sense unless you understand the problem and its context.

EXERCISES

Read the introductory sections of "Effects of Peer Presence on Sex-Typing of Children's Play Behavior" and "Perceptions of Social Control Among Black College Students," which appear immediately following the questions. Scan each report, rereading sections as necessary to answer the questions. Write your answers and compare them with the feedback for exercises at the end of this chapter.

1. Identify the problem/hypothesis of the study. Name the variables. Based on reading the problem/hypothesis in context, is this an association study or a difference study? Explain.
2. Is the problem/hypothesis researchable using scientific method-ology? What data must be collected to answer the question or test the hypothesis? Explain.
3. Does the abstract mention the problem, methodology, results, and conclusions? Is the abstract appropriate in length? Does it use com-plete sentences? Is it written in the past tense?
4. What need or justification for the study is pointed out in the context? With respect to the literature that is reviewed, does the justification seem reasonable? Explain.
5. Are the variables mentioned in the title? Is the scope of the study indicated? Is the most important word or phrase first? Is the title relatively short and free of unnecessary words?

Effects of Peer Presence on Sex-Typing of Children's Play Behavior

LISA A. SERBIN, JANE M. CONNOR, CAROL J. BURCHARDT, AND CHERYL C. CITRON

State University of New York at Binghamton

Effect of peer presence on the sex-typed toy choices of 3- and 4-year-olds was investigated in a repeated measures experimental design. Twenty-six girls and thirty-six boys were tested under three conditions: (a) alone; (b) in the presence

of a same-sex peer; and (c) in the presence of an opposite-sex peer. Amount of time spent playing with three feminine- and three masculine-stereotyped toys was recorded. For both boys and girls, play with "sex role-inappropriate" toys was significantly lower in the presence of an opposite-sex peer than in the solitary condition. Across conditions boys exhibited less play with opposite-sex-typed toys than girls. Rate of play with opposite-sex-typed toys increased in successive trials for both sexes. These results indicate that the presence of an opposite-sex peer functions as a discriminative stimulus for avoidance of "sex role-inappropriate" play in preschoolers and suggests that preschoolers may have a history of differential reinforcement for sex-typed play in the presence of peers.

Sex-typing of children's play behavior has been widely reported in classroom, home, and experimental settings. Observational studies suggest that sex-typed behavior in the preschool classroom may be directly reinforced by differential attention, praise, and punishment (e.g., Fagot & Patterson, 1969; Serbin, O'Leary, Kent, & Tonick, 1973). Further support for the differential reinforcement hypothesis comes from experimental demonstrations of stimulus control over rates of sex-typed play. That is, the presence of an adult or peer, if associated with reinforcement of sex-appropriate and/or punishment of sex-inappropriate play, should reduce rates of play with toys culturally stereotyped as appropriate for the opposite sex. Results consistent with the hypothesis have been reported by Hartup, Moore, and Sager (1963) who observed that the presence of a female adult increased preschoolers' selection of sex role-"appropriate" toys when compared to behavior in a solitary condition. A similar pattern has been reported by Rekers (1975) in a study of cross-gender identified boys.

The importance of peers as an influence in the development of sex-typed play behavior has been suggested by several studies. Kobasigawa (1968) reported that modeling of sex-inappropriate play by same-sex peers can disinhibit this behavior in an observing child. However, observational studies suggest that peers usually act in ways which would encourage children to conform to sex role stereotypes. In an observational study of classroom play behavior, Fagot and Patterson (1969) reported that peers primarily interacted with each other during play involving sex-appropriate toys. Ross (1971) reported that boys encouraged peers of both genders to choose sex role-appropriate toys at an experimental "toy store." Such findings suggest that due differential reinforcement, peers, like adults, come to function as discriminative stimuli for sex role conformity. Using college students, Bem and Lenny (1976) have demonstrated that the presence of a peer, especially a peer of the opposite sex, inhibits behavioral flexibility and leads to increased sex role conformity. If such stimulus control is found as early as the preschool period. this would suggest that (a) children learn very early that they may be rewarded and/or punished by peers for conformity and nonconformity, respectively, to sex stereotypes, and (b) that peer presence may play an important role in limiting children's play to sex-"appropriate" activities.

The present study was designed as an experimental test of the hypothesis that peers function directly as discriminative stimuli for preschoolers' sex-typed play behavior, inhibiting exploration of toys culturally labeled as appropriate for the opposite sex. An experimental design, in which children were observed in a playroom alone, with same-sex peers, and with opposite-sex peers, was used. It was predicted that peer presence would inhibit play with toys culturally labeled as appropriate for the opposite sex. . . .

REFERENCES

Bem, S. K., & Lenny, E. Sex typing and the avoidance of cross-sex behavior. *Journal of Personality and Social Psychology,* 1976, **33,** 48–54.

Fagot, B. I., & Patterson, G. R. An in vivo analysis of reinforcing contingencies for sex-role behaviors in the preschool child. *Developmental Psychology,* 1969, **1,** 563–568.

Hartup, W. W., Moore, S. G., & Sager, G. Avoidance of inappropriate sex-typing by young children. *Journal of Consulting Psychology,* 1963, **27,** 467–473.

Keppel, G. *Design and analysis: A researcher's handbook.* Englewood Cliffs, N.J.: Prentice-Hall, 1973.

Kobasigawa, A. Inhibitory and disinhibitory effects of models on sex-inappropriate behavior in children. *Psychologia.* 1968, **11,** 86–96.

Maccoby, E. E., & Jacklin, C. N. *The psychology of sex differences.* Stanford, Calif.: Stanford Univ. Press, 1974.

Rekers, G. A. Stimulus control over sex-typed play in cross-gender identified boys. *Journal of Experimental Child Psychology,* 1975, **20,** 136–148.

Ross, S. A. A test of the generality of the effects of deviant preschool models. *Developmental Psychology,* 1971, **4,** 262–267.

Serbin, L. A., O'Leary, K. D., Kent, R. N., & Tonick, I. J. A comparison of teacher response to the pre-academic and problem behavior of boys and girls. *Child Development,* 1973, **44,** 796–804.

Perceptions of Social Control Among Black College Students

Charles E. Babbit, *Edinboro State College*

Harold J. Burbach, *University of Virginia*

One of the major themes of protest in the past decade revolves around the issue of social control. Although there are many variations on this theme, the basic problem can be stated quite simply: a growing number of collectivities (e.g., blacks, chicanos, women, and students) are challenging the existing control mechanisms of society in an attempt to acquire a greater amount of control over their social lives. In many instances, however, institutional authorities are failing to answer these challenges effectively and are thereby leaving many members of minority groups frustrated and alienated.

Among those institutions which stand accused of being unresponsive to the control needs of its minority participants are colleges and universities. Supportive of this assertion are the works of writers such as Harper,[1] Powell,[2] and Pruitt,[3] which contend that institutions of higher education are failing

[1]Frederick D. Harper, "Black Revolt on the White Campus," *Journal of College Student Personnel,* X (September, 1969), 291–295.

[2]Joanne Powell, "Higher Education for the Black Student," *Journal of College Student Personnel,* XI (January, 1970), 8–14.

[3]Anne S. Pruitt, "Black Poor at White Colleges—Personal Growth Goals," *Journal of College Student Personnel,* XI (January, 1970), 3–7.

to invite the full participation of black students in their organizational life. And at the empirical level, Lyons,[4] in a recent national survey, found that while black students wanted more control over the decision-making process, several schools dismissed or expelled practically all of their matriculating black students who tried to achieve this end through demonstrations.

While most of the writings on the subject directly or indirectly indict the larger, predominantly white institution, there is very little evidence to indicate whether or not the smaller, predominantly black school is doing much better. The present investigation was motivated by the belief that there is a need for such information. Specifically, our purpose was to compare the perceptions of social control among black students across three settings: a large urban university, a medium sized urban college, and a small urban center.

Social control is defined as "the process of specifying preferred states of affairs and revising ongoing processes so as to move in the direction of these preferred states."[5] Viewed in terms of people, the process of control in organizations involves *authorities* who function to commit resources and guide organizational operations to effect particular ends and *partisans* who are subject to the decisions made by authorities.[6] In college and university settings, most positions of authority are occupied by administrators and faculty while students are, for the most part, cast in the partisan role.

The authority structure of a college or university is comprised of both formal and informal components. The formal structure consists of an extensive set of norms which are formally stated as laws and organizational roles with specified rewards or punishment for conformity or violation. With few exceptions, the formal mechanisms of control are in the hands of the faculty and administration. In the informal structure norms are not formally stated and are enforced through acts of social pressure such as praise or ridicule by other partisans in the system. As student partisans enter the system and come under the influence of the authority structure, they correspondingly develop some general perceptions regarding its legitimacy and worth. Of concern here is the question of whether these collective perceptions among black student partisans are, as many critics assert, more negative in the large university than in the smaller, less complex educational settings.

[4]James E. Lyons, "The Response of Higher Education to the Black Presence," *Journal of College Student Personnel*, XIII (September, 1972), 388–394.

[5]Amitai Etzioni, *The Active Society* (New York: The Free Press, 1968), p. 45.

[6]William A. Gamson, *Power and Discontent* (Homewood, Illinois: Dorsey, 1968).

FEEDBACK FOR EXERCISES

Our answers to the exercises are given in this section. The wording of your responses may differ, but the meaning should closely approximate these answers. Write answers to the questions for one or more reports in Appendix A if you need additional practice.

"Effects of Peer Presence on Sex-Typing of Children's Play Behavior"

1. The hypothesis is stated in the last paragraph as follows:

   The present study was designed as an experimental test of the hypothesis that peers function directly as discriminative stimuli for preschoolers' sex-typed play behavior, inhibiting exploration of toys culturally labeled as appropriate for the opposite sex.

It is stated more specifically in the final sentence:

It was predicted that peer presence would inhibit play with toys culturally labeled as appropriate for the opposite sex.

The variables are "peer presence" and "play behavior." This is a difference study that focuses on a possible cause-and-effect relationship between the variables. Specifically, researchers want to know what effect peers have on the choices children make regarding masculine/feminine stereotyped toys.

2. The problem is researchable using scientific methodology. Data can be collected by arranging for children to play alone, with same-sex peers, or with opposite-sex peers. Their choice of toys can be noted by observation while they play under these conditions.

3. The abstract does mention the problem, the methodology, and the results and conclusions. The abstract contains about 170 words, uses complete sentences, and is written in the past tense.

4. The study's justification is primarily as a replication of similar studies with the variables. However, Serbin and her associates emphasize that their study is to be an "experimental test of the hypothesis," indicating that they are going beyond the studies cited in the review. In other words, the goal of their study is control, while previous research studies sought explanation. They also state the need to check whether the results of the study with college students are true with preschool children. The justification seems reasonable in view of the cited research.

5. Both variables, "peer presence" and "sex-typing of behavior," are mentioned in the title. The scope of the study is indicated by the phrase, "children's play behavior." As a first word, "effects" is not very important, but the title is relatively short and free of unnecessary words. To conform to the criteria, the report could be titled: "Peer Presence: Effects on Sex-Typing of Preschool Children's Play Behavior."

"Perceptions of Social Control Among Black College Students"

1. The problem statement appears in the third paragraph as follows:

Specifically, our purpose was to compare the perceptions of social control among black students across three settings: a large urban university, a medium sized urban college, and a small urban center.

The variables are "perceptions of social control" and "types of institutions." The problem statement focuses on a possible cause-

and-effect relationship between types of institutions and perceptions of social control.

2. The problem is researchable using scientific methodology. Types of colleges can be differentiated according to the size of enrollment as these researchers did. Perceptions of social control can also be measured.

3. No abstract is given in the report.

4. This study is justified by the researchers as a replication effort. Babbit and Burbach indicate that previous research was conducted at predominantly white institutions. They want to find out whether similar results are found among black students. Their justification seems reasonable.

5. Both variables are mentioned in the title, with "social control" prominently displayed. However, "types of colleges" is not so clearly indicated. Scope is indicated by the phrase, "college students." Although "perceptions" is not a very important first word, the title is relatively short and free of unnecessary words. This title, which conforms to the criteria, is perhaps clearer: "Social Control as Perceived by Black Students in Three Types of Colleges."

RECOMMENDED REFERENCES

Davitz, J. R., & Davitz, L. L. *Evaluating research proposals in the behavioral sciences* (2nd ed.). New York: Teachers College Press, 1977. Although the book is basically a guide for evaluating research proposals, the information about problems and hypotheses may sharpen your understanding of these concepts.

Eckhardt, K. W., & Ermann, M. D. *Social research methods.* New York: Random House, 1977. Appendix 1 offers information about the construction of titles, abstracts, and contexts of research reports.

Gephart, W. J. *The problem and problem delineation techniques.* Bloomington, Ind.: Phi Delta Kappa, 1968. Two sections, "What does 'problem' mean?" and "A suggested resolution," are worth reading if you'd like a slightly more sophisticated approach to understanding problem statements.

Locke, L. F., & Spirduso, W. W. *Proposals that work: a guide for planning research.* New York: Teachers College Press, 1976. This book contains specimen plans for research projects. Perhaps its greatest value to the beginning research student is the helpful critiques that are presented with the proposed research plans. Sections on the literature review show how reviews are organized and the functions of the cited literature.

3

Reading Method Sections: Subjects

Following the introduction to the research report is a method section. Here researchers describe the people who participated in the study (subjects), the instruments used to collect data, how treatments (if any) were administered, and how the data were collected. Sometimes the method section also includes information about data analysis. The major purpose of this part of the report is to explain the methodology used to answer the problem or test the hypothesis.

If you become an active researcher, you will be much more concerned with details of procedures than you are now. Even so, reading about decisions that must be made to answer research questions should help you appreciate the complexities of research. This chapter introduces research design and methods of selecting and assigning subjects in research studies. Chapters 4 through 6 will continue the discussion of other aspects of methods, including instrumentation, data collection, and data analysis.

Chapter objective.   After you have completed this chapter, you should be able to assess the appropriateness of *subject selection* and *subject assignment procedures* in selected research reports.

BACKGROUND AND OVERVIEW OF RESEARCH DESIGN

Problem Statement and Methodology

When the problem statement is read in its context, it tells what kind of methodology should be used for its solution. Descriptive methodology is used for association studies and for some difference studies. Experimental methodology, however, is used for most difference studies. Another approach, historical methodology, is less common in education. See Appendix E for a brief discussion of this topic.

In association studies, researchers may try to find out whether there is a relationship among variables, and if so, what direction the relationship takes and how strong it is. These investigators seek explanation as their goal. On other occasions, however, this information may already be known to researchers, and their intention is to use the relationship in a prediction study. Both these situations require **descriptive methodology.** This method uses existing situations for data collection and does *not* require any manipulation of variables by the researchers. What is required is very careful measurement of the variables and appropriate interpretation of the results.

In difference studies, researchers choose between control and explanation as their goal. The choice depends on whether investigators can manipulate one of the variables under study. Where manipulation is possible, control can be the goal and **experimental methodology** is appropriate. In experimental studies, researchers actually alter the quality of one of the variables to see whether this causes any differences in another variable. Most researchers would probably like to use experimental methodology since it is the only approach that gives solid information about cause-and-effect relationships. If manipulation is *not* possible, then explanation is the goal, and a form of descriptive methodology must be used.

Remember the problem cited in Chapter 2 concerning test anxiety and intelligence? It was stated this way: "Will lowering test anxiety result in higher intelligence scores?" The researchers want to know whether manipulating the independent variable, test anxiety, will have an effect on the dependent variable, intelligence. (Manipulating the independent variable is also called "treatment administration.") Depending on the care with which the study is planned and carried out, researchers may be able to answer their question and shed some light on a cause-and-effect relationship between test anxiety and intelligence.

Consider a second problem mentioned in Chapter 2: "Will increasing socioeconomic status raise intelligence levels?" How do researchers manipulate socioeconomic status? The answer is that usually they don't. Changing the socioeconomic status of a group of people would be costly and time-consuming. Not many researchers could afford to work on a project with such a requirement. Furthermore, it could be unethical to alter someone's socioeconomic status. There is, however, a way to deal with the question that uses descriptive methodology and gives an answer about a possible cause-and-effect relationship.

Using the descriptive approach, a group of people with a range of intelligence scores could be located. Then researchers would gather information about socioeconomic status to see whether the people with higher intelligence scores differ from those with lower intelligence scores. The variation in socioeconomic status already exists as a characteristic of the people in the study, and is therefore not manipulated by the researchers. Precisely because the researchers are not able to exert control in the situation, the results may suggest a possible cause-and-effect relationship but they neither prove nor disprove its existence. Researchers who use this technique are not able to rule out the contribution of other variables to the results. Geographic location, race, cultural habits, and many other variables can affect intelligence. Socioeconomic status is only one of the possible causes of differences in intelligence.

Maybe you now realize more clearly why all studies cannot use experimental methodology. Variables such as aggression, anxiety, and even motor ability are not easily manipulated. How can researchers induce any of these conditons and remain within the ethical constraints that must be put on experimentation? Usually these variables can be studied in humans only by descriptive methodology.

Components of Research Design

Regardless of which methodology is used, researchers must plan procedures very carefully to get evidence for answering their research problems. We refer to the generalized procedures of a study as the **research design** and to the major divisions within the design as components. The list below illustrates these definitions. Five components are named and some questions that researchers must answer are mentioned. Chapters 3 through 6 will answer these questions from the perspective of consumers of research. The components and questions include the following:

Subjects: What is the population from which the subjects (people) for the study are selected? How are they selected? How are subjects assigned to groups? How are treatments assigned to groups?

Instrumentation: Which instruments are selected for data collection? Are these instruments commercially published or constructed by the researchers? Are the measurements both valid and reliable for the problem of the study?

Treatment: In experimental studies, what are treatment and no treatment? Which variables are held constant? Who administers the treatment?

Data collection: Where are data collected? When are data collected? Are directions standard for all subjects? Who collects data?

Data analysis: How are raw data summarized and organized? How are data analyzed? Who does the data analysis?

Researchers do not arrive at answers to these questions easily. They study all aspects of their problem very carefully and make decisions they believe will give the most valid answers. To do this, they try to control as many sources of variance as possible. They would like to be sure that whatever variations they introduce into a research situation are not contaminated by variations that get into the project without their knowledge. We refer to different kinds of variance by the terms *systematic* and *error variance.*

Systematic variance is the variation that experimenters introduce through manipulation of the independent variable in administering the treatment. It is called "systematic" because researchers hope that most of the variation is in the direction intended by the manipulations. Systematic variance can also be introduced in an unplanned fashion, just by the procedures of the research effort.

Error variance, on the other hand, refers to variation that comes about by errors in sampling or through chance variation among the persons in the study. Although no project is free of error variance, researchers try to minimize it. When you read Chapters 3 through 6, you will read about ways of reducing error variance and unplanned systematic variance.

BACKGROUND FOR READING METHOD SECTIONS: SUBJECTS

Populations and Samples

When a research question is formulated, there is almost always a group of people about whom the problem is being asked. Let's return to one of the problems in Chapter 2 for an example. Researchers want to know whether exercises to reduce test anxiety will raise scores on intelligence tests. They probably have in mind some group about whom they would like to have this question answered, such as college students, eighth-graders or high school students. This group is the population for whom the problem is being considered.

A **population** is simply a group that has one or more characteristics in common, such as right-handed people, middle-school students, first-born children, Spanish-surnamed elementary students in Smith County, or freshmen at Dunklin County Junior College. Notice that a population can vary widely in size. The group of all right-handed persons is much larger than the freshman class at Dunklin County Junior College.

Another consideration in the selection of participants is the relevance of the problem to the population. Although it would be informative to explore test anxiety and intelligence in blue-eyed senior citizens, other populations are more directly involved with the variables. To return to our example, even if the researchers want to answer the question for people in general, the population actually used will probably be both available and germane to the problem, such as high school students at nearby Lincoln High School. The people used in the study, known as the **subjects** (not victims, as some have suggested), will be members of this target population.

In most cases the entire population is not used as subjects. When you consider the size of populations such as first-born children or middle-school students, it is easy to see that collecting information from this many people is simply not feasible. Even for a somewhat smaller population, such as students at Lincoln High School, the time and expense involved may prohibit the use of all students. Therefore, part of the population is selected to represent the whole. This smaller set of people is the **sample.** If Lincoln High has 2,400 students, the researchers might select 10% or 240 students to represent the population, a manageable number for the study. The key word here is *represent*, because whatever is true for the sample will be implied to be true for all Lincoln High students. A sample that is representative allows researchers to apply or generalize the results to the entire population. Sample results can't be used this way unless the sample is very similar to the population. If a sample is representative, the research results are very likely to have **generalizability,** which means they are true for all members of the population, including those not in the sample. The sample selected from Lincoln High, then, must be typical of the entire student body. This concern for generalizability is very important in research, and you will read about it again when hypothesis testing is discussed in Chapter 6.

Sampling Procedures

Sampling is the process of choosing a set of subjects from a population. Researchers try to conduct sampling so that the sample closely resembles the population. Common sense suggests that the researchers probably won't get a representative sample if they use the first 240 students who arrive at school on a certain day. Why should early-risers be considered representative of all students? (For that matter, some of us feel that early-risers have a warped view of the world anyway!) Suppose the son of one of the researchers is captain of the Lincoln football team. Couldn't he just round up a few members of the team? Obviously this might be convenient, but there are better ways to select a sample, ways that would enable the answers to the research problem to be applied to all students at Lincoln High School.

Samples can be chosen in several ways. In selecting the method for a particular study, researchers must decide whether to use a scientific or a nonscientific sampling procedure. This choice is extremely important for proper interpretation of the results. Scientific sampling is done by one of several methods to ensure that the sample is as typical of the population as circumstances permit. In other words, it increases the confidence that the results obtained from the sample are similar to those that would be obtained from using the whole population in the study. Nonscientific sampling usually involves picking subjects by convenience, which does not promote the same confidence in results.

There are four basic types of scientific sampling methods: simple random, stratified random, cluster, and systematic sampling. In research where a scientific method was used to select the sample, you will probably find one of these labels mentioned.

Simple random sampling. In **simple random sampling,** everyone in the population has an equal chance of being picked for the sample. There are no favorites, no teacher's pets or researchers' offspring, except by chance selection. All subjects are selected at random, so the choice of one subject does not in any way influence the selection of any other individual. If any specific person or group is included or excluded from the study because of a researcher's familiarity with the subjects and their characteristics, bias contaminates the sample, making it deliberately unlike the population in some way. By using simple random sampling, researchers try to ensure that only chance differences prevent the sample from being an accurate representation of the entire population.

Let's return to the researchers who want to see whether intelligence scores can be influenced by participation in exercises to reduce test anxiety. To obtain a simple random sample from Lincoln High School, they could place all student names in a container and take out 240 names. This would be the sample, free of any intentional or unintentional bias on the part of the researchers. Although the sample would not be exactly like the population, any differences between population and sample would be due to chance alone. Researchers could expect that approximately the same proportions of freshmen, sophomores, juniors, and seniors would be in the sample as in the population. For the same reasons, it would be probable that the sample includes about the same percentages of high and low intelligence levels as exist in the population. Even though it is very likely that this sample would be representative, it is possible for simple random sampling to produce a sample with some characteristics that are not proportional to those of the population.

In Lincoln High School each of the four classes has 600 students. Suppose the sample drawn from the container was composed of 15 freshmen, 80 sophomores, 72 juniors, and 73 seniors. Although this distribution of classes in the sample is not likely, it could occur. If the investigators believe that freshmen are more likely to suffer from test anxiety than "seasoned" upperclassmen, they may want to see that all classes are equally represented in the sample. Therefore, another sampling technique may be used.

Stratified random sampling. A variation of the simple random technique, called **stratified random sampling,** allows researchers to be certain that the sample is evenly balanced by classes. In this kind of sample, the population is divided into strata (layers) on some known basis before the sample is picked at random. If the total sample is going to be a percentage of the population, like the 10% chosen for Lincoln High School, researchers select that percentage of each strata of the population. Since each class at Lincoln High has 600 members, 10% (or 60 students) would be chosen at random from each class. This would make a total sample of 240, the number the researchers want.

Of course, a population can be stratified in many ways. The important thing is for stratification to be relevant to the problem. In their investigation of intelligence and test anxiety, researchers may want to have all levels of IQ evenly represented in the sample. In this case the population would be stratified by IQ levels before the sample is chosen.

It's likely that students who are chosen using simple or stratified random sampling will come from every part of the high school population, meaning that many classes will be interrupted. The principal could require the researchers to use whole classes to minimize disruption. This would call for another variation of sampling, based on groups instead of individuals.

Cluster sampling. When the unit of sampling changes from the individual to a group of people, **cluster sampling** is being done. The groups identified may be all the schools within a district, all the households on a city block, all the classrooms of a given grade, and so on. Groups are drawn by random selection as in simple random sampling. However, in cluster sampling all the individuals within the cluster or group are subjects for the research project. In the study at Lincoln High School, all first-period classes could be used as groups. If each class contained an average of 20 students, then 12 classes could be selected at random for the sample.

Cluster sampling has advantages and disadvantages. When a population is very large, selecting groups instead of individuals may be the most feasible method. This also results in the efficient use of time and money in a research effort. Nevertheless, the representativeness of subjects drawn by cluster sampling is open to question. The use of intact groups increases the chances of having a sample that is not typical of the entire population.

Systematic sampling.   Another variation of random sampling is **systematic sampling**. Ordinarily this method uses lists of names or identification numbers. Once the size of the sample is known and the first person is selected using a random method, the remaining persons in the sample are chosen on some type of systematic basis, such as every seventh person or every other person. After the first subject is identified, the location of all other sample members is automatically determined. If the researchers at Lincoln High wanted to use systematic sampling, they could take the student directory and select every tenth name in the book to produce their sample of 240. This would certainly be easier than putting the names of all students in a container and drawing a sample. The drawback to systematic sampling is that it might skip some important portions of the population who are grouped together on the list.

These four types of sampling do not exhaust the alternatives in selecting subjects. Researchers may use more than one type of sampling if a combination produces a more representative sample. Researchers at Lincoln High could combine cluster and stratified sampling by choosing three freshman, three sophomore, three junior, and three senior classrooms to make up their sample, thus using classroom clusters with grade-level strata.

Convenience sampling.   In **convenience sampling,** samples are drawn with no randomization. These samples may be intact classrooms or readily available groups. Note how this procedure is different from the cluster sampling example we discussed. When the researchers were told to randomly pick whole classes instead of individual students, they had to use cluster sampling. If they were simply offered the use of 12 physical education classes, this would be convenience sampling with no hint of randomization. Convenience sampling is handy, and it may be the only possibility available to researchers. When it is used, however, the results cannot be used accurately to describe the population. Thus, the generalizability of results is greatly limited.

Table 3.1 compares the advantages and disadvantages of these five methods of sampling. You may want to try your hand at seeing how well you understand sampling procedures by completing Checkpoint 3.1.

Assigning Subjects and Treatments

What is done with the sample after it is selected? The answer depends on the kind of study. If the problem focuses on the association between variables, the sample will probably be kept intact. In difference studies, however, the sample may be either subdivided or kept intact.

Subjects in experiments are frequently assigned to experimental or control groups by methods similar to random sampling procedures. This **random assignment** occurs whenever subjects are placed within groups, or groups are assigned to particular experimental conditions by a chance process. It is *not* the same thing as random sampling, which refers only to the method used to draw subjects from the population. Random assignment and random sampling are desirable because they help eliminate potential biases that could influence the results of the study. Both are categorized as methods of **randomization,** which are procedures designed to distribute variation within subjects and experimental conditions by chance alone.

On other occasions researchers draw stratified samples and use each layer as a group to be subdivided. Let's go back to Lincoln High for an example. Assume the researchers have selected a stratified sample of 240 students, 60 from each of four classes. They may then assign students at random to two groups by putting half the subjects from each class in each group. Then each group will contain 120 subjects—30 freshmen, 30 sophomores, 30 juniors,

Table 3.1
COMPARISONS OF SAMPLING METHODS

Method of sampling	Advantages	Disadvantages
Scientific		
Simple random	Is representative of population except for chance differences	May be difficult to precisely identify entire population
Stratified random	Allows researcher to take into account population characteristics that may influence the study	May be difficult to identify exact membership in each strata
Cluster	Provides more efficient randomization of very large populations than simple randomization	Is not appropriate in all situations; changing unit to cluster may make it hard to collect data from all individuals in clusters; data from clusters may not be representative of population
Systematic	Allows representative sampling using a less time-consuming method than simple or stratified randomization	Making first selection fixes all other selections; is not quite as free of bias as simple or stratified randomization
Nonscientific		
Convenience	Subjects are available without too much trouble	Subjects may not be representative of population to which researcher wants to generalize results

Identify the method of sampling.

1. A state decides to field-test its new competency assessment program in a small percentage of school districts. The names of all school districts are put into a large container. The districts selected from the container by a random procedure will participate in the field test.
2. Curmudgeon Teachers College wants to know whether training in stress management will improve the self-esteem of new teachers. They take a list of all their teacher education graduates who began teaching in the past two years and select every tenth person on the list.
3. A group of researchers decides to investigate the relationship between creativity and the need to achieve in students from a large urban middle school. Since 40% of the student body is chicano, 45% anglo, and 15% black, they randomly select one eighth of the total students in each ethnic group for the sample.
4. At another middle school, the same researchers are asked to use only the eight art classes for their study of creativity and need to achieve.
5. A vocational education teacher wants to see if a new career counseling program will influence student preferences for certain careers. There are 100 students in vocational education classes. She selects subjects by drawing 36 numbered slips from a hat containing the numbers 1 to 100, and uses the students listed beside each of those 36 numbers on the vocational education computer printout of student names.

ANSWERS: 1. simple random 2. systematic 3. stratified random 4. convenience 5. cluster

and 30 seniors. Random assignment can be made by the flip of a coin or some other chance procedure.

Next the researchers will designate one of the two groups as the treatment group, or the experimental group. These subjects will participate in exercises to reduce test anxiety. The second group, known as the control group, does not participate in these exercises. Usually the decision as to which group receives treatment is also made by a random procedure, such as another toss of the coin. This eliminates one more possibility for researcher bias.

The sample may be kept intact for difference studies so that subjects serve as their own control group. That is, subjects may be tested under one condition, usually following a treatment, and then tested later under other conditions. Measures can be made repeatedly for as many conditions as the design contains. This type of repeated measures procedure is most often used when it is difficult to secure large numbers of subjects.

In research reports sample size is almost always mentioned. One of your concerns as you read reports is whether the number of subjects is appropriate for the problem, since the size of a sample influences the researchers' likelihood of making accurate conclusions about the hypothesis. A look at several reports will show variations in the number of subjects. Studies of growth and development require the observation of large numbers of people in order to establish norms. Research involving exceptional children, on the other hand, may use fewer subjects because this population is much smaller. These examples show how the purpose of a study may dictate the selection of a relatively large or small sample.

Often there are no exact criteria by which a reader can quickly judge the optimum sample size in a given study. There are formal ways to determine the adequacy of sample size if specific features of a research situation are known, including the magnitude of the hypothesized association or difference, and the strictness of the standards that the researchers set for making a correct conclusion about their hypothesis. More will be said about this way of judging sample size in connection with data analysis (in Chapter 6).

Consideration of sample size can be done informally, based on general information about a research study. A sample should be large enough to represent the population accurately. If a sample is too small to represent the whole population, the results of the study cannot be accepted with much confidence. Four or five students from a large school can't be typical of the entire group. Of course, in every sample there will be some amount of **sampling error**—the degree to which the sample and the population differ with respect to the variables under investigation. In general, the larger the sample, the more likely it is to represent the population. This assumes, of course, that the sample is drawn scientifically. Size alone will not compensate for a lack of scientific accuracy.

READING AND ANALYZING METHOD SECTIONS: SUBJECTS

Content and Form

Typically the first part of the method section describes subjects. The amount of information given varies from one report to another, with some researchers sketching only the number of subjects and a minimal amount of background information. Other researchers describe their subjects in detail. Average age, IQ, number of males and females, socioeconomic levels, or ethnic composition are sometimes given in the description. Usually characteristics that have a bearing on the problem are included.

Suggestions for Reading and Analysis

When you read the subjects portion of major research reports, you probably won't have much difficulty finding a description of the population and sample. Thesis and dissertation advisers, as well as grant evaluators, are famous for seeing that these kinds of details are included. The task may not be so easy when you read journal research reports, however. In some reports there is no mention of a population or sampling procedures used in selecting subjects.

Description of the population is essential, since the whole point of the study is to answer a question about a given population. If you don't find a clear definition of the population, it will be impossible to apply the results of the study to a population. Furthermore, it is easier to judge the appropriateness of the sampling technique if you have an idea of the size or relevant characteristics of the population. A sample of 50 in an association study may sound tremendous until you learn that the population is 100,000. If the sample consists of two randomly selected 25-pupil classrooms out of 4,000 such classrooms, you may have even further doubt about the generalizability of the results.

Here are some suggestions for looking at sample sizes. If a study has 30 or more subjects, the sample size is probably adequate, unless you have reason to believe that the population is extremely large or so varied that 30 subjects could not represent the important characteristics of the population. Furthermore, when a sample is split, the number of subjects in each group or stratum needs to fairly represent the population, so your concern as a reader should be directed to the size of these subdivisions. In general, when you see very small samples or subdivisions, think about the generalizability of the results. When a population consists of people who are very much alike, it will take fewer subjects to be representative, and you might conclude that the researchers were justified in using a small sample. If, however, the population appears to contain considerable variation among its members, you should be more skeptical of a tiny sample.

Sometimes the results of the study must be interpreted as though the entire population or a convenience sample were used. This is necessary when the population is not well defined, the sampling procedures are not described, or the procedures are inappropriate to the population. In these cases, the results are true only for the actual subjects in the study. It is only with great care that the results could be presumed to resemble results obtained from other groups very much like the actual subjects of the study.

It is not unusual to make errors in analyzing subject information. One mistake is to assume the existence of a population when it is not described. This can lead to faulty interpretation and generalization of results. A second and closely related error is to assume that a random method of sampling was used when no method is stated. It is possible to confuse random sampling with the random assignment of subjects. You should note whether the word *random* applies to the selection of the subjects (the sample) or to a way of placing subjects into groups after the sample is drawn. A good rule of thumb is to assume nothing. If researchers have taken the trouble to randomly select a sample or to randomly assign subjects to groups, they will usually tell you so in plain language.

As you read a report, you can use the criteria listed below as guidelines for analyzing and evaluating the subject information in a report. Each criterion refers to a feature that should be present in a well-written research report. The criteria can help you determine the trustworthiness of the results and prevent errors in analysis.

Criteria for subjects portions of reports include the following:

1. *Populations and subjects for studies should be clearly described.* All characteristics of the population that may influence the research problem should be mentioned. If the population is stratified, descriptions and the relative proportions of each stratum need to be included. When samples are used, any relevant characteristics not mentioned in the population description should be noted.

2. *Sampling procedures, if any, should be suitable for the problem and clearly described.* Specific sampling procedures should be appropriate for the kind of problem and mentioned by name. Methods of assigning subjects and treatments to groups should be detailed. Scientific (randomized) methods are preferable to nonscientific methods.

3. *The sample sizes indicated should be appropriate for the populations and kinds of studies.* Samples need to be big enough to represent the characteristics of the population. Fewer subjects will serve as a representative sample for a uniform population than for a varied population. Any time samples are subdivided into smaller units, judgments of size should be related to the representativeness of each division.

4. *In difference studies the assignment of subjects and treatments to groups should be made randomly whenever possible.* Although randomization does not eliminate all unwanted variance, potential sources of bias are reduced. Using randomization techniques strengthens the research design.

SUMMARY

The problem statement in a research study determines the goal of science sought and the choice of methodology. When control is the goal, experimental methodology is commonly used. This involves the manipulation of an independent variable to see what changes result in a dependent variable. If the research problem seeks explanation or prediction, descriptive methodology is chosen to identify the strength and direction of the relationship between the variables. Descriptive methods are also used in difference studies in which the independent variable has already been applied and no manipulation can take place.

The design of a research study includes activities in several areas. Each component of the overall design is chosen to minimize unwanted variance.

Decisions include selecting subjects and instrumentation, planning and carrying out treatment, and collecting and analyzing data.

Subject selection and assignment procedures are the main ways that researchers control variance. Furthermore, these procedures influence the kind of statistical analysis that can be used for the project data. The population or group of persons considered in the problem should be identified. Usually only a portion of this population, called the sample, is selected to represent the population in the study. Ideally samples are chosen scientifically through some randomized process. This ensures that all members of a population are equally likely to be chosen and that the choice of one member in no way influences the choice of any other member. Methods for selecting samples include the scientific procedures of simple random sampling, stratified random sampling, cluster sampling, and systematic sampling. Nonscientific or convenience sampling is used when scientific methods are not possible.

The assignment of subjects to groups and to treatments should ideally be done in some random fashion, even when subjects were not randomly selected. Sample size should be large enough for the sample to be representative of the population.

Information about subjects is usually found in the first part of the method section of a research report. Populations and subjects must be clearly described, and the sampling procedures should be identified. Note whether scientific or nonscientific procedures were used, and whether the sample size is appropriate for the population and kind of study. When subjects are assigned to groups or treatments, this should be done randomly, if possible.

EXERCISES

Read the information about subjects (and other subsections as needed) of "Effects of Peer Presence on Sex-Typing of Children's Play Behavior" and "Perceptions of Social Control Among Black College Students," which appear immediately following the questions. The introductory sections of these reports are at the end of Chapter 2. Write your answers and compare them with the feedback for exercises at the end of this chapter.

1. Describe the population from which the sample was drawn. If the population is not mentioned, indicate that this is the case.
2. Describe the subjects for the study unless they have been described in statements about the population. Which technique (if any is named) was used to select the sample? Does using this technique provide an adequate sample for data collection? Give reasons for your answer.
3. In difference studies, were subjects assigned to groups or treatments? If yes, were random methods used? Explain. (You may need to read the procedures section for this information.)

4. Does the sample size appear to be appropriate for the population? Explain.
5. Based on the information given, to what population can the results of the study be generalized? Explain.

Serbin et al., *Effects of Peer Presence on Sex-Typing of Children's Play Behavior*

METHOD

Subjects

Twenty-six girls and thirty-six boys, mean age 51 months (age range 40–60 months), participated in the study. Children were students at a university child study center and attended two or three 2.5-hr. preschool classes per week. Children were primarily middle class, from both blue and white collar families; approximately 20% were from lower SES backgrounds. Approximately 15% of the children were from minority (black and oriental) families. Prior to the study, the subjects had been enrolled in preschool from 1 to 11 months, with an average of 5 months previous attendance.

Procedures

All subjects participated in three conditions: solitary, same-sex peer, and opposite-sex peer. This constituted a 2 (sex) $\times$ 3 (conditions) factorial design with repeated measures on the second factor. Subjects in the solitary condition were taken into a small room containing a row of six toys. Three of the toys were male stereotypic and three female stereotypic. Male and female toys were alternated and consisted of the following: plastic soldiers, small dolls and doll furniture, miniature firetrucks, a plastic tea set, toy airplanes, and an ironing board and iron (with clothes to iron). Children in this condition were instructed as follows: "There are some toys in this room for you. You can play with any of the toys you want to. I will be working at my desk (in the adjoining room), while you are playing. In a little while, I'll come in and we'll do some drawing, then we'll go back to the classroom." The child was then left alone in the room for 3 min.

The procedure for the same- and opposite-sex peer conditions was identical to that for the solitary condition, except that a same- or opposite-sex peer remained in a corner of the room at a desk, drawing a picture. The order of conditions was varied, with random assignment of subjects to each of the six possible orders. In the peer present conditions, children were told that they could play with the toys while waiting their "turn" to crayon. Each child served as a "peer" while the next subject was tested and was then returned to the classroom. The three exposures to the experimental situation which each child received were spaced 3 to 5 days apart. In the peer present condition children were instructed: "_____ (name of peer) is finishing a picture at the desk. You will have a chance to draw when he/she is done. While you are waiting your turn, you can play with these toys. You can play with any of the toys you want to. I will be working at my desk (in the adjoining room) while you are playing. In a little while, I'll come in and we'll do some drawing and then we'll go back to the classroom." Peers were instructed: "Now it's your turn to draw. When you are finished, we'll go back to class. Be sure to pay attention to your drawing, and let _____ (subject) play by him/ herself for a little while."

Observational System

Observations were made from behind a one-way glass mirror. An undergraduate observer (from a total pool of eight available observers) recorded the toy(s) a child was touching, every 5 sec. (i.e., 36 observations per session).

Talking by either the subject or the peer was recorded. Interobserver agreement was periodically assessed on approximately 10% of the experimental trials and was computed by the formula below, on an interval by interval basis:

$$\frac{\text{Agreements on occurrence}}{\text{Agreements and disagreements on occurrence.}}$$

Interobserver agreement ranged from 95 to 100% on the specific toys and behavioral measures of talking and playing. No hypotheses were given to the observers regarding the effects of peer presence.

Babbit and Burbach, *Perceptions of Social Control Among Black College Students*

METHOD

Instrument and Analysis

The absence of a scale to measure social control within educational settings made it necessary to develop one for this research. Basic to this undertaking is the assumption that all student partisans develop an attitudinal perspective on the authority structure of their college or university. Proceeding on this assumption, and drawing on the conceptual literature on the subject, three indexes comprised of 10, 12, and 13 items were formulated to tap perceptions of social control as they are focused on the administration, faculty, and student body respectively. Following is a representative item from each index:

Administration. In general, the administration of this school is fair in dealing with student problems.

Faculty. Most faculty at this school are ready and willing to help the individual student when they (sic) need it.
Student Peer Group. The social pressures at this school frequently force the individual to go along with things they (sic) may not want to go along with.

Without a criterion measure of social control, it was necessary to rely on the argument that the scale items have face validity. In addition, an item-to-total analysis revealed that all items were significantly correlated ($p < .01$) with the underlying criterion of the scale thus providing evidence for the scales' construct validity. When corrected by the Spearman-Brown prophecy formula, the respective split-half reliability coefficients for the peer, faculty, and administration social control indexes were .83, .79 and .75.

The response set consists of a Likert-type continuum upon which the respondent is asked to indicate his degree of agreement or disagreement with each statement. Each item is scored on a 1 to 4 basis, with 1 being assigned to the response indicative of the most positive attitude toward the authority structure and 4 to the most negative. The total score for each individual is obtained by summing across all items in a particular index.

Our analysis is aimed at determining whether there are differences in levels of social control among black students in the three educational settings selected for examination. First, scores were obtained for the total sample on each index, and a correponding mean and standard deviation were computed for each subsample representative of the urban center, college, and university settings. The *t*-test was then used to compare the group means.

Subjects and Data

The three settings were all located in a single metropolitan area in the northwestern region of the state of New York. The university was a large (approximately 23,000), urban, predominantly white institution with an excellent academic reputation. The college was also urban, largely white, considerably smaller (approximately 8,000), and somewhat less academically prestigious than the university. Although both institutions can be regarded as urban, it should be noted that both are located on the periphery of the city, unlike the urban center which is situated in the core area itself.

The fact that it was a two-year institution distinguished the urban center from the college and university. A recent innovation of the state university system, the urban center began operation in November, 1965, with an enrollment of 48 students. Its rolls expanded to 671 students by the fall of 1967, to 737 by 1970, and presently has an enrollment of approximately 850. The center offers college-level courses in language arts, science, mathematics, English, and the social sciences. In addition, it provides a variety of remedial courses together with a broadly based vocational education program. In short, it is the purpose of the urban center to prepare students for either senior level colleges and universities or the world of work.

Sixty black subjects were randomly selected from the freshman and sophomore classes of each institution, thus constituting a total sample of 180. All subjects were from the same metropolitan area, were of lower or lower-middle socioeconomic status, and had similar educational backgrounds. In an effort to maximize the return rate, black personnel from the respective institutions were enlisted and paid to personally contact and administer the research instruments to each subject while guaranteeing them their anonymity. Data were collected in the spring of the year after the freshmen had had nearly one year and the sophomores nearly two years of contact with their respective institutions. The number of instruments completed by subjects from the urban center, college, and university was 49, 55, and 56, respectively.

FEEDBACK FOR EXERCISES

This section is intended to let you know how well you answered the exercises. Although the wording of your answers will differ, the meaning should be similar to the following answers. You may answer the exercises for one or more reports in Appendix A if you need additional practice.

"Effects of Peer Presence on Sex-Typing of Children's Play Behavior"

1. The population from which the sample was drawn is not clearly specified.
2. The subjects in the study were students at a university child study center who attended two or three 2.5-hour classes each week. There were 26 girls and 36 boys with a mean age of 51 months. Children came from mixed racial backgrounds and primarily middle-class families. No sampling techniques are mentioned.
3. Yes. Subjects served as their own controls in this project. They were assigned to each of three treatments using a random method.
4. Since the population is not specified, there is no way to say whether the sample size is appropriate.
5. The results of this study can be generalized to all children at the university child study center where the study was done. The results may apply to comparable populations of preschoolers in other child study centers provided the general conditions of socioeconomic class, sex, and racial backgrounds are considered.

"Perceptions of Social Control Among Black College Students"

1. The population from which the sample was drawn consisted of all the black freshmen and sophomores at each of the three institutions located in northwestern New York.
2. The subjects were from the same metropolitan area, were of lower or lower-middle socioeconomic status, and had similar educational backgrounds. The subjects represent a stratified random sample from the population, with the strata being the types of colleges. This technique is appropriate for the problem since it assured representativeness of the population.
3. No. Subjects were used as an intact group. They had already undergone treatment by virtue of being enrolled in the different types of colleges.
4. The sample size appears to be appropriate for the population, although 60 students from the population of the urban center (total enrollment of 850) is a higher percentage than 60 students from the university (total enrollment of 23,000). Having 60 students in each group probably allows generalization about group differences.
5. It seems safe to say that the results of this study can be generalized to the freshmen and sophomore black students at the three institutions involved. The results may be generalizable to other institutions that have characteristics similar to those included in this study.

RECOMMENDED REFERENCES

Chein, I. An introduction to sampling. In C. Sellitz, L. S. Wrightsman, & S. W. Cook, *Research methods in social relations*, (3rd ed.). New York: Holt, Rinehart & Winston, 1976. This information, which appears in Appendix A, is a very readable account of the major concepts related to subject selection described in this chapter.

Choppin, B. Interpreting research: sampling. *Educational Research*, 1974. *16*, 218–221. This article notes important sampling considerations and cites actual examples of the effects of sampling inadequacies.

Eckhardt, K. W., & Ermann, M. D. *Social research methods: perspective, theory and analysis.* New York: Random House, 1977. Part Five, "Sampling and Sampling Designs," offers additional information on simple random, stratified random, and cluster sampling.

Marks, E. S. Some sampling problems in educational research. *Journal of Educational Psychology*, 1951, *42*, 85–96. Marks discusses each of the major sampling techniques, pointing out possible difficulties in their application to real-world situations. He emphasizes the need to use sampling procedures that are appropriate to the research problem.

Slonim, M. J. *Sampling.* New York: Simon & Schuster, 1960. Published originally as *Sampling in a Nutshell*, this is one of the most easily read sources on sampling. We think you'll enjoy the light-hearted discussions of the major concepts in sampling.

Sudman, S. *Applied sampling.* New York: Academic Press, 1976. Each of the subject selection procedures is described in a chapter of its own in this very readable book.

Warwick, D. P., & Lissinger, C. A. *The sample survey: Theory and practice.* New York: McGraw-Hill, 1973. Chapter 4, "Sampling and Estimation," may help those who would like additional examples of various sampling techniques.

4

Reading
Method Sections:
Instrumentation

This chapter continues the discussion of methodology in research studies, specifically focusing on instrumentation. Since an entire branch of education is devoted to the study of measurement and evaluation, it would be impossible for this book to give all the information you may need on this topic. We will provide some general guides and direct you to other sources for additional information.

If you already know about tests and measurements, you may scan the background section of the chapter. However, whether you read for details or review, keep in mind that you will apply this information in reading and analyzing research reports at the end of the chapter.

Chapter objective.   Upon completion of this chapter you should be able to *assess the appropriateness of the instrumentation* in selected research reports.

BACKGROUND FOR READING METHOD SECTIONS: INSTRUMENTATION

Instrumentation in Research Design

As we are using the term, **instrumentation** refers to decisions researchers make about collecting data. The main concern is the careful selection of instruments appropriate for the particular research problem. Sometimes this selection is made from commercially published instruments; at other times researchers must devise an instrument from scratch. Regardless of the route taken, both the validity (truthfulness) and the reliability (stability and consistency) of the results from instruments must be checked prior to using the instrument in the project. The sections that follow give more details about these aspects of instrumentation.

Categories of Instruments

Chapter 1 mentioned that educational research often involves one or more of these variables: achievement, intelligence, aptitude, personal-social adjustment, attitudes and interests, motivation, and motor tasks. Each can be measured more than one way. We have loosely categorized the kinds of instruments used to measure variables as tests, scales, inventories and surveys, observation reports, sociometric techniques, and interviews.

Researchers may select commercially prepared instruments or develop their own measuring devices. Tests, scales, inventories, surveys, and observation reports are published commercially; they are also often developed by researchers to fit special cases. Usually interview schedules, sociometric techniques, and observation methods are constructed for a particular project. Table 4.1 gives an overview of categories and sources of instruments for measuring selected variables in educational research. Detailed information about each category is presented in the sections that follow.

Tests. Widely used as measurement devices, tests can probably be used to collect data about most variables in educational research. According to Sax, a test is "any planned, intrusive procedure or series of tasks used to obtain observations" (1980, p. 634). Tests may involve the performance of all kinds of tasks, both verbal and motor. What they have in common, according to the definition, is that the person taking the test knows that observations are being made about him or her.

Verbal tests. These tests usually involve pencil and paper work with words and symbols, although there are also punch-out cards and computer-assisted administration procedures. In all verbal tests the formats are fairly well standardized. Subjects either select responses (as in multiple-choice or true-false) or generate them (as in essay, short answer, or math problems).

Performance tests. In contrast, performance tests require the subject to demonstrate certain behaviors while the examiner looks on. Performance tests are frequently used in driver education, shop, and science classes. For example, a biology teacher may be very particular about how students conduct dissections, make slides, or mount specimens. To measure these performances, the teacher makes notes or completes a checklist for the behaviors witnessed while students perform the tasks.

Table 4.1

CATEGORIES AND SOURCES OF INSTRUMENTS
FOR MEASURING SELECTED VARIABLES IN EDUCATIONAL RESEARCH

Categories of Instruments	Variables						Usual sources of instruments	
	Achievement	Intelligence	Aptitude	Attitudes, interests	Personal-social adjustment	Motor tasks	Commercial	Researcher-designed
Tests	+	+	+		+	+	+	+
Scales		+	+	+	+		+	+
Inventories and surveys				+	+		+	+
Observation reports				+	+	+	+	+
Sociometric techniques					+			+
Interviews				+	+			+

Tests may be commercially prepared or developed by researchers to fit the problem of the study. Whenever commercial tests are used, some of the difficulties of writing tests are avoided. For instance, commercial tests are expected to have clear directions for administration and scoring. When researchers develop their own tests, however, these procedures may be a little unclear. Norms or expected performance levels are probably available for most commercial instruments but are usually not known for tests developed by researchers. In addition, since commercial tests were written by "experts," the items may be constructed better than those in some researcher-developed tests. Most commercial tests have been subjected to validity and reliability checks, and this information is available to potential users.

This discussion may sound like a pitch for using commercial tests, but that is not our intention at all. There *are* studies for which no commercial test is appropriate—for example, short-term achievement or some performance-oriented situations. If a commercial test is not well suited to the research problem, it has no advantage for the researcher because it may be invalid or unreliable for the project. We simply note that commercial tests have some positive features. Selected standardized achievement, intelligence, aptitude, and personal-social adjustment tests are described in Appendix B.

Scales. Instruments called scales are typically used to quantify the measurement of variables such as intelligence and personal-social adjustment, including self-concept, test anxiety, dogmatism, and the like. The form of scales varies from one instrument to another. Three commonly used forms are Likert-type, equal-appearing intervals (Thurstone-type), and semantic differential scales.

Likert-type scales. These consist of several simple statements related to one concept—for example, anxiety, attitudes toward school work, or interest in research. The subject is asked whether he or she "strongly agrees" (SA), "agrees" (A), is "undecided" (U), "disagrees" (D), or "strongly disagrees" (SD) with each of the statements. See Figure 4.1. The spaces have values 1–5, with 5 usually being assigned to the most positive position. In scoring, the values of all the attitude statements are added. A high total score reflects a positive attitude.

Attitude Statement

	SA	A	U	D	SD
I like reading about research.	____	✓	____	____	____
Research is something I'd like to do.	____	____	✓	____	____
I'd rather watch TV than read research reports	____	____	____	____	____

FIGURE 4.1 Likert-type scale items.

Equal-appearing intervals. Also called Thurstone-type scales, equal-appearing intervals are a little more complicated than Likert-type scales. Statements in this type of instrument have been evaluated by "experts" who assign a value to them after a careful sorting procedure. Subjects are asked to mark the statements with which they agree. Figure 4.2 is modified slightly from the Dutton Arithmetic Scale (Dutton, 1956). Scale values are not included with the statements given to the subjects. Values of the statements that each subject picks are averaged to give a score for that person. A high score signifies a positive attitude.

Semantic differential scales. These scales consist of pairs of bipolar adjectives (cold-hot, good-bad, etc.) at opposite ends of a row of seven spaces (Osgood, Suci, and Tannebaum, 1975). These spaces are assumed to be numbered 7, 6, 5, 4, 3, 2, 1, or in the opposite sequence, depending on which end the positive adjective appears. In one of these seven spaces the subject places a mark to indicate his or her feelings about the particular object or concept named above the set of spaces. Marks for each pair of adjectives are summed; a high score indicates a positive position. See Figure 4.3 for an example of a semantic differential scale.

These three scales are frequently used in educational measurement, although there are also other types of scales. Researchers may devise their own instruments involving these techniques or use commercially produced scales. Some selected published scales for measuring personal-social adjustment are described in Appendix B.

Inventories and surveys. These instruments are often used to measure aspects of attitudes and interests or personal-social adjustment variables. Sax indicates that an inventory is "usually a series of items having no 'correct' answer but that measure individual differences in affect" (1980, p. 624). Inventories and surveys are self-report instruments, with the scores sometimes translated onto profile sheets. Subjects are asked to answer questions with either yes or no. Inventories may have either a single score or part scores,

Scale Value	Attitude Statement
9.5	_____ 1. I think about mathematics problems outside of school and like to work them out.
3.7	_____ 2. I don't feel sure of myself in mathematics.
8.6	_____ 3. I enjoy seeing how rapidly and accurately I can work mathematics problems.

FIGURE 4.2 Equal-appearing intervals scale items.

1. sharp   __ : ✓ : __ : __ : __ : __ : __ :   dull
2. passive   __ : __ : __ : __ : __ : __ : ✓ :   active
3. strong   __ : __ : ✓ : __ : __ : __ : __ :   weak
4. rugged   __ : __ : __ : __ : __ : __ : __ :   delicate
5. unpleasant __ : __ : __ : __ : __ : __ : __ :   pleasant
6. good   __ : __ : __ : __ : __ : __ : __ :   bad
7. attractive __ : __ : __ : __ : __ : __ : __ :   unattractive
8. light   __ : __ : __ : __ : __ : __ : __ :   heavy
9. slow   __ : __ : __ : __ : __ : __ : __ :   fast

FIGURE 4.3   Semantic differential scale.

depending on the inventory and its purpose. A personal adjustment inventory could have items similar to those in Figure 4.4.

There are many personality and interest inventories offered by commercial publishers. Inventories are usually general in scope and cover a lot of territory. To illustrate, the Ohio Vocational Interest Survey elicits responses from students about their interest on 24 different scales related to 114 "worker trait groups" (Rothney, 1972). Other published surveys and inventories are described in Appendix B.

Observation reports.   These reports are used to measure personal-social adjustment, attitudes, or interests. However, unlike inventories and surveys, which are self-reports, observation instruments require someone to observe the behavior and make a record. This record may be in the form of an anecdotal record, frequency recording, checklist, or rating scale (Cartwright and Cartwright, 1974). Because most situations that require observation are unique, researchers usually have to design their own instruments, although there are a few commercially prepared checklists and rating scales.

	Yes	No
I often feel embarrassed.		✓
Self-discipline is one of my strongest traits.	✓	
I avoid conflict whenever possible.		
I am tired most of the time.		

FIGURE 4.4   Items from a personal adjustment inventory.

Anecdotal records. Used most commonly in unstructured situations, anecdotal records furnish a report of verbal statements and actions taken by the subjects. If value judgments are made at all, they are placed in a separate category and labeled "interpretations." The observer usually includes a description of the setting, names or letters to identify subjects, and the date.

Anecdotal records may be used to gather preliminary information about behaviors that later can be translated into more structured observation reports. Because of the time required to use and interpret the results, anecdotal records are not often selected as the main instrument in gathering research data. See Figure 4.5 for an example of an anecdotal record.

Frequency recordings. As the name implies, the frequency of behaviors is recorded with tallies on a list of behaviors for each subject observed. According to a predetermined plan, an observer marks those behaviors that occur. Plans include marking at specified time intervals, marking as often as the behavior changes, or marking each behavior that occurs within a specified time interval. Under any of these plans, the result is a cumulative number of behaviors within a defined time period. You may draw your own conclusions about the frequency recording shown in Figure 4.6.

Checklists. A checklist contains a list of behaviors that are marked as present or absent by the observer during a given time period. These instruments are used to record data for individual subjects. See Figure 4.7. As the example indicates, the checklist simply tells whether or not a behavior was observed. No indication is given about the extent of the behaviors.

Rating scales. These instruments not only tell whether the behavior was observed, as checklists do, but also indicate the degree to which it was shown. The extent of the behavior is indicated by a scale that has either verbal descriptions (see Figure 4.8a) or numbers with assigned values (see Figure 4.8b). An observer marks the point on the scale that corresponds to the

Name of subject:	Archimedes
Date:	250 B.C.
Location:	Street in Greece
Observations:	Subject was seen running in the street, draped in a towel, with soap bubbles dripping off his elbows. Subject was yelling in a loud voice, "Eureka! I've found it!"
Interpretation:	The guy is a nut!

FIGURE 4.5 An anecdotal record.

Name of subject: ___F. SMEDLEY___

Date: ___3/19___

Time observed: ___10:45 — 11:15 AM___

Behaviors observed during research methodology class

Yawns ___卌 卌___

Head nods ___III___

Stares out window ___卌 I___

Looks at watch ___卌 卌___

Doodles on paper ___卌___

FIGURE 4.6 A frequency recording.

observed behaviors. Note that rating scales can be used with a small group of subjects, perhaps five to seven. Rating scales can also be used with individuals.

Sociometric techniques. To gather data about peer appraisals, sociometric techniques may be chosen (Gronlund, 1959). These techniques allow researchers to study the interactions between group members as well as their communication patterns and the choices they make. Questions like these are asked: With whom would you most like to work? Whom would you like to have as neighbors? With whom would you share recreation facilities? Choices are plotted on a matrix opposite the name of the chooser (see Figure 4.9).

After the matrix is marked, the choices are analyzed according to one-way or simple choices, two-way or mutual choices, and no choices. In this example, the Stepmother chose the Prince as did each of the Stepsisters; these are simple or one-way choices. Cinderella's choices of the Prince and the Fairy Godmother represent mutual, two-way preferences since they also picked her. Everyone was chosen in this situation. The "Total times chosen"

Name of subject: ___F. SMEDLEY___

Date: ___3/17 — 3/20___

Work and study habits

Turns work in on time ___YES___

Completes assignments ___NO___

Follows directions ___NO___

Exhibits interest in learning ___NO___

FIGURE 4.7 A checklist.

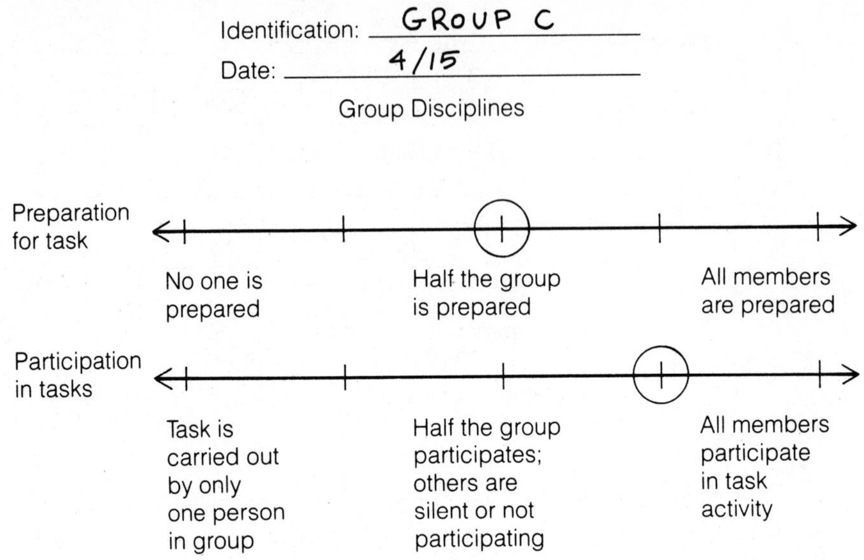

Identification: __GROUP C__
Date: _____4/15_____

Group Disciplines

Preparation
for task

No one is
prepared

Half the group
is prepared

All members
are prepared

Participation
in tasks

Task is
carried out
by only
one person
in group

Half the group
participates;
others are
silent or not
participating

All members
participate
in task
activity

FIGURE 4.8a   Rating scale with verbal descriptions.

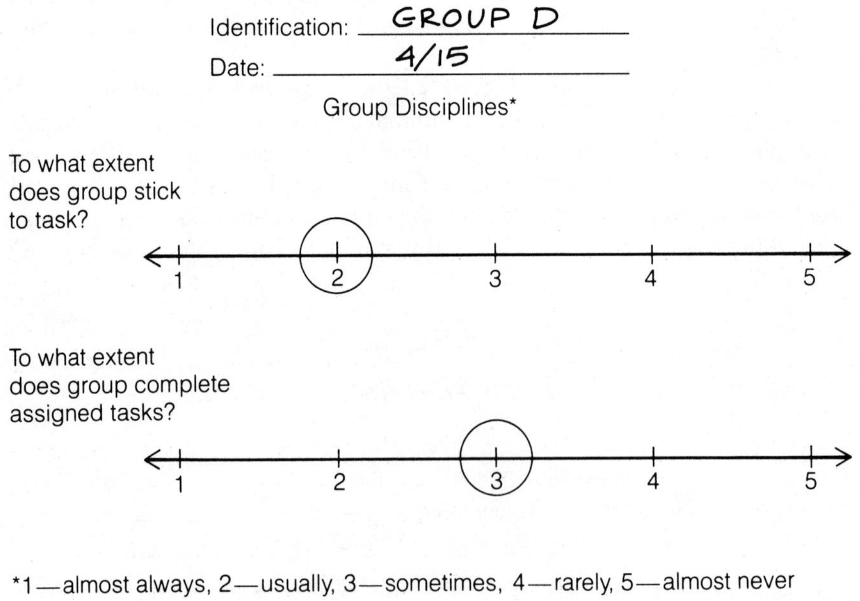

Identification: __GROUP D__
Date: _____4/15_____

Group Disciplines*

To what extent
does group stick
to task?

1   2   3   4   5

To what extent
does group complete
assigned tasks?

1   2   3   4   5

*1—almost always, 2—usually, 3—sometimes, 4—rarely, 5—almost never

FIGURE 4.8b   Rating scale with numerical values.

Question: Whom do you like?

Chooser \ Choice	Cinderella	Stepmother	Stepsister I	Stepsister II	Prince	Fairy Godmother
Cinderella					✓	✓
Stepmother			✓	✓	✓	
Stepsister I		✓		✓	✓	
Stepsister II		✓	✓		✓	
Prince	✓					
Fairy Godmother	✓					
Total times chosen	2	2	2	2	4	1

FIGURE 4.9   Matrix for sociometric choices.

section of the matrix shows the Prince as the star and the Fairy Godmother as the least popular character. In research studies, patterns resulting from choices may give the researchers information to answer questions related to topics such as prejudice, class leadership, and social acceptance.

Sociometric matrices are almost always designed by researchers who must draft the question(s) that will be posed to subjects. After the information is collected, it is entered in the matrix. Then the number and kinds of choices are analyzed in terms of the problem statement.

Interviews. As a tool for collecting research data, interviews are less common than tests or scales because the interviewer must meet with the respondents, usually one at a time. Interviews are used in studies involving attitudes, interests, or personal-social adjustment. Since the topics being explored may deal with sensitive issues, the content of the questions and the ways they are asked must elicit true and dependable information from the respondents. Researchers must develop questions that are pertinent to a particular setting. The development of the interview may take a long time because it frequently includes pretesting the questions and rewording them based on the results of trial runs.

Interviews may be either unstructured or structured, depending on the kind of questions selected. Unstructured questions are open-ended, allowing the respondent freedom in thinking about and answering them. Figure 4.10a illustrates some open-ended questions. The classification or categorization of answers to open-ended items is left up to the interviewer and may be a difficult and time-consuming task.

Structured interviews, on the other hand, use closed questions. Questions and alternative answers are read by the interviewer to the respondent, who must select the option that most nearly represents his or her answer to each question. In this way the classification of answers is decided before the data are collected. Open-ended questions can be restructured by adding alternative answers as shown in Figure 4.10b. In both kinds of interviews, a prescribed set of questions called an interview schedule is used. The interviewer is free to modify the content, wording, or sequence of the questions in an unstructured interview. However, the interviewer does not have this freedom in a structured situation.

Researchers sometimes use interviews in conjunction with other data collection instruments. Initial information from respondents can be obtained through surveys or other types of self-reports. Interviews may then be conducted in follow-up studies to collect in-depth information on a topic.

Under some circumstances, researchers write a set of questions similar to the interview schedule and mail it to subjects as a survey or questionnaire.

Which type of in-service training do you like best?

Whichever ones allow me to leave early.

How well does your supervisor appreciate your work efforts?

That depends on the kind of work involved. Sometimes a lot; other times only a little.

FIGURE 4.10a   Open-ended items.

Which of these types of in-service training do you like best?

_____ A speaker who discusses problems that are similar to mine

_____ Someone who lectures about the do's and don't's in my field

__✓__ A group discussion in which my peers and I talk about our problems and "get it off our chests"

_____ A supervisor works beside me trying to understand my strengths and weaknesses and gives helpful suggestions

How well does your supervisor appreciate your work efforts?

_____ Very much

__✓__ Much

_____ Enough

_____ Little

_____ Very little

FIGURE 4.10b   Closed questions.

There are time and cost advantages in getting information this way. However, without face-to-face contact, some respondents ignore the questions; therefore the researcher is left with incomplete data. Follow-up letters to nonrespondents sometimes help, although these requests may also be ignored. The interviewer is in a much better position to get complete data than the person who sends questionnaires. Since only those individuals who really want to send back their questionnaires will do so, the data from a questionnaire may contain more biases than data from interviews.

Checkpoint 4.1 allows you to see how well you've understood the discussion of instrumentation. Take time to do it now.

Levels of Measurement of Data

The instruments we described yield a wide variety of data. Unstructured interviews and anecdotal records can give unwieldy information that is useful only after careful sorting and classification. Other instruments, such as checklists or rating scales, produce data that are more manageable but of very different kinds. Generally, data from rating scales are more complex than those from checklists. The characteristics of these different kinds of data determine their particular level of measurement. The levels of mea-

CHECKPOINT 4.1

Identify the category of instrumentation from which you would most likely select an instrument to measure variables in these situations.

1. The program director would like to know how graduates feel about the training they received as part of a particular program of studies.
2. A teacher would like to find out which of three groups made the greatest progress in a year of social studies instruction.
3. A school psychologist plans to visit classrooms to see which reinforcement techniques teachers are using with students.
4. A counselor is interested in finding out the extent to which clients interact with their peers in structured settings.
5. A vocational education teacher plans to help students with career choices.

ANSWERS: (Your answers may be different from these.) 1. interviews (or questionnaires) 2. tests (achievement) 3. observation reports (checklists) 4. sociometric techniques 5. inventories and surveys

surement are a way to categorize data according to the quality and complexity of the information they represent. There are four levels, called *nominal, ordinal, interval,* and *ratio,* arranged in a hierarchy. Each level has specific features which data must have to be labeled according to that level.

Nominal. Data at the simplest level of measurement are called **nominal,** because they merely distinguish between individuals, with no inherent values attached to the distinctions. Examples of nominal data are answers to the background questions researchers often ask at the beginning of interviews, tests, and attitude scales. Subjects are asked to mark appropriate boxes to indicate their sex, level of schooling, range of income, and other information. These data may be used by the researcher to classify responses. Nominal data simply name characteristics.

Ordinal. At the **ordinal** level, data are more complex than at the nominal level because they not only may indicate distinctions between subjects or responses but also the relative importance of the data. Likert-type rating scales, for instance, measure the attitudes of subjects toward one concept. The marks for "strongly agree" to "strongly disagree" imply a definite ranking or preference on the part of the subject. Rating scales that use the numbers 1–5 to stand for ratings between "almost always" and "almost never" also yield ordinal data. "Almost always" is probably better (or worse) than "usually," and "usually" is better (or worse) than "sometimes." There is a qualitative difference between the rankings, but it is not necessarily uniform across the scale. For these reasons, performing arithmetic operations on ordinal data can lead to inappropriate data conclusions.

Interval. Data having all the characteristics of nominal and ordinal data, plus the added feature of equal distances between the unit value points, are called **interval** data. That is, not only are characteristics named and assigned importance, but also the distances between the marks or ranks are equal. This quality of interval data permits researchers to perform arithmetic operations on the data, such as averaging or adding a constant. Test scores, frequency counts, and total scale values from equal-appearing scales are examples of interval data. Notice that a test score of 85 is 5 points more than a score of 80 and 5 points less than a score of 90.

Ratio. When data have the characteristics of all the previously mentioned levels, plus the advantage of a zero beginning point, they are called **ratio** data. Since human characteristics are usually present in varying quantities but are rarely absent, there are few examples of ratio data in the behavioral sciences. What is the meaning of a zero on a test? Does it mean, as some have suggested, that the person knows nothing about the subject of the test? Or does it mean that what the person knows was not measurable by the test? We can think of very few examples that offer ratio data. Frequency recordings can yield ratio data, however. Suppose Fred Smedley yawns 10 times in research class; Sally Cissel, 20 times; and Kathy Cooper, not at all. Sally yawns twice as much as Fred and 20 times as often as Kathy.

Knowing levels of measurement is very important in the choice of data analysis procedures. Generally speaking, researchers like to get interval data because they can then select more powerful statistical tools for analyzing data than they can with nominal or ordinal data. Measurement of data will be discussed further in Chapter 6 when we explain data analysis procedures. Meanwhile, you may want to use Checkpoint 4.2 to see how well you understand levels of measurement.

Standards for Instrument Selection

The previous discussion of instruments illustrates the variety that is available to researchers. Whether a commercial or researcher-made instrument is used, however, there are two major standards for the selection process. One of these is the **validity** or truthfulness of the results. The other is **reliability** or the consistency and stability of the measurements.

A brief example will illustrate both these ideas. Imagine a steel ruler 50 centimeters long. If you use the ruler to measure the dimensions of a window frame, the results will be valid because the ruler is measuring length, which is what it is supposed to measure. If you try to determine the weight of the window frame using the ruler, the measurement would not be valid; that is, rulers aren't supposed to measure weight.

Moreover, you can expect to find approximately the same dimensions for the window frame if it is measured repeatedly. The consistency of these measures (dimensions) demonstrates the reliability of measurements made with the ruler. If the ruler were made of thin stretchy rubber instead of steel, you could get a different measure every time it was used, indicating unreliability. Let's carry these ideas further and apply them in the context of selecting instruments for research purposes.

Validity. Four types of validity are used in educational and psychological measurement: construct, content, face, and criterion-related validity (American Psychological Association, 1974). Each will be described briefly. For additional information, see measurement and evaluation textbooks, especially Gronlund (1981), Sax (1980), and Tuckman (1975).

Construct validity. The question of whether an instrument measures the concept it claims to measure is referred to as its construct validity. A construct is a hypothetical idea such as motivation, aggression, intelligence, or test anxiety. Words like these are sometimes used to explain what is meant by several related behaviors. For example, a coach may say that a player is "motivated" who does some of these things: is prompt for practice sessions, is suited out at all times, stays late to work on skills, and bombards the coach with requests to be a starter in an upcoming game. These behaviors are collectively described as "motivation."

To have construct validity, an instrument must measure the construct according to its definition in the psychological literature. A test anxiety instrument, for example, must measure this construct as it is defined by those who study test anxiety. One research problem mentioned in Chapter 2 was: "What will be the effects of a perceptual-motor development program on the eye-hand coordination of kindergarten children?" Eye-hand coordination is a construct that describes the generalized ability of joining hand actions with those of the eyes. Some examples are: positioning a tennis racket (or baseball bat, fielder's glove, or hand) so that it comes in contact with an oncoming ball, moving hands in rhythm to a music selection that is being read with the eyes, and moving fingers on a typewriter while the eyes are looking at the copy page. Since these behaviors are too complex for most kindergarteners, simpler ones would be selected to measure this construct in a preschool setting. Tracing the perimeter of a two-dimensional shape, catching a play-

---

CHECKPOINT 4.2

Identify the level of measurement with which each of these data are associated.

1. class standing—first in class, second, etc.
2. male-female designations
3. student identification numbers
4. marks such as excellent, very good, etc.
5. scores representing total points such as 70, 82, 95, etc.

ANSWERS: 1. ordinal 2. nominal 3. nominal 4. ordinal 5. interval

ground ball, and lacing shoes are behaviors that are appropriate for young children.

Content and face validity. Content validity concerns how well the instrument measures the objectives or content of the variable studied in the research problem. More specifically, content validity directly influences the representativeness of the results as a measure of the variable. Chapter 2 introduced this problem: "Do counterconditioning procedures improve the spelling performance of upper elementary students?" Since spelling performance is the variable being measured, the researcher should select an instrument with an adequate sampling of easy to difficult words that are appropriate for fifth-graders. Adequate sampling requires knowledge of the whole content of spelling words for fifth-graders. Using only easy words or only hard words would not give valid results of spelling ability.

Although it is of less importance than content validity, face validity also applies to the content of instruments. It has to do with how well an instrument by its surface characteristics appears to deal with the desired content. Subjects in a study may need to believe that an examination or interview is relevant for its stated purpose. Otherwise they may approach the data collection with suspicion or a lack of seriousness which could adversely affect their responses. If an instrument is supposed to measure vocational preferences, for example, subjects expect to see items containing references to work-related situations.

Content validity requires the careful analysis of an instrument to be sure that the content is both representative and suitable for the purpose of the project. Often this takes knowledge of some fairly sophisticated measurement concepts. Face validity, on the other hand, can usually be determined by a rather simple inspection of the instrument.

Both of these types of validity may be desirable in an instrument, but having one does not guarantee that the other is also present. An instrument can have face validity but lack content validity, or vice-versa. A reading test might be a good measure of college-level reading skills but lack face validity because the items are juvenile in content. An interview schedule appearing to be closely related to the research purpose may have little content validity because of the narrow range of the questions.

As the reader of a research report, you can determine the face validity of an instrument based on what the researchers say about it or from sample items included in the report. It is difficult, however, to determine the content validity of an instrument unless the researchers carefully describe how they determined that their instrument was valid as a measure of the variable of interest.

Criterion-related validity. To establish this type of validity, measures from one instrument are compared with measures on a related task. For example, students in a typewriting class can be asked to take a test that consists of typing a selection of specified length and complexity under timed conditions.

Since this behavior is important in most secretarial positions, measures from the typing class are related to a criterion behavior outside the immediate setting of the class. Results of the typing test have criterion-related validity when they can be used to predict performance in secretarial positions.

Criterion-related validity is most often a concern of association studies in which performance on one measuring device is used to predict performance on a second measurement. As a case in point, consider this question from Chapter 2: "How well does prealgebra aptitude predict success in Algebra I?" Researchers would use a prealgebra aptitude test, which is supposed to measure a person's ability to deal with algebra. Such a test would have criterion-related validity to the extent that it could be used to predict success when students actually took Algebra I.

Each example mentions both a purpose and a setting for using an instrument. This is done to make you aware that validity is always specific to a particular use (Gronlund, 1981). An instrument that is valid for one research situation might not be valid for another. Hence, researchers must keep in mind both the variable to be measured and the setting in which the measurement will take place when instruments are selected, if valid measures are to be made.

This means that researchers must know their problem inside and out, have a very clear picture of the variables under consideration, and understand how to operationalize these variables in meaningful ways. Under some circumstances, researchers must produce an instrument that can be used to measure the variable satisfactorily. In other cases, they will have to search the manuals of commercially published instruments to learn whether an instrument is valid for the particular problem in its setting.

Reliability. The consistency or dependability of measures obtained from an instrument is referred to as **reliability**. Researchers want instruments whose measures are consistent time after time. This may mean dependability from one data collection to another, from one part of the instrument to another part, or from one form of an instrument to another form.

Reliability is estimated by correlating two or more sets of measurements. To establish the reliability of an instrument, one set of scores is correlated with a second set, giving a coefficient, usually r, that ranges $+1.00$ to -1.00. (See Appendix C-2.) The closer the coefficient is to $+1.00$, the less error variance in the measurements. Hence, an instrument with $r = .80$ gives more reliable results than an instrument with $r = .50$.

As this example indicates, there will always be some mismatch between the measures that are correlated to produce the reliability coefficient. Some variation in results can be expected as a reflection of built-in weaknesses in the instrument. For example, the test may contain too few items, directions for administration or scoring may be poorly worded, or the content may be inconsistent. Although it is not possible to eliminate these errors entirely, they must be minimized to increase reliability.

The three most commonly measured qualities of reliability are stability, equivalence, and internal consistency. A measure of the *stability* of scores can be calculated with a test-retest method. A group of people is given an instrument, and after a predetermined period of time, the same instrument is administered again. The two sets of scores are then correlated to give an estimate of the stability of the scores over the time between administrations of the instruments. This estimate will be inaccurate if the subjects remember their responses from the first to the second administration. Instruments that show stability are appropriate in relatively long-term projects or in any other project in which stability over time is important.

A measure of the *equivalence* of scores can be calculated by the equivalent forms method. A group of people is given an instrument at one sitting, followed closely by a second instrument that is similar in construction, length, difficulty, and other characteristics. The two sets of scores are correlated, with the resulting coefficient indicating how well both forms are measuring the same aspects of behavior. This quality of reliability may be important in studies that test subjects before and after treatment.

Both stability and equivalence can be obtained by using the equivalent forms method and allowing more time to elapse between administrations of the test. A high correlation coefficient in this case indicates that both forms of the instrument probably measure the same content and are reliable samples of the general content of the test.

Internal consistency can be estimated by the split-half technique, or by one of the Kuder-Richardson (K-R) formulas or Cronbach's alpha. In all cases the reliability can be estimated from a single administration of the instrument. Using the split-half method, responses from half the items (usually the odd-numbered items) are correlated with responses from the other half (the even-numbered items). The resulting correlation coefficient is usually corrected by the Spearman-Brown formula to estimate the reliability of the full-length instrument. In other methods, item responses are correlated between all possible splits of the entire instrument, and the coefficient represents the average reliability of the measures obtained from all possible subdivisions of the instrument.

A high correlation coefficient from any of these methods indicates that the test has homogeneous test items, which suggests that subjects would score about the same on both halves of a test (if the split-half method is calculated) or on any given sample of the test items (if a K-R or Cronbach's alpha is used). Internal consistency is especially important when subjects may not have time to complete the instrument. This type of reliability is frequently sought for instruments used in short-term projects.

Researchers are concerned with estimating the reliability of instruments prior to using them in data collection because they want to be sure their observations are accurate. Since decisions about their research hypotheses will be based on data collected from subjects, the reliability of the observations directly influences the credibility of the results.

The particular quality and degree of reliability sought depends on the nature of the variables being measured. For example, an intelligence test, with items of increasing difficulty, is better checked for internal consistency by the split-half method than by a procedure which determines all possible splits. Test designers would not expect scores from easier items usually found at the beginning of an intelligence test to be consistent with scores from the harder items at the end of the test. The reliability coefficient from an intelligence or achievement test would have to be in the range of .80 and up to be acceptable to most researchers. On the other hand, a reliability coefficient from a measure of attitudes or personal-social adjustment may be lower and still be acceptable. Generally intellectual ability and acquired learning are more stable than variables which directly involve mood and emotion.

When reliability is sought for the direct observations made of subjects, *interrater reliability* is the concern. Sometimes data are collected from observation of subjects. In these cases, persons who observe the performances of subjects must be in agreement in order for their observations to be considered reliable. The similarities of their ratings or observations are compared with the dissimilarities in a simple formula. The result is an index number ranging from 0 to 1, and it is interpreted like any other reliability coefficient. Frick and Semmel (1978) describe a variety of ways to measure the agreements among observers, and they give guidelines for acceptable indexes.

Interrater reliability can be calculated for whatever quality of reliability the situation demands. If several raters are used, their observations need to be equivalent. When ratings are taken over a period of time, stability is important. In other situations such as those where samples of behavior are rated, internal consistency may be crucial.

READING AND ANALYZING METHOD SECTIONS: INSTRUMENTATION

Content and Form

When you read reports, you may have to search for an explanation of the instruments. Although there may be a part of the method section titled "Instrumentation" or "Test Procedures," information about these topics may be described along with other procedures without being in a special section.

The amount of information given varies from one report to another. When researchers use very familiar, commercially prepared instruments, they usually don't say much about them. On the other hand, if the instruments are not well known or if they have been developed for the study, a considerable amount of information may be included. Often in these cases, researchers show examples of the kinds of items, primarily to help readers understand how the instrument fits as a measure of the variable. Typically, there is a lengthy discussion of the development procedures, reliability tests, and other matters.

Suggestions for Reading and Analysis

Once you have found the instrumentation information in a research report, you should try to relate the variables of the problem statement to the instruments. There will not be a one-to-one correspondence because some variables are not measured—for example, treatments in experiments. However, there will be at least one variable that is measured.

Read the information about instruments very carefully and try to decide whether they are appropriate for measuring the variables, particularly for the subjects selected for the project. For example, the Stanford-Binet Intelligence Test has a good reputation as a dependable measure of intelligence. It is not as appropriate for adults as for children, however, since its norms are derived primarily from its use with children.

As we pointed out earlier, there probably won't be much information on content validity, but you may be able to make a judgment about the face validity of instruments. It may also be difficult to evaluate either construct or criterion-related validity. These types of validity *can* be checked, however, if you read either the manual for an instrument or perhaps the reviews in a standard reference. (See the Recommended References.) If your major purpose in reading research reports is to track down instruments for measuring variables that you want to investigate, spend extra time reading about the instruments in sources beyond the report itself.

Furthermore, we suggest that you search the report for information about reliability. Very often when researchers use commercial instruments, they simply indicate the reliability coefficient and method of estimation (split-half, alpha, K-R, or Spearman-Brown). When researchers develop their own instrumentation, they frequently describe the procedures used to estimate reliability. These may include evaluating the instruments in a preliminary or pilot study. In any case, researchers should communicate estimates of the reliability of their instruments.

Sometimes readers make mistakes in reading about instrumentation. A common error is believing that a commercial instrument is better than one developed by a researcher. There's an aura about standardized tests that may prevent some people from recognizing the need for researcher-made instruments. Another mistake is failing to be concerned about which instrument was used to measure a certain variable. To be more specific, administering a standardized achievement test both before and after treatments (as required in some difference studies) is probably not going to detect much difference unless there is a long time between the "before" and "after." A standardized test is just not sensitive to small changes that may occur in student learning. Finally, some readers don't look for information about unfamiliar instruments. They just accept the researcher's word that the choice was appropriate. We hope you will avoid these mistakes as you read reports.

Often the credibility of the study may hinge on the instruments. Because instrumentation is important, here are some criteria for judging these procedures in research reports.

1. *Instrumentation should be valid for collecting data on the variables in the study. Validity information should be clearly stated.* Instruments must be valid measures of the variables of the study and suitable for use with the subjects selected for the project. Formal evidence of validity is definitely preferred.

2. *Instrumentation should provide reliable data for the study. Reliability estimates should be clearly stated.* Indicators of reliability add to the credibility of instrumentation, particularly when unfamiliar commercial or researcher-made instruments are used. A reliability coefficient should be reported that reflects the type of reliability suggested by the problem—internal consistency, stability, equivalence, or interrater reliability.

SUMMARY

Choices about instrumentation are crucial to the success of a research project. Because of this, researchers must carefully select the instruments that best fit their research problems.

Seven loosely defined categories of instruments are tests, scales, inventories and surveys, observation reports, sociometric techniques, and interviews. Tests can be used to measure most variables in educational research, while other instruments are probably appropriate for measuring only a few of the variables. Sociometric techniques, for example, are best used to measure variables involving personal-social adjustment. Tests, scales, inventories and surveys, and observation reports are commercially available and are appropriate for some research settings.

Data from instruments in any of the categories fit into one of four increasingly complex measurement levels: nominal, ordinal, interval, or ratio. Ratio data are not often obtained in education because they have a zero beginning point. Researchers usually prefer to classify their data as interval, since this permits the arithmetic operations required in the more powerful statistical tests. Nominal and ordinal data may be restricted to less powerful statistical tests.

Each instrument selected should be valid and reliable for the research problem. The instrument must not only give truthful data that are consistent for answering the research question but also meet the validity requirements of the situation. An instrument that is valid and reliable in one situation may not meet these standards in other circumstances.

Instrumentation is reported in the method section of research reports, sometimes in titled subsections or mixed with other procedures. Usually researchers name a relatively familiar commercially prepared instrument or explain some of the procedures used in preparing their own instruments. Don't decide automatically that the instrument chosen was necessarily the most appropriate one for the study. To avoid this mistake, carefully check the authors' statements about validity and reliability.

Read the instrumentation subsections of "Effects of Peer Presence on Sex-Typing of Children's Play Behavior" and "Perceptions of Social Control Among Black College Students," which appear following the questions. The introductory sections of these reports are located at the end of Chapter 2. Write your answers and compare them with the feedback for exercises at the end of this chapter.

1. Identify the instruments by name or type that were used to collect data in this study. Which variables were measured by each of these instruments?
2. Describe briefly any information the researchers give regarding the validity of the instrument(s). Explain whether this information convinces you that the instrumentation is valid.
3. Describe briefly any information the researchers give regarding the reliability of the instruments. Explain whether this information convinces you that the instrumentation is reliable.
4. Based on the information given, is the instrumentation suitable for providing data to answer the research problem? Explain.

Serbin et al., *Effects of Peer Presence on Sex-Typing of Children's Play Behavior*

METHOD

Subjects

Twenty-six girls and thirty-six boys, mean age 51 months (age range 40–60 months), participated in the study. Children were students at a university child study center and attended two or three 2.5-hr preschool classes per week. Children were primarily middle class, from both blue and white collar families; approximately 20% were from lower SES backgrounds. Approximately 15% of the children were from minority (black and oriental) families. Prior to the study, the subjects had been enrolled in preschool from 1 to 11 months, with an average of 5 months previous attendance.

Procedures

All subjects participated in three conditions: solitary, same-sex peer, and opposite-sex peer. This constituted a 2 (sex) X 3 (conditions) factorial design with repeated measures on the second factor. Subjects in the solitary condition were taken into a small room containing a row of six toys. Three of the toys were male stereotypic and three female stereotypic. Male and female toys were alternated and consisted of the following: plastic soldiers, small dolls and doll furniture, miniature firetrucks, a plastic tea set, toy airplanes, and an ironing board and iron (with clothes to iron). Children in this condition were instructed as follows: "There are some toys in this room for you. You can play with any of the toys you want to. I will be working at my desk (in the adjoining room), while you are playing. In a little while, I'll come in and we'll do some drawing, then we'll go back to the classroom.'' The child was then left alone in the room for 3 min.

The procedure for the same- and opposite-sex peer conditions was identical to that for the solitary condition, except that a same- or opposite-sex peer remained in a corner of the room at a desk, drawing a picture. The order of conditions was varied, with random assignment of subjects to each of the six possible orders. In the peer present conditions, children were told that they could play with the toys while waiting their ''turn'' to crayon. Each child served as a ''peer'' while the next subject was tested and was then returned to the classroom. The three exposures to the experimental situation which each child received were spaced 3 to 5 days apart. In the peer present condition children were instructed: ''_____(name of peer) is finishing a picture at the desk. You will have a chance to draw when he/she is done. While you are waiting your turn, you can play with these toys. You can play with any of the toys you want to. I will be working at my desk (in the adjoining room) while you are playing. In a little while, I'll come in

and we'll do some drawing and then we'll go back to the classroom.'' Peers were instructed: ''Now it's your turn to draw. When you are finished, we'll go back to class. Be sure to pay attention to your drawing, and let _____(subject) play by him/herself for a little while.''

Observational System

Observations were made from behind a one-way glass mirror. An undergraduate observer (from a total pool of eight available observers) recorded the toy(s) a child was touching, every 5 sec. (i.e., 36 observations per session). Talking by either the subject or the peer was recorded. Interobserver agreement was periodically assessed on approximately 10% of the experimental trials and was computed by the formula below, on an interval by interval basis:

$$\frac{\text{Agreements on occurrence}}{\text{Agreements and disagreements on occurrence.}}$$

Interobserver agreement ranged from 95 to 100% on the specific toys and behavioral measures of talking and playing. No hypotheses were given to the observers regarding the effects of peer presence.

Babbit and Burbach, *Perceptions of Social Control Among Black College Students*

METHOD

Instrument and Analysis

The absence of a scale to measure social control within educational settings made it necessary to develop one for this research. Basic to this undertaking

is the assumption that all student partisans develop an attitudinal perspective on the authority structure of their college or university. Proceeding on this assumption, and drawing on the conceptual literature on the subject, three indexes comprised of 10, 12, and 13 items were formulated to tap perceptions of social control as they are focused on the administration, faculty, and student body respectively. Following is a representative item from each index:

Administration. In general, the administration of this school is fair in dealing with student problems.
Faculty. Most faculty at this school are ready and willing to help the individual student when they (sic) need it.
Student Peer Group. The social pressures at this school frequently force the individual to go along with things they (sic) may not want to go along with.

Without a criterion measure of social control, it was necessary to rely on the argument that the scale items have face validity. In addition, an item-to-total analysis revealed that all items were significantly correlated ($p < .01$) with the underlying criterion of the scale thus providing evidence for the scales' construct validity. When corrected by the Spearman-Brown prophecy formula, the respective split-half reliability coefficients for the peer, faculty, and administration social control indexes were .83, .79 and .75.

The response set consists of a Likert-type continuum upon which the respondent is asked to indicate his degree of agreement or disagreement with each statement. Each item is scored on a 1 to 4 basis, with 1 being assigned to the response indicative of the most positive attitude toward the authority structure and 4 to the most negative. The total score for each individual is obtained by summing across all items in a particular index.

Our analysis is aimed at determining whether there are differences in levels of social control among black students in the three educational settings selected for examination. First, scores were obtained for the total sample on each index, and a corresponding mean and standard deviation were computed for each subsample representative of the urban center, college, and university settings. The *t*-test was then used to compare the group means.

Subjects and Data

The three settings were all located in a single metropolitan area in the northwestern region of the state of New York. The university was a large (approximately 23,000), urban, predominantly white institution with an excellent academic reputation. The college was also urban, largely white, considerably smaller (approximately 8,000), and somewhat less academically prestigious than the university. Although both institutions can be regarded as urban, it should be noted that both are located on the periphery of the city, unlike the urban center which is situated in the core area itself.

The fact that it was a two-year institution distinguished the urban center from the college and university. A recent innovation of the state university system, the urban center began operation in November, 1965, with an enrollment of 48 students. Its rolls expanded to 671 students by the fall of 1967, to 737 by 1970, and presently has an enrollment of approximately 850. The center offers college-level courses in language arts, science, mathematics, English, and the social sciences. In addition, it provides a variety of remedial courses together with a broadly based vocational education program. In short, it is the purpose of the urban center to prepare students for either senior level colleges and universities or the world of work.

Sixty black subjects were randomly selected from the freshman and sophomore classes of each institution, thus constituting a total sample of 180. All subjects were from the same metropolitan area, were of lower or lower-middle socioeconomic status, and had similar educational backgrounds. In an effort to maximize the return rate, black personnel from the respective institutions were enlisted and paid to personally contact and administer the research instruments to each subject while guaranteeing them their anonymity. Data were collected in the spring of the year after the freshmen had had nearly one year and the sophomores nearly two years of contact with their respective institutions. The number of instruments completed by subjects from the urban center, college, and university was 49, 55, and 56, respectively.

FEEDBACK FOR EXERCISES

This section is intended to let you know how well you answered the questions in the exercises. Although the wording of your answers will differ, the meaning should be similar to the following. Write answers to the exercises for one or more of the reports in Appendix A for additional practice.

"Effects of Peer Presence on Sex-Typing of Children's Play Behavior"

1. Data were collected using a researcher-designed observation report, probably a frequency recording. This observational system was used to measure the choices of toys according to the sex stereotypes associated with them.
2. The researchers make no specific comment about the validity of their instruments. However, their detailed explanation makes clear that the observational system does measure what it's supposed to measure, which is children's play behavior.
3. The reliability of the instrumentation is indicated by the information on interobserver agreement. Apparently the observers were trained prior to the project. The researchers point out that their agreement ranged from 95% to 100% on the specific toys and behavioral measures of talking and playing during experimental trials. This information seems to indicate that the measurements made during the project were reliable.
4. The instrumentation seems highly suitable for collecting data for this research problem. The observational system satisfies the criteria for validity and reliability in this particular situation.

"Perceptions of Social Control Among Black College Students"

1. The researchers designed a Likert-type scale to measure the perceptions of social control by the administration, faculty, and student body.
2. The researchers claim that their instrument has both face and construct validity. We agree that the instrument probably does have

face validity, but additional information is needed to make a judgment about construct validity.

3. Split-half reliability coefficients ranging from .75 to .83 are reported for the measures of social control. These r values are clearly in an acceptable range for reliability estimates.

4. The instrumentation seems suitable for collecting data in this research project. A closer tie between the meaning of "social control" as defined psychologically and items in the scales (indexes) would clarify whether the instrument has construct validity.

RECOMMENDED REFERENCES

Buros, O. K. (Ed.). *Mental measurements yearbooks* (Vols. 1–8). Highland Parks, N.J.: Gryphon Press, 1938–78. New editions of this work are published every few years. They contain information about tests published throughout the English-speaking world; test reviews; and bibliographies on the construction, use, and validity of specific tests.

Buros, O. K. (Ed.). *Personality tests and reviews*. Highland Parks, N.J.: Gryphon Press, 1970. Similar in format to the *Mental Measurements Yearbooks,* this volume concentrates on nonprojective and projective tests. A total of 370 tests currently in print are indexed along with 134 tests now out of print.

Buros, O. K. (Ed.). *Tests in print II*. Highland Parks, N.J.: Gryphon Press, 1974. This reference contains a comprehensive bibliography of tests; a classified index to the contents of *Mental Measurements Yearbooks*; a comprehensive bibliography through 1971 on the construction, use, and validity of specific tests; and a classified scanning index.

Cartwright, C. A., & Cartwright, G. P. *Developing observational skills*. New York: McGraw-Hill, 1974. This book offers extremely practical suggestions on making and using observation reports.

Edwards, A. L. *Techniques of attitude scale construction*. New York: Appleton-Century-Crofts, 1957. As the title implies, this book is intended to assist in the preparation of attitude scales. The guidelines, however, can also be applied in judging the adequacy of scales used in data collection.

Fishbein, M. (Ed.). *Readings in attitude theory and measurement*. New York: Wiley, 1967. Part II consists of 23 readings on attitude measurement, including standardized, multidimensional, and alternative measurement techniques, together with readings on problems and prospects in attitude achievement. Information should be helpful as background for almost any type of attitude measure.

Gorden, R. L. *Interviewing: Strategy, techniques, and tactics* (rev. ed.). Homewood, Ill.: Dorsey Press, 1975. This book offers both theoretical and practical information on interviewing. Since its fog index is low, it can be read easily by anyone who wants more information on interviewing.

Gronlund, N. E. *Sociometry in the classroom*. New York: Harper, 1959. This book is a very readable guide to the use and interpretation of sociometric methodology in educational settings. It provides detailed "how-to" information as well as discussions of the validity and reliability of those techniques.

Gronlund, N. E. *Measurement and evaluation in teaching* (4th ed.). New York: Macmillan, 1981. This textbook aids anyone seeking help on constructing tests and other measurement devices or evaluating standardized tests.

Interviewer's manual, Survey Research Center. Ann Arbor: Institute for Social Research, University of Michigan, 1969. This guide to interviewing is practical and helpful for all aspects of preparation and actual interview procedures.

Lanyon, R. I., & Goodstein, L. D. *Readings in personality assessment.* New York: Wiley, 1971. The readings furnish important background information on different approaches to personality measurement procedures. The fog index is high in certain parts.

Osgood, C.; Suci, J.; & Tannebaum, P. *The measurement of meaning.* Urbana: University of Illinois Press, 1975. For additional information on the semantic differential scale, this book offers comprehensive information.

Rokeach, M. *The open and closed mind.* New York: Basic Books, 1960. Background information and results of experiments with dogmatism scales are outlined. The California F Scale, which has been used in research studies, is reproduced in Appendix B of this book.

Sax, G. *Principles of educational and psychological measurement and evaluation* (2nd. ed.). Belmont, Calif.: Wadsworth, 1980. The author gives detailed information on the construction and selection of a wide range of instruments. The humor is delightful!

Tuckman, B. W. *Measuring educational outcomes: Fundamentals of testing.* New York: Harcourt Brace Jovanovich, 1975. Four parts are included in this text on measurement: planning a test, constructing a test, evaluating a test, and using published tests. A particular strength is the quantity of illustrations of the main ideas.

5

Reading
Method Sections:
Procedures

Three components of research design are described in this chapter: treatment administration, data collection, and data analysis procedures. Treatment administration is important in experiments, and data are collected in all studies. Although data analysis is part of research design, it is only introduced in this chapter in preparation for a more detailed discussion in Chapter 6.

Research design is reconsidered in this chapter. The procedures you read about in Chapters 2 through 4 should begin to fit together when you read about designs. You will learn the meaning of validity of designs, as well as detailed information about designs for both association and difference studies. At that point and with a few suggestions, you are asked to examine the final parts of the procedures sections of some reports.

Chapter objective.   After completing this chapter, you should be able to: *assess the appropriateness of treatment administration procedures, data collection procedures,* and *overall design procedures* in selected research reports.

BACKGROUND FOR READING METHOD SECTIONS: PROCEDURES

Treatment Administration

In experimental studies, researchers must decide how treatment will be handled. **Treatment** includes all the operations, exclusive of data collection, that subjects will undergo. Operations are relatively simple in studies with only one group of subjects because the treatment is given to all participants. In multigroup studies, however, the treatment procedures are more complicated since researchers may vary either the amount or the duration of treatment among groups of subjects. They may also decide whether every group gets a treatment.

Decisions about treatment are extremely important in research design, since they determine the systematic variance that the researchers introduce. Treatment is what the researchers hope will produce the hypothesized results and indicate a cause-and-effect relationship. Therefore, researchers try to plan treatment administration procedures carefully.

Frequently in educational studies, one method of instruction is compared with other methods to see which is most effective in terms of student achievement, attitudes, or some combination of dependent variables. On many occasions the problem compares a new approach with the traditional one, which is often dubbed the "control." The new approach may be described in detail, while the traditional approach is given a one-line description or, worse yet, a description such as "the control group had no experimental treatment introduced." Researchers need to give very clear definitions of treatment and no treatment, or levels of treatment.

Deciding who will administer treatment is sometimes a problem, especially when a large number of personnel are needed. Using treatment administrators with dissimilar qualifications can create differences in results. For instance, using student teachers as well as regularly certified teachers might pose some doubts about whether the treatment or the people giving the treatment brought about changes in dependent variables. To avoid difficulties, researchers must try to minimize the differences between treatment administrators as much as possible.

Data Collection

Data collection refers to all the operations related to getting information from subjects for the answer to a research problem. It is the implementation of the researchers' selection of instrumentation procedures.

Data collection procedures are important in research design, for they can introduce error variance if they are carried out in a haphazard fashion. Even the most careful selection of instruments may be rendered useless if the persons who administer them fail to follow directions, omit certain sections, or otherwise foul up data collection. Well-planned and executed data collection procedures are necessary to ensure that the results from the instruments selected for the study are reliable.

Collecting data is a major task in all studies but particularly in association studies. Frequently there are several measurements on each subject. Unless all measures are taken in one sitting, it may be hard to get data from every subject. In difference studies researchers sometimes collect pretest data before beginning treatment. They always collect data at the end of treatments in difference studies.

In both kinds of studies, collection methods should fit with sampling and instrumentation procedures. Researchers must choose physical settings, time schedules, and personnel that are appropriate for the instruments selected and the number of subjects involved.

All groups should take the instruments as close to the same time as possible. Giving a test earlier or later to one of the groups in a study can affect the reliability of the results. If possible, the same person should collect all data. If more than one person is involved, each should have the same training for the role and have a standard set of instructions. These actions help ensure against unwanted variance.

Data Analysis—An Introduction

Data analysis refers to all the operations done on data collected from subjects. Raw data are always organized and summarized. Usually data analysis also involves selecting, using, and interpreting statistical tests. We said "usually" because there is another way of analyzing data that is not reported very often. This alternative is replication of the study to see whether there is support for the research hypothesis.

The ways of organizing and summarizing data depend on the level of measurement of the data. (See Appendix C-1.) The summarized data are analyzed to see if they provide answers to the research questions of the study.

To make inferences from the subjects to any larger group requires statistical testing. The choices of these tests depend on the kind of study, whether association or difference, and the method of selecting subjects.

When subjects for the study are drawn from a population using one of the scientific methods, researchers are on much safer ground in making inferences about the results of statistical tests than they are with a convenience sample. Most statistical tests assume that subjects are randomly drawn from a population or randomly assigned to groups within a total sample. Data analysis procedures will be described in greater detail in Chapter 6.

BACKGROUND: RESEARCH DESIGN REVISITED

Designs for Association Studies

Two types of designs will be discussed in this section, for correlation and prediction studies. Both designs are very simple because there are no treatments to administer, although all other components of research design must be planned.

Correlation studies.   Association studies intended to test hypotheses about relationships between variables are called **correlation studies.** Their results indicate the magnitude and direction of the relationship. Correlation studies are particularly useful in the exploratory phases of problems. Rosenshine and Furst (1973), for example, explain how correlational studies were used to determine which kinds of classroom interaction behaviors were worth pursuing further in experimental studies.

In other instances there may be a genuine need to assess the strength or direction of a relationship among variables. Is there a relationship between a teacher's preferred teaching style and his or her personality characteristics? Is there a relationship between a student's learning style and the amount of time spent on task activities? These and other questions need answers about the possible relationship between the variables before additional research can be done.

Variance is controlled in correlation studies only through careful attention to sampling, data collection procedures, and interpretation of the results. Researchers must select representative samples, locate valid and reliable instruments, and standardize data collection procedures. Since there are no treatments involved, any variance in the study cannot be traced to the manipulation of a variable.

The design itself consists of the selection of subjects and instruments followed by the collection of data on two or more variables that are thought to be related. Data are usually collected for the different variables in relatively close time proximity. Simple correlation designs require a minimum of two variables, while more complex designs explore relationships among several variables.

Prediction studies.   When association studies take advantage of established relationships between variables, they are called **prediction studies**. In these studies, one or more variables, called predictors, are used to make predictions about another variable, known as the criterion. For example, people who are at least moderately successful in high school can be expected to be successful in other endeavors as well. Studies have shown that the best predictor of success in college is the degree of success in high school (Baird, 1970).

One of the differences between designs for correlation and prediction studies is the amount of time that elapses between data collection points. As an example, assume researchers are attempting to predict success or non-success in a given area of graduate study based on scores from the Graduate Record Examination. They must collect data from the GRE and then wait until students have attempted to go through those graduate programs before collecting the second set of data. This period of time may be a year or several years. Published prediction studies often involve several predictor variables and one or two criterion variables. Researchers may attempt to show how GRE results, undergraduate grade point average, and a general intelligence test score (the predictor variables) combine to predict success in graduate school (the criterion variable). In effect, the combination of predictors is usually better than any single one of the variables.

Like correlation studies, prediction designs are simple. There are data collection points for the predictor variables, separated by a time interval for data collection on the criterion variable(s). Of course, if measures of the predictor and criterion variables are available at the outset of the study, little or no time lapse occurs between data collection on each variable. See Appendix C-2 if you need more information about the way correlation and prediction are related.

Designs for Difference Studies

Five designs will be discussed in this section: (1) true experiments, (2) quasi-experiments, (3) preexperiments, (4) *ex post facto* designs, and (5) factorial designs. Each of these designs has unique features that make it particularly useful for certain research problems. Variations of some designs are also discussed briefly. One way of classifying research designs is by the kind of methodology used.

Designs that use experimental methodology
- true experiments
- quasi-experiments
- preexperiments

- factorial true experiments
- factorial quasi-experiments

Designs that use descriptive methodology
- ex post facto studies
- factorial ex post facto studies

True, quasi-, and preexperimental designs all require experimental methodology, whereas an ex post facto design uses descriptive methods. Factorial designs can use either of these methods.

There is a hierarchy of "goodness" associated with these designs based on how well they control variance. Results from designs with better control of variance can be accepted with greater confidence since these designs rule out many alternative explanations of the outcomes. Experimental studies allow researchers to look for relationships between possible causes and effects by manipulating a variable that is believed to be the cause. Furthermore, most experiments use comparison groups to show what happens when subjects do not receive treatment or receive different levels of treatment.

Chapter 3 described the advantages of using random sampling methods in selecting subjects for the experiment. We also noted that further randomizing procedures should be used whenever possible in assigning subjects and treatments to groups. The overriding concern in all these procedures is to control error variance, which is more likely to be present if less scientific methods are used. Table 5.1 outlines this information about variance in difference studies.

In the discussion that follows we will describe designs for difference studies in their approximate order for controlling variance, from strongest to weakest. True experiments are described first, followed by quasi- and preexperiments. Then there is discussion of ex post facto designs, which are not experiments at all. Finally, we describe factorial designs, which can control variance well or poorly depending on their construction.

True experimental designs. The classic approach to research is seen in **true experimental designs,** which test the effect of one variable manipulated by the researcher on one (or more) dependent variable(s). Suppose a group of swimming coaches want to know whether to adopt a new technique as a standard procedure for speed swimmers. They may form two groups of swimmers; one is instructed by the new technique, while the second continues with traditional instruction. Swimmers in both groups are then timed on a series of laps. The effectiveness of the new technique is judged by comparing the average speed of the treatment group with the average speed of the control group. In this way any differences in speed between the two groups may possibly be attributed to the treatment.

What makes this a true experiment? A manipulated variable, the random assignment of subjects and treatments, and the use of comparison groups are three benchmarks of true experiments. In this example the coaches could put the names of all the subjects in a hat and then draw names to form the groups. This would give each swimmer an equal chance of being selected for the new treatment. Furthermore, they should then flip a coin to determine which group will receive the treatment. Unless the coaches take some precautions to assign subjects and treatments randomly, they may introduce bias into the experiment. Also, it's highly desirable that they use a random technique to select the subjects from the population of swimmers. This, however, is not a requirement for a true experimental design. It simply offers one more opportunity to eliminate bias.

There are several true experimental designs. At the option of the researchers, subjects may or may not take a pretest. Since randomization procedures tend to make the groups similar, a pretest is not absolutely necessary. However, if the researchers are interested in the changes subjects make during the course of the experiment, a pretest is required. See Figure 5.1 for information about a true experiment, posttest-only design.

A second variation of the classic true experimental design involves the use of four groups rather than two. It is called the Solomon four-group design, and involves two groups that receive experimental treatment and two control groups (Solomon, 1949). In each of these pairs, one group takes a pretest and the other group does not. Although this design combines the advantages of the pretest-posttest and the posttest-only designs, it may be hard to locate the relatively large numbers of subjects needed for four groups. Figure 5.2 shows how this design works.

Table 5.1
VARIANCE IN DIFFERENCE STUDIES

Design	Degree of control	Method of control			
		Assignment of subjects to groups	Assignment of treatment to groups	Selection of subjects from population	Number of groups of subjects
True experimental	High	Random	Random	Random (preferred) or nonrandom	At least two
Quasi-experimental	Moderate	Nonrandom	Random	Nonrandom	Usually two
Pre-experimental	Very low	Not applicable	Not applicable	Usually nonrandom	Usually one, sometimes two
Ex post facto	Low	Not applicable	Not applicable	Usually nonrandom	At least two
Factorial True	High	Random	Random	Random (preferred) or nonrandom	At least four
Quasi	Moderate	Nonrandom	Random	Nonrandom	At least four
Ex post facto	Low	Not applicable	Not applicable	Usually nonrandom	At least four

Quasi-experimental designs. Sometimes all the conditions for an experiment are not possible. This is especially true when an experimenter conducts research in schools. Frequently individual students cannot be taken at random from classes to participate, although intact classes can be used. **Quasi-experiments** should be selected in these cases. In this kind of design, the independent variable can be manipulated, comparison groups are available, and treatment can be assigned randomly. Although the assignment of subjects to groups is not random, the intact groups should be as nearly alike as possible; that is, comparing an "advanced" group of subjects with a "beginning" group is not good research practice. Other procedures in this design are carried out as if it were a true experiment.

Variations of quasi-experiments are counterbalanced, time series, and repeated measures designs. In **counterbalanced designs** there are usually two groups, a manipulated variable with two values (may be treatment/no treatment, or treatment A/treatment B), and the random assignment of treatment to groups. In this design each group gets both treatments but in the opposite sequence. If the first group gets treatment A and then treatment B, the second group gets treatment B and then treatment A. This design minimizes the effect of carry-over or interference from one treatment to the other. Figure 5.3 diagrams the operations of a simple counterbalanced design.

A **time series design** involves making several measurements of the dependent variable before introducing the treatment, and then making several more measurements. Researchers who use this design expect that the pattern of the measurements may be interrupted by the introduction of the treatment. Measurements prior to treatment identify the consistency of subject performance. When the treatment is given, its effect is determined by seeing whether the subjects alter their previous pattern of performance or remain about the same. Occasionally this design is used to study single subjects

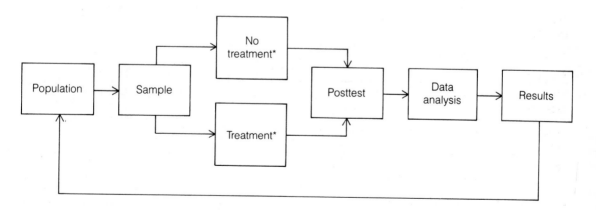

*Random assignment to groups

FIGURE 5.1 True experiment, posttest-only design.

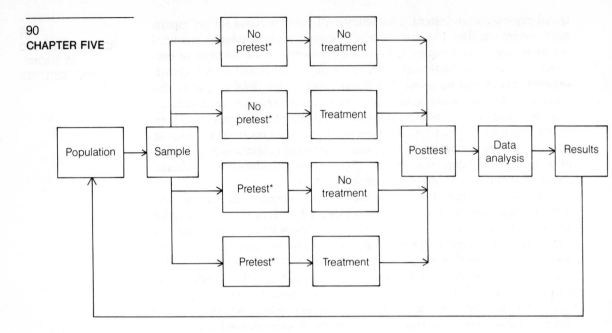

*Random assignment to groups

FIGURE 5.2   True experiment, Solomon four-group design.

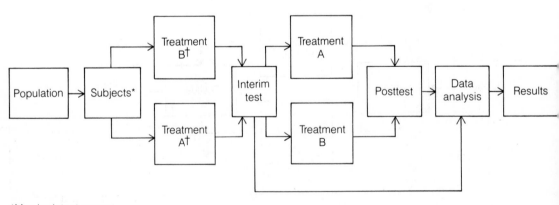

*May be intact groups

†Random assignment

FIGURE 5.3   Quasi-experiment, counterbalanced design.

rather than groups; however, reports of such research are rare. This design may or may not have a control group; the design is stronger when a control group is used, however. Figure 5.4 shows how a time series design works.

In a **repeated measures design,** subjects serve as their own controls. This means they are exposed to both treatment and no treatment, with measures taken on the dependent variable under both conditions. Sometimes the subjects may go through more than one cycle of treatment and no treatment during the course of the experiment. Comparisons are made between data collected following the treatment and no treatment conditions. This design is better than a design with no control group at all. See Figure 5.5 for information about repeated measures designs.

Quasi-experiments do not control variance as well as true experiments. Their control comes from manipulation of the independent variable, the use of comparison groups, and random assignment of treatment groups. If one or more of these conditions is missing, researchers have a design with even less control.

Preexperimental designs. As the name indicates, a **preexperimental design** is not really an experiment. Some references do not consider this design worthy of discussion except to say how poor it is (Kerlinger, 1973; Campbell & Stanley, 1963). There is almost no control of variance; hence, the results are extremely questionable. Manipulation of the independent variable may be the only characteristic of an experiment in this design.

In a preexperiment either one or two groups of subjects are used. They may or may not be pretested before having the treatment applied to one group. Following the posttest an interpretation of the scores is made. Since there is frequently no control group and sometimes no pretest, researchers cannot be sure whether gains in test scores are due to the treatment or to other things in the study. This design has the most serious weaknesses of any we have described.

Ex post facto designs. These designs are used in studies that test the effect of one variable selected by researchers on one or more dependent variables.

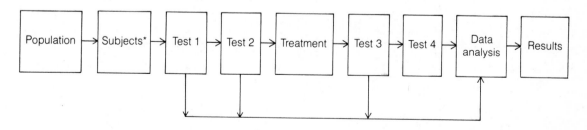

*May be intact groups

FIGURE 5.4 Quasi-experiment, a time series design, no control group.

The word *selected* is important in the previous sentence because it signifies the basic difference between true experiments and *ex post facto* designs. In **ex post facto studies,** researchers locate people who have already experienced the independent variable and then study its possible effects in terms of the dependent variable(s). Note the past tense: people who *have already experienced* the variable. The meaning of *ex post facto* is *after the fact.*

This design is chosen, for example, when researchers want to know about the effects of aggressive behavior on task performance. Aggression is a variable that cannot easily be manipulated within ethical limits. Researchers may create a highly controversial situation if one group of people is trained to be aggressive while a control group does not receive this treatment. The ethics of experimentation (about which we will say more in Chapter 8) usually do not permit this kind of research activity. The best that researchers may be able to do is measure a sample of people who differ in terms of aggressive behavior. This sample is subdivided into two or more groups according to the degrees of aggressiveness shown. Next the investigators measure subjects' task performance and note whether there are differences between the groups on this variable that might possibly be related to aggression. See Figure 5.6 for an example of an *ex post facto* design.

Variance cannot be as well controlled in *ex post facto* studies as it is in experimental studies. Since there is no manipulated variable, there can be no random assignment of subjects and treatments to groups. Using a control group is the only way to control variance in this design. Because of these characteristics, *ex post facto* designs are used when explanation or prediction is the goal.

Factorial designs.   Investigation of more than one independent variable at a time is possible in **factorial designs.** They are better than two true experiments because researchers can see whether there is interaction between the independent variables, called "factors," in terms of the dependent variable. **Interaction** occurs when one independent variable in combination with another independent variable causes a different effect than the simple total of their separate effects.

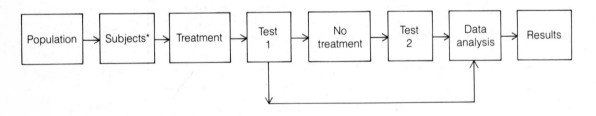

*May be intact group

FIGURE 5.5   Quasi-experiment, repeated measures design.

Suppose the swimming coaches mentioned in the true experiment wish to study not only the new technique but also the length of time of swimming instruction. Perhaps longer or shorter periods of instruction would help the speed of swimmers. A factorial design would allow them to study both these variables simultaneously. The simplest factorial design requires four groups of subjects, one group for each combination of factors. Group A receives the new technique in a long instructional period; group B, the new technique in a short period; group C, the traditional technique in a long period; and group D, the traditional technique in a short period. See Figure 5.7 for a graphic display of these groups.

A factorial design permits researchers to answer these questions:

1. Does the kind of instruction interact with the length of instruction to influence the speed of swimmers? Compare A with B with C with D.
2. Does the kind of instruction influence the speed of swimmers? Compare A and B with C and D.
3. Does the length of the instructional period influence the speed of swimmers? Compare A and C with B and D.

Although questions 2 and 3 could be answered if the researchers conducted true experiments, question 1 can be answered only with a factorial design.

In carrying out this design, the coaches would select subjects for four groups. Then each group would be randomly assigned to a kind of treatment, new or traditional, and an instructional period, long or short. This example uses a *true factorial design* with two independent and manipulatable variables, comparison groups, and the random assignment of subjects and treatments to groups.

In some settings researchers may not be able to design the project in quite this fashion. Sometimes the second independent variable is not manipulatable, meaning that subjects cannot be assigned at random to groups. In this case a *quasi-factorial design* is used. For example, suppose the second in-

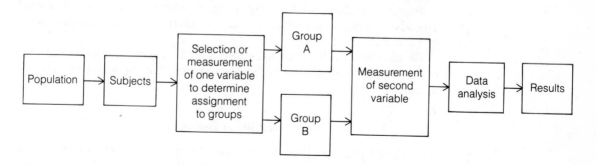

FIGURE 5.6 *Ex post facto* design.

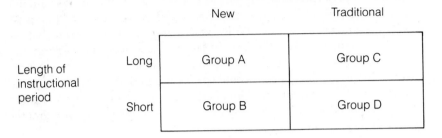

FIGURE 5.7   Groups of subjects in a simple factorial design.

dependent variable is IQ, sex, age, or some other selected variable. Under these circumstances the random assignment of subjects is extremely difficult because one of the IQ groups, sex groups, or other groups may not be representative of the population. Researchers may divide the subjects by IQ (or sex, age, etc.) and then randomly assign them to groups. Researchers usually use as many randomizing procedures as possible to improve their confidence in the results.

When neither of the independent variables can be manipulated, a *factorial ex post facto design* may be selected. It's conceivable, for example, that researchers could want to know whether aggressive behavior interacts with age or sex on task performance. A factorial design permits the study of two or more of these variables simultaneously. After both factors have been selected rather than manipulated, the factorial *ex post facto* works just like any other factorial design.

Factorial designs can be more complex than the 2 by 2 design described. If the swimming coaches have both males and females, for instance, they may want to know whether the sex of the subjects interacts with the new technique and the length of instruction. The design becomes 2 by 2 by 2 (2 kinds of instruction, 2 lengths of instructional periods, 2 sexes), requiring eight groups of subjects. The careful use of factorial designs offers one of the better opportunities for answering complex issues in educational research. The advantages and disadvantages of the difference designs are displayed in Table 5.2.

Checkpoint 5.1 is intended to help you recall some of the primary features of designs for association and difference studies. Take time to work through it now.

Validity of Designs

At this point you have probably concluded that a lot of hard work goes into planning a research project. Conceptualizing the problem and planning the methodology take a great deal of time and energy. Obviously, then, research-

Table 5.2
COMPARISONS BETWEEN DESIGNS FOR DIFFERENCE STUDIES

Design	Advantages	Disadvantages
True experimental (variations: posttest only, Solomon four-group)	Control is goal; can confirm cause-and-effect relationships	Only one independent variable explored at a time; may be difficult to assign subjects to groups
Quasi-experimental (variations: counterbalanced, time series, repeated measures)	Control is goal; may be relatively easy to locate intact groups of subjects	Because subjects are not assigned randomly to groups, comparisons may be invalid
Preexperimental	Very easy to locate one group of subjects; even two groups can usually be managed	Almost no variance is controlled
Ex post facto	Explanation or prediction is goal; best way to study some variables that are not manipulated	Cause-and-effect relationships cannot be confirmed
Factorial	Two or more independent variables can be investigated simultaneously	Requires many subjects

ers want to be as sure as possible that the results from a project give true answers to the research problem. As you look at research results, ask the same question that every researcher must ask: *Are the results valid?* Don't be misled into thinking this is easily answered. There are no surefire answers. Results are always more or less valid rather than completely valid or invalid. Part of the reason for this indefinite answer is the wide-ranging concerns that make up the concept of validity. Validity in research designs is truthfulness in the same sense that we spoke of validity in instrumentation. However, many aspects of the entire research project either contribute to the overall validity or threaten it by weakening the validity in some way.

Campbell and Stanley (1963) wrote a classic work on validity describing two general kinds: *external* and *internal*. Other researchers (Bracht & Glass, 1968; Jurs & Glass, 1971; Cook & Campbell, 1979) have added information on the validity of designs. In the sections that follow, we will give simple meanings for these two kinds of validity so you will understand the reasons for the major differences between designs.

External validity.   When researchers want to know whether their results are applicable to persons who did not actually participate in the study, they are concerned with the **external validity** of the results. The central focus of

CHECKPOINT 5.1

Identify the kind of study (association or difference) and the design (correlation, *ex post facto*, true experiment, etc.)

1. The director of speech therapy in a large school system is faced with a shortage of therapists. In this system, students usually have individual therapy sessions, but the number of clients (students) has risen sharply. In an effort to handle all the students who need therapy, a research project is begun to see whether small-group therapy is as effective as individual therapy, and if the ages of the subjects have an effect on their progress in therapy. Since there are 600 students who need therapy, the director decides to randomly select a sample of 150. These subjects are separated into two groups by their median age, with those above the median designated as older students and those below the median as younger students. Half the subjects in each of these two groups are randomly assigned to receive group therapy, while the remaining half have individual therapy.

2. Members of the district association of business teachers are concerned about the declining abilities of high school students to take and transcribe shorthand accurately. They have a hunch that listening abilities are related to performance in this area of business education. They agree to give a standardized test of listening ability to all students enrolled in their classes as well as a shorthand test. They plan to check out their hunch using the collected data.

3. Students enroll in Introduction to Psychology at a state university by computer, which results in a random assignment to class sections. Instructors in the psychology department want to find out whether videotaped lectures are as effective in terms of student achievement as live lectures. Half the classes are randomly assigned to watch videotaped lectures, while the remaining half attend live lectures. At the end of the semester, achievement is registered on a comprehensive final exam.

ANSWERS: 1. difference; factorial quasi-experiment 2. association; correlation 3. difference; true experiment

external validity is the generalizability of the results from the sample to the population that the sample is supposed to represent. The results of the study are always true for the subjects or actual participants in the study. However, inferences about the results for other groups similar to the subjects may or may not be true, depending on sampling procedures. Chapter 3 indicated that researchers can properly generalize findings to a population only when the subjects have been randomly selected from that population. This aspect of external validity is important for both association and difference studies.

Four factors mentioned by Campbell and Stanley (1963) are the following:

1. *Reactive or interactive effects of testing and treatment.* When subjects are given pretests, they may become aware of ideas,

thoughts, and considerations related to the treatment. This new sensitivity may prevent them from being representative of the population from which they were selected. Hence, generalizing the results of the experiment to the population from which the sample was drawn may not be advisable.

2. *Interactive effects of selection biases and treatment.* Characteristics of the subjects may make them more or less susceptible to the treatment. To the extent that selection biases operate, they may make the sample sufficiently different from the population that generalizing to the population is difficult.

3. *Reactive effects of experimental procedures.* In some research situations the physical and emotional atmosphere is changed as a result of the treatment. Conceivably changes in the atmosphere may affect the subjects' performance on the variables studied. When this is true, the results are probably not applicable to members of the population who did not participate in the experiment.

4. *Multiple-treatment interference.* When more than one treatment is used with a group of subjects, the effects of previous treatments may contaminate the results. Findings would be generalizable only to other groups that had similar treatments in the same sequence.

Factors that affect external validity are largely uncontrolled in most experimental designs. Campbell and Stanley (1963) point out that the interaction of testing and treatment is uncontrolled in true pre/posttest, quasi-experimental, and one-group pre/posttest preexperimental designs, because in each of these designs a pretest is given. In the true experiment, posttest-only subjects are not pretested.

None of the designs controls for the interaction of selection of subjects with treatment or for reactive arrangements. Both these factors represent possible sources of concern when results are generalized.

Internal validity. The central question of **internal validity** is whether the independent variable is responsible for changes in the dependent variable. Researchers must be sure that changes in the dependent variable did not happen because of other variables that were not controlled in the experiment. For a research design to be internally valid, it must control factors that might account for changes in the dependent variable. This control enables researchers to assume that the independent variable has caused any observed differences. Since internal validity is a concern only in cause-and-effect relationships, it is confined to experimental studies.

Many factors can affect internal validity. These may or may not be under the researchers' control. According to Campbell and Stanley (1963), the following factors may threaten the internal validity of experimental designs:

1. *Contemporary history.* On some occasions the subjects in a research project may have experiences outside the research setting that are responsible for changes in the dependent variable.

2. *Maturation processes.* Biological or psychological changes in the subjects during the time span of the experiment may account for changes in the dependent variable.

3. *Pretesting procedures.* Subjects who take a pretest in an experiment may learn things from the testing experience that will improve their posttest measures on the dependent variable.

4. *Measuring instruments.* Deviations in the procedures for collecting data can account for changes in the dependent variable.

5. *Statistical regression.* If subjects on the extreme ends of sampling distributions are used in experiments, their second set of scores may be closer to the mean due to regresison effects rather than the independent varable.

6. *Differential selection of subjects.* Subjects in comparison groups may be different from each other in terms of the dependent variable at the onset of the experiment. When this is true, changes registered at the conclusion of the experiment may not be attributable to the independent variable.

7. *Experimental mortality.* If subjects drop out of the experiment before it is completed, comparisons of group results might unduly favor one group over others. Changes in the dependent variable in these circumstances cannot be so directly attributed to the treatment or lack of it.

8. *Interaction of selection with maturation, history, and other factors.* Factors that are not accounted for in the experiment can affect the dependent variable, even when the comparison groups seem to be alike at the beginning of an experiment. Some designs require several groups. If intact groups are used (as in quasi-experiments), there could be biases operating within the experiment that could bring about changes in the dependent variable. These changes would not be the result of the independent variable.

These factors are largely controlled in true and quasi-experiments (Campbell and Stanley, 1963). Since randomization procedures are used in assigning subjects and treatments to groups, some of these threats are less menacing. whatever biases could creep into the experiment are probably canceled by these procedures. A couple of exceptions should be pointed out in the case of quasi-experiments. Campbell and Stanley note that statistical regression could be a threat in quasi-experiments. Consider that intact classes are assigned to treatments at random. If the composition of the classes is such that a large number of subjects represent the extremes of the sampling distribution, their posttest scores could reflect the regression effect rather than changes due to the independent variable. By the same kind of reasoning, there could be a threat in terms of the interaction of selection with other factors, such as maturation or history. Therefore, selective biases may be at work in some quasi-experiments, favoring one group over others.

Almost none of the threats to validity are controlled in preexperiments. Usually there are few or no randomization procedures and sometimes there is no control group. In the one-group, pretest-posttest design, only the selection of subjects and subject mortality are controlled. Since there is only one group, the experimenter can probably control the number of subjects well. Because of severe threats to validity, it would be difficult to interpret the results of a preexperiment as a valid answer to a problem.

For a graphic presentation of the designs and factors that threaten validity, see Table 5.3, which is adapted from the work of Campbell and Stanley (1963). As you study this chart, be aware that it is not intended to substitute for additional reading and consideration about a particular design's researchers. Their choices are determined by fitting the design with the most appropriate controls to their problem and the situation in which it is investigated.

READING AND ANALYZING METHOD SECTIONS: PROCEDURES

Content and Form

After researchers describe the subjects and instruments for the study, the remainder of the method section is usually devoted to general information about other procedures. Although there is no standard way of subtitling this information, you may sometimes find one of these headings: "procedures for independent (or dependent) variable," "design," or simply "procedures." Whatever the title, there should be information about treatment administration in experimental studies and about data collection in all reports. Sometimes there is a small section about data analysis procedures, although these are more frequently described in the results section.

Authors differ in the amount of detail they include about procedures. As we stated previously, the variation is sometimes due to the editorial policy of the journal. Sometimes there just isn't enough space for details concerning procedures. At other times researchers decide how completely they will describe procedures.

Suggestions for Reading and Analysis

We suggest that you be very sure you understand the problem of the study before beginning to read the procedures section. Clarify whether the researchers are seeking explanation, prediction, or control as the goal of the study. Remember that you will not find information on treatment administration unless the goal is control.

In experimental studies researchers should give details on treatment administration procedures. The activities of both the treatment group(s) and the no treatment or control group(s) need to be very clear. Look for information about who administered the treatment(s) and whether the personnel had training needed for the particular treatment they gave.

Table 5.3
VALIDITY OF DESIGNS

	True Experimental			Quasi-experimental			Preexperimental	
	True pre/posttest	True posttest	Solomon four-group	Quasi-experiment	Counter-balanced	Time series	Preexperimental pre/posttest	Preexperimental posttest
Factors that affect internal validity								
• History	+	+	+	+	+	−	−	+
• Maturation	+	+	+	+	+	+	−	?
• Testing	+	+	+	+	+	+	−	+
• Instrumentation	+	+	+	+	+	?	?	+
• Regression	+	+	+	?	+	+	+	+
• Selection	+	+	+	+	+	+	+	−
• Mortality	+	+	+	+	+	+	−	−
• Interaction of selection and maturation, selection and history	+	+	+	−	?	+		−
Factors that affect external validity								
• Interaction of testing and treatment	−	+	+	−	?	−	−	−
• Interaction of selection and treatment	?	?	?	?	?	?	−	
• Reactive effects	?	?	?	?	?	?	?	
• Multiple-treatment interference				?	−	?		

Abbreviations: +, factor controlled; −, definite weakness; ?, possible source of concern; and *blank*, factor is not related.
Adapted from D. T. Campbell & J. C. Stanley, *Experimental and Quasi-Experimental Designs for Research*, Chicago: Rand McNally, 1963. Reprinted by permission of the American Educational Research Association.

Check whether the treatment conforms to the meaning of the independent variable mentioned in the problem statement and its context. For example, researchers may want to know about the effects of cross-age tutoring on the self-concepts of participants. If the treatment consists of simply using peers to tutor each other, we seriously question whether that's an adequate way to deal with "cross-age tutoring" as an independent variable, even if the age range within the classrooms involved is two or three years. Cross-age tutoring usually refers to a broader age range. Although researchers do operationalize variables for a study according to their own judgment, their definitions must be examined carefully to see that the sense of the variable is not lost.

When treatments are discussed, researchers usually describe ways of accounting for extraneous variables. As you read, try to determine whether any variables were not controlled that should have been. Examples are the length of treatments for the different groups and the qualifications of personnel involved in administering treatment. If these kinds of things are not comparable for all groups, think about the impact of their lack of equivalence on the outcome of the study.

Details of data collection should be included for all studies. The kind of data, how they were gathered, and who did the collection should be reported. Ideally, enough details should be given to enable another researcher to replicate the study. When special instruments such as interviews, sociometric devices, and tests were used, researchers need to furnish information concerning the qualifications and training of the personnel who collected the data.

Finally, you should be able to figure out which design was used even if it is not specifically mentioned in the study. In doing this, you are making a tentative judgment about how well the project was planned and how much confidence to place in the results. Take this matter of confidence seriously. For example, unless researchers specifically say that subjects were assigned randomly to groups, proceed on the basis that they probably were *not* assigned randomly. The flow chart in Figure 5.8 can help you decide which of the main designs were used in reports of difference studies. Read the problem and procedures section carefully. Then ask and answer questions in the order shown. This method will help isolate the general names of the research designs.

As you consider the design that was used, think about how well it provides data to answer the problem of the study. Would another design furnish better data for a solution? This question is hard to answer. Although we've touted the advantages of true experiments and factorial designs in this chapter, sometimes a quasi-experiment may be just as appropriate. Consider the case of a high school mathematics teacher who has five classes of Algebra I every day. Suppose this person is interested in comparing how laboratory and traditional approaches affect student attitudes. It really may not matter whether this particular researcher can assign subjects to groups. Assuming that students are assigned to classes fairly randomly, comparing intact groups

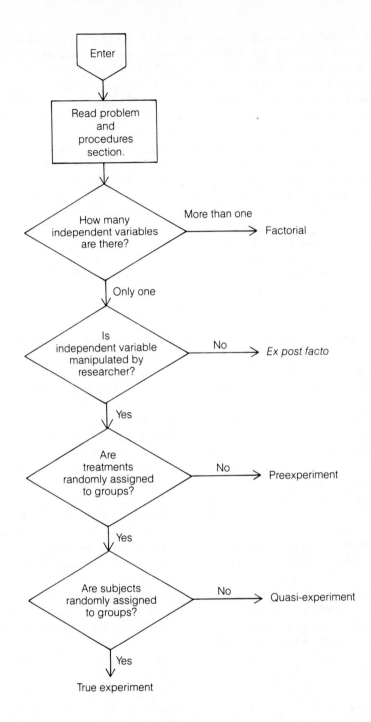

FIGURE 5.8 Flow chart for deciding which design was used in difference reports.

with other intact groups in a quasi-experiment is satisfactory. The results of this project for this problem and this particular teaching situation should be about as valuable as those from a true experiment.

When you read the procedures section, try to watch for a couple of pitfalls. Always be aware of the problem of the study as you read. This will help you notice how each of the variables is dealt with—whether it is manipulated, selected, or measured. You should look in the procedures section to be sure that the researchers account for all the variables mentioned in the problem.

You should also be careful not to accept the design procedures uncritically. If the researchers fail to describe the population from which the sample was taken, don't be afraid to say that the results may not be valid for every similarly described sample. If researchers say that a particular instrument was used to measure a certain variable, be careful as you interpret the results. For example, word recognition tests do not measure reading comprehension any more than computation tests measure mathematical reasoning. We suggest that you take what you read with a grain of salt!

Criteria for evaluating the procedures subsections of research reports include the following:

1. *Treatment administration in experiments should be appropriate for the problem and clearly defined.* The relationship between the procedures and the independent variable must be very clear. The procedures section should define operationally all activities in both treatment and no treatment groups. In addition, authors should indicate who administered the treatments, their qualifications, and the time schedules for treatment administration.
2. *Data collection procedures should be clearly defined.* Highlights of data collection procedures should be given, including pre- and posttesting or the administration of multiple instruments. Researchers should indicate who collected data and a time sequence for collection.
3. *When all the procedures are considered together, you should be able to figure out which design was used.* Subject selection and assignment to groups, assignment of treatments to groups, data collection procedures, and treatment administration constitute the main components of a research design. Based on this information, you should be able to decide which design was used and point out any strengths and weaknesses of that design for the particular problem.

SUMMARY

Treatment administration procedures are included in the method section of experimental research reports. Researchers should define both treatment and no treatment, or levels of treatment, so you can see whether there really were differences in the administration of the independent variable. Additional information about treatment administrators and their qualifications is also useful.

Data collection procedures for all studies are reported in the method section, including information about the schedule of data collection and the personnel who made the collections. Data analysis procedures cover all aspects of handling and treating collected data.

Designs for correlation and prediction studies are very simple since there is no manipulation of a variable. Both kinds of studies require that data on at least two variables be collected and analyzed. In correlation studies, researchers look for cues to the strength or direction of the association between variables. In prediction studies, researchers look to see whether a known association between variables can be used for prediction purposes. Variance in both kinds of designs is controlled by the careful actions of the researchers in sampling, data collection, and analysis.

Designs for difference studies are more complex than those for association studies due to treatment administration procedures. True experiments assign subjects and treatments randomly to groups, manipulate at least one variable, and use comparison groups. Quasi-experiments have these same features except that intact groups are used. Therefore, they do not control variance as adequately as true experiments. In quasi-experiments treatment should be randomly assigned. Preexperiments provide even less control than quasi-experiments. Preexperiments may or may not have a comparison group, and they usually use intact groups that are not randomly assigned to treatment. These designs do, however, involve manipulation of a variable.

Ex post facto designs, though used in difference studies, employ descriptive methodology and seek explanation or prediction rather than control. Designs for these studies are appropriate when researchers cannot manipulate the independent variable.

Factorial designs are used when researchers wish to study how two or more independent variables or factors affect dependent variables either singly or in interaction. Depending on whether the variables can be manipulated, factorial designs can represent an extension of true or quasi-experiments or *ex post facto* studies. Factorial designs are more complex than studies with a single independent variable.

All parts of design procedures work together to determine the validity of the research design by controlling variance. External validity refers to the generalizability of results from the subjects in the sample to the population they represent. Internal validity is assurance that the independent variable is actually responsible for any observed changes in the dependent variables, meaning that internal validity is a particular concern of experimental studies. Designs differ in their control of threats to validity.

Descriptions of procedures for treatment administration and data collection appear in the method section among other information. When you start to read about procedures, be sure you understand the problem of the study and the goal of science to be met. Check to see whether all variables in the problem statement are operationally defined in this section. Look also for any uncontrolled variables that could affect the outcome of the study. By analyzing the sampling procedures and data collection schedule, you should be able to figure out which design was used. Evaluating the strengths and weaknesses of the design allows you to interpret the results of the study.

EXERCISES

Read the method section of "Effects of Peer Presence on Sex-Typing of Children's Play Behavior" and "Perceptions of Social Control Among Black College Students," which appear immediately following the questions. The introductory sections of these reports are at the end of Chapter 2. Write your answers and compare them with the feedback for exercises at the end of this chapter.

1. In experiments, how well are the treatment administration procedures described? For example, are the procedures complete? Do they fit the problem?
2. In all studies, how well are data collection procedures described? For example, are procedures complete? Do they fit with the selection of subjects and instruments? Is the time sequence indicated? Explain.
3. Name the design used in the study. Describe it briefly.
4. Based on the information about sampling, instrumentation, data collection, and treatment administration (where used), how appropriate are the design procedures for answering the problem of the study? Explain.

Serbin et al., *Effects of Peer Presence on Sex-Typing of Children's Play Behavior*

METHOD

Subjects

Twenty-six girls and thirty-six boys, mean age 51 months (age range 40-60 months), participated in the study. Children were students at a university child study center and attended two or three 2.5-hr preschool classes per week. Children were primarily middle class, from both blue and white collar families; approximately 20% were from lower SES backgrounds. Approximately 15%

of the children were from minority (black and oriental) families. Prior to the study, the subjects had been enrolled in pre-school from 1 to 11 months, with an average of 5 months previous attendance.

Procedures

All subjects participated in three conditions: solitary, same-sex peer, and opposite-sex peer. This constituted a 2(sex) X 3(conditions) factorial design with repeated measures on the second factor. Subjects in the solitary condition were taken into a small room containing a row of six toys. Three of the toys were male stereotypic and three female stereotypic. Male and female toys were alternated and consisted of the following: plastic soldiers, small dolls and doll furniture, miniature firetrucks, a plastic tea set, toy airplanes, and an ironing board and iron (with clothes to iron). Children in this condition were instructed as follows: "There are some toys in this room for you. You can play with any of the toys you want to. I will be working at my desk (in the adjoining room), while you are playing. In a little while, I'll come in and we'll do some drawing, then we'll go back to the classroom." The child was then left alone in the room for 3 min.

The procedure for the same- and opposite-sex peer conditions was identical to that for the solitary condition, except that a same- or opposite-sex peer remained in a corner of the room at a desk, drawing a picture. The order of conditions was varied, with random assignment of subjects to each of the six possible orders. In the peer present conditions, children were told that they could play with the toys while waiting their "turn" to crayon. Each child served as a "peer" while the next subject was tested and was then returned to the classroom. The three exposures to the experimental situation which each child received were spaced 3 to 5 days apart. In the peer present condition children were instructed: "_____(name of peer) is finishing a picture at the desk. You will have a chance to draw when he/she is done. While you are waiting your turn, you can play with these toys. You can play with any of the toys you want to. I will be working at my desk (in the adjoining room) while you are playing. In a little while, I'll come in and we'll do some drawing and then we'll go back to the classroom." Peers were instructed: "Now it's your turn to draw. When you are finished, we'll go back to class. Be sure to pay attention to your drawing, and let_____(subject) play by him/herself for a little while."

Observational System

Observations were made from behind a one-way glass mirror. An undergraduate observer (from a total pool of eight available observers) recorded the toy(s) a child was touching, every 5 sec. (i.e., 36 observations per session). Talking by either the subject or the peer was recorded. Interobserver agreement was periodically assessed on approximately 10% of the experimental trials and was computed by the formula below, on an interval by interval basis:

$$\frac{\text{Agreements on occurrence}}{\text{Agreements and disagreements}}$$
$$\text{on occurrence.}$$

Interobserver agreement ranged from 95 to 100% on the specific toys and behavioral measures of talking and playing. No hypotheses were given to the observers regarding the effects of peer presence.

METHOD

Instrument and Analysis

The absence of a scale to measure social control within educational settings made it necessary to develop one for this research. Basic to this undertaking is the assumption that all student partisans develop an attitudinal perspective on the authority structure of their college or university. Proceeding on this assumption, and drawing on the conceptual literature on the subject, three indexes comprised of 10, 12, and 13 items were formulated to tap perceptions of social control as they are focused on the administration, faculty, and student body respectively. Following is a representative item from each index:

Administration. In general, the administration of this school is fair in dealing with student problems.
Faculty. Most faculty at this school are ready and willing to help the individual student when they (sic) need it.
Student Peer Group. The social pressures at this school frequently force the individual to go along with things they (sic) may not want to go along with.

Without a criterion measure of social control, it was necessary to rely on the argument that the scale items have face validity. In addition, an item-to-total analysis revealed that all items were significantly correlated ($p < .01$) with the underlying criterion of the scale thus providing evidence for the scales' construct validity. When corrected by the Spearman-Brown prophecy formula, the respective split-half reliability coefficients for the peer, faculty, and administration social control indexes were .83, .79 and .75.

The response set consists of a Likert-type continuum upon which the respondent is asked to indicate his degree of agreement or disagreement with each statement. Each item is scored on a 1 to 4 basis, with 1 being assigned to the response indicative of the most positive attitude toward the authority structure and 4 to the most negative. The total score for each individual is obtained by summing across all items in a particular index.

Our analysis is aimed at determining whether there are differences in levels of social control among black students in the three educational settings selected for examination. First, scores were obtained for the total sample on each index, and a corresponding mean and standard deviation were computed for each subsample representative of the urban center, college, and university settings. The *t*-test was then used to compare the group means.

Subjects and Data

The three settings were all located in a single metropolitan area in the northwestern region of the state of New York. The university was a large (approximately 23,000), urban, predominantly white institution with an excellent academic reputation. The college was also urban, largely white, considerably smaller (approximately 8,000), and somewhat less academically prestigious than the university. Although both institutions can be regarded as urban, it should be noted that both are located on the periphery of the city, unlike the urban center which is situated in the core area itself.

The fact that it was a two-year institution distinguished the urban center from the college and university. A recent innovation of the state university system, the urban center began operation in November, 1965, with an enrollment of 48 students. Its rolls expanded to 671 students by the fall of 1967, to 737 by 1970, and presently has an enrollment of approximately 850. The center offers college-level courses in language arts, science, mathematics, English, and the social sciences. In addition, it provides a variety of remedial courses together with a broadly based vocational education program. In short, it is the purpose of the urban center to prepare students for either senior level colleges and universities or the world of work.

Sixty black subjects were randomly selected from the freshman and sophomore classes of each institution, thus constituting a total sample of 180. All subjects were from the same metropolitan area, were of lower or lower-middle socioeconomic status, and had similar educational backgrounds. In an effort to maximize the return rate, black personnel from the respective institutions were enlisted and paid to personally contact and administer the research instruments to each subject while guaranteeing them their anonymity. Data were collected in the spring of the year after the freshmen had had nearly one year and the sophomores nearly two years of contact with their respective institutions. The number of instruments completed by subjects from the urban center, college, and university was 49, 55, and 56, respectively.

FEEDBACK FOR EXERCISES

This section is intended to let you know how well you answered the questions in the exercises. Your wording may differ, but your thoughts should be similar. You may answer the exercises for one or more reports in Appendix A if you need additional practice.

"Effects of Peer Presence on Sex-Typing of Children's Play Behavior"

1. Treatment administration procedures are generally well described. There is no indication of who administered the treatments, but details are included about the content and duration of each treatment. These procedures fit the problem.
2. The data collection procedures are well described. The situation in which the observers collected data and exactly what kinds of data they reported are included. Observers were also unaware of the hypotheses of the study.
3. This study used a quasi-experimental factorial design with play condition as one of the independent variables (manipulated) and sex of the subjects (selected) as a second independent variable. It

is a repeated measures design with the same subjects participating in each condition.

4. The design procedures seem to be appropriate for answering the problem of the study. The treatments (play conditions) allow for the collection of data about whether "peers function directly as discriminative stimuli for preschoolers' sex-typed play behavior." Collecting data by direct observation seems well suited to the problem.

"Perceptions of Social Control Among Black College Students"

1. Not applicable; this study was not an experiment.
2. Data collection procedures are well described. The report indicates that black persons were paid and trained to administer the instruments to the subjects. This reflects particular care in collecting data. The authors do not explain what happened to the data for 20 students who were selected but were not included in the count. The time sequence is indicated in the report. Actually there was only one instrument for each subject, which simplified the time sequence very much.
3. This study used an *ex post facto* design. Perceptions of social control (dependent variable) were studied in relation to types of college (independent variable). However, no manipulation of the independent variable was possible.
4. The design procedures seem to be appropriate for answering the problem of the study. Researchers were able to get information about black student perceptions of social control in three types of college settings.

RECOMMENDED REFERENCES

Campbell, D. T., & Stanley, J. C. Experimental and quasi-experimental designs for research. In N.L. Gage (Ed.), *Handbook of research on teaching*. Chicago: Rand McNally, 1963. Note: The section described is also available as a separate publication. This information is classic and should be read by anyone seriously considering the design of a major research project. The discussion of all major designs and appropriate statistical tests is well written.

Cook, T. D., & Campbell, D. T. *Quasi-experimentation: Design and analysis issues for field settings*. Chicago: Rand McNally, 1979. Chapter 2, "Validity," is particularly helpful in understanding external and internal validity. There are two additional kinds of validity: statistical conclusion and construct validity. The discussion of quasi-experimental designs is one of the most definitive. If you read it all, you'll probably get more than you bargained for.

Gottman, J. M., McFall, R. M., & Barnett, J. T. Design and analysis of research using time series. *Psychological Bulletin*, 1969, *72*, 299–306. The authors explain how time series designs can be used in different settings, especially those in which control groups may not be available or measurements of the dependent variable are gathered over time.

Leonard, W. H., & Lowery, L. F. Was there really an experiment? A quantitative procedure for verifying treatments in educational research. *Educational Researcher*, 1979, 8(6), 4–7. The authors outline a procedure for the verification of treatment in the context of a research project in high school biology. The procedures are generalizable to other subject areas and probably would help a reader of research reports to critique treatment administration procedures.

6

Reading
Results Sections

In research reports, the results section follows the method section. Results should tell you how the researchers analyzed their data to test hypotheses. Since researchers plan data analysis along with other procedures, they sometimes include this information in a special part of the method section. This is more common in theses, dissertations, and other long research reports than in shorter reports. In journal reports, however, data analysis is usually discussed in the results sections.

This chapter is intended to develop a preliminary understanding of data analysis necessary for reading research reports. Selected data analysis techniques are discussed from a nonmathematical perspective. Because so many variations of the basic procedures are cited in research reports, several related procedures are also mentioned

It is not intended that you have a thorough understanding of every procedure mentioned in this chapter. No background in statistics is assumed, although you will probably find it helpful to consult Appendix C at certain points.

Chapter objective. After you complete this chapter, you should be able to *assess the appropriateness of the choices of significance tests, interpret probability statements,* and *assess the adequacy of results for answering the research questions* in selected research reports.

BACKGROUND FOR READING RESULTS SECTIONS

Data Analysis Procedures

To obtain research results, data from individual subjects must be checked, assembled into meaningful units, and analyzed. In brief, data analysis procedures include the following:

1. preparing data from subjects for analysis—checking to see that data are complete, sorting the data by groups, possibly changing data from higher to lower levels of measurement and performing other related operations
2. summarizing data from the subjects into meaningful units, known as descriptive statistics—seeing if hypothesized associations (or differences) are found (Appendix C contains information about descriptive statistics)
3. applying appropriate inferential statistics—determining whether the associations (or differences) found occurred by chance
4. interpreting the results—deciding whether and how well the information answers the research question

In most research efforts all these procedures focus on the use of inferential statistics. In the sections that follow, an overview of inferential statistics is followed by a more detailed description of the first three procedures as they are applied in data analyses. Interpreting results is the subject of Chapter 7.

Overview of Inferential Statistics

Purpose.   Researchers want to know if the results provide answers to their research questions. Their concern is whether the results have **significance,** which is a judgment about the importance or worth of the findings. If researchers are interested in the worth of the results only for the subjects of the study, summarizing the data from the subjects would be sufficient. Most of the time, however, researchers want to know that the results are meaningful in a broader frame of reference. Can the findings be applied to people beyond those in the sample? Making judgments about the generalizability of results is what **inferential statistics** is all about. In fact, the term *inferential* is used because inferences about a population are based on information from a sample. When researchers use inferential statistics, they are trying to answer this question: Is the observed association (or difference) real, or did it happen because of chance variation in the population?

The mathematical procedures used in inferential statistics are called **statistical tests.** Although many different statistical tests are available for a variety of research situations, there are basically two categories of tests: parametric and nonparametric. Researchers are most likely to choose a **parametric test** if the data meet these conditions: (1) all observations are independent, meaning no observation influences any other observation; (2) the data are at least interval in level; (3) the data represent a normal distribution (see Appendix C-1 for more information); and (4) the variance is homogeneous. Even when data do not conform to all these standards, parametric tests may sometimes be used. For example, unless very small samples are involved, the assumption of a normal distribution is not terribly important. Furthermore, if all groups in the study contain equal numbers of subjects, the assumption of homogeneous variance does not have to be met.

When these four conditions cannot be met or safely discounted, **nonparametric tests** should be used. These tests are designed to use nominal or ordinal measurements. They make no assumptions about the distribution or variation of the population. If interval data are obtained but researchers decide that the distribution is not normal or the variance is not homogeneous, the data may be changed to a lower level and a nonparametric test used for the analysis.

It is necessary to distinguish between parametric and nonparametric tests because they differ in their capacity to test hypotheses. Generally, parametric tests are more powerful than their nonparametric counterparts. This means that parametric tests are more likely to help researchers detect the presence of the hypothesized relationship between variables if it actually exists. Researchers usually try to use parametric tests whenever possible.

How Inferential Statistics Work

To use inferential statistics, researchers must carry out the following six steps:

1. Consider the null hypothesis that must be rejected in order to accept the research hypothesis.
2. Select an inferential test that is appropriate for the problem, the level of data of the study, and the sample.
3. Select a level of significance for the results.
4. Use data from the subjects in the mathematical formula for the inferential test.
5. Compare the results of the statistical test with critical values of that test at the predetermined level of significance.
6. Retain or reject the null hypothesis.

We will discuss each of these steps in some detail.

Step 1. Consider the null hypothesis that must be rejected in order to accept the research hypothesis. Chapter 2 discussed the purpose and form of a research hypothesis as a tentative statement of the solution to a problem. In general, a **null hypothesis** implies that any observed relationship between variables is due solely to chance variation in the population. Here are some examples of both kinds of hypothesis statements:

Research	Null
1. First-graders who are taught with the multisensory approach to reading instruction will learn a greater number of words than comparable first-graders taught with the auditory-visual approach to reading instruction.	1. There is no difference in the number of words learned by first-graders who are taught with the multisensory approach and those taught with the auditory-visual approach to reading instruction.
2. Kindergarten children in a perceptual motor development program will perform differently on eye-hand coordination tasks than similar kindergarteners who receive no perceptual motor training.	2. Kindergarten children in a perceptual motor development program will perform the same on eye-hand coordination tasks as similar kindergarteners who receive no perceptual motor training.
3. There is a moderately high positive correlation between self-concept scores and ratings on public-speaking abilities of high school students.	3. There is no correlation between self-concept and public-speaking ability in high school students.

The reason for this emphasis on the null hypothesis rather than the research hypothesis is rooted in the mathematical logic behind hypothesis testing. People do research because they want scientific answers to questions about relationships between variables. This requires the statement in the form of a research hypothesis of what researchers expect as the answer to their question. If any anticipated research hypothesis is not true, then the null hypothesis is the most accurate statement that can be made about the variables. The strictness of the scientific method requires researchers to retain the null as the most likely hypothesis unless it can be rejected based on the analysis of data. From a statistical standpoint, the purpose of a research study is to retain or reject the null hypothesis. When this hypothesis is tested, researchers learn how probable it would be to get the results they have found if the null hypothesis were actually true.

However, if the results are so unusual thay they would be quite unlikely to happen just because of random variation in the population, the null hypothesis can be rejected. As you can imagine, researchers generally want differences or correlations to be large enough to reject null hypotheses in favor of the alternative research hypotheses. Results are said to be statistically significant when they are of a magnitude to permit the rejection of the null hypothesis.

Step 2. Select an inferential test. Statistical tests that are appropriate for association and difference studies are discussed later in this chapter. Descriptions of these tests include discussion of the level of data required and the descriptive statistics needed for each test.

Step 3. Select a significance level. The **level of significance** is a probability level. Selected by researchers, the level is intended to minimize the danger of retaining a false hypothesis or rejecting a true one. Keep in mind that there is no way to be 100 percent sure about the results. So most of the time, researchers set either 5% or 1% probability (written $p = .05$ or $p = .01$) as a margin of error. This means that they are willing to reject the null hypothesis and retain their research hypothesis if they can be confident that their results are so rare that the same result would occur by chance alone no more than 5 times in 100 (or 1 time in 100) within the same population.

Researchers set this probability of error at a level that they can live with according to the consequences of such an error. Usually they are willing to gamble that the results are statistically significant when, in fact, they are not. In most educational research, there is little danger in being mistaken about statistically significant results 1% or 5% of the time. Occasionally, however, the potential consequences of such an error could be so undesirable that the probability level is set higher, such as 1 in 500 or 1,000 times. Such a strict level of significance is more common in research where treatments are very costly or risky.

Step 4. Use data in the statistical test. Data from the subjects of the project are fed into the mathematical formula for the statistical test.

Step 5. Compare results of the statistical test with critical values of the test at the predetermined level of significance. After the calculations are complete, researchers are ready to examine the results in relation to critical values for that particular statistical test. A critical value is usually the smallest value for the test outcome that researchers can get in order to reject the null hypothesis in favor of the research hypothesis. Such values, recorded in tables for each test, were obtained by repeated calculation of the statistical tests, using different sample sizes and numbers of groups. The critical values therefore take into account typical variations that would be expected, and they are expressed in terms of their probability of occurrence by chance. Researchers locate the table for the particular test they used and note the significance level. Then they look at whether the calculated test outcome is as great or greater than the tabled value.* If it is, the result is "statistically significant" within the predetermined probability of error.

Step 6. Retain or reject the null hypothesis on the basis of the comparison. If the results are so unusual that they would rarely be seen by chance variation in the population, then researchers usually conclude that their hypothesized relationship between variables actually exists and is responsible for the association (or difference) that is observed. Retaining (or failing to reject) the null hypothesis indicates that the results of the study could have happened by chance.

Data Analysis in Association Studies

Chapters 2 and 5 discussed the purposes and designs for two kinds of association studies. One kind of association study is concerned with assessing the strength and direction of the relationship between variables through correlation techniques. The second kind involves using one or more variables as predictors of another variable or set of variables. These studies are called correlation and prediction studies, respectively.

Simple correlation and regression, the basic techniques used in many studies, are described briefly in the paragraphs that follow. There are many variations of these techniques to fit the particular requirements of the data and research problem. For your reference, Appendix C-2 gives brief descriptions of several kinds of correlation.

Simple correlation. The first step is to choose a correlation technique that matches the level(s) of measurement. Data are plugged into the mathematical formula of the chosen technique resulting in a correlation coefficient that summarizes data from the subjects. To make inferences about the correlation for the population, researchers may perform a statistical test using the correlation coefficient, to see if it is statistically significant. Tests for this purpose, such as the *t*-test, are essentially the same as those used in difference studies,

---

* Mann-Whitney *U*-tests work in the opposite direction. The calculated values should not exceed tabled values.

and will be described later in this chapter. An easier approach is to compare the calculated coefficient from the subjects with critical values for that coefficient at the predetermined level of significance. These tables make it unnecessary for researchers to perform their own statistical test of the correlation.

Simple regression analysis. The previous paragraphs explained one option for making inferences from the sample to the population. **Regression,** a form of prediction, is an alternative for making inferences from the sample to the population. If a statistically significant correlation is found between variables, researchers can predict the value of one of these variables when the corresponding value of the second variable is known. The known variable is called the *predictor* variable; the unknown variable is the *criterion*. To do regression accurately, predictions should be made only for subjects in the same population as those for which the statistically significant correlation coefficient was calculated. (For more information about regression, see Appendix C-2.)

Multivariate data analyses. Frequently association studies involve more than two variables. When this is the case, **multivariate data analyses** must be used, which involve a set of more complex data analysis procedures than those previously described. Some of these are multiple regression, discriminant analysis, and canonical correlation, which are all prediction techniques. One multivariate correlation technique is factor analysis. In the remainder of this section, these data analyses will be described briefly in terms of how they work and the situations for which they are appropriate.

Multiple regression and discriminant analysis are used in studies that have two or more predictor variables and a criterion variable. Each predictor variable must have some correlation with the criterion variable. In multiple regression, an equation is used that weights each predictor variable in terms of its ability to predict. The result from this equation is a squared multiple correlation coefficient R^2, which can have values between 0 and $+1.00$.

R^2 values are interpreted in the same way as squares of other coefficients of correlation (r, rho, etc.) If $R^2 = .47$, researchers know that about 47% of the variance in the criterion variable is acccounted for by the combined predictors. However, the predictors taken *singly* probably have less common variance with the criterion variable. So combining the predictors gives more information about the joint variation of variables than using each predictor alone. That's why multiple regression is frequently applied in prediction studies.

Discriminant analysis, a variation of multiple regression, is used when the criterion variable is the group membership of the subjects. Groups can be based on any kind of classification—occupation, sex, achievement level, and others. The purpose of this analysis is to predict group membership of the subjects based on the predictor variables.

When there are several predictor variables and several criterion variables, canonical correlation should be the chosen statistical test. This procedure is applicable when the purpose of the study is to learn about the strength of the overall relationship between the predictor and criterion variables, and to determine which specific variables among both the predictor and criterion variables account for most of the relationship between the two sets.

Factor analysis is used to identify the number and nature of broad factors underlying a cluster of variables. This technique can also be applied in testing hypotheses about the relationships among variables. Factor analysis is a highly complex technique that requires sophisticated mathematical procedures.

Data Analysis in Difference Studies

Difference studies were described in Chapters 2 and 5 according to their purposes and designs. You will recall that most of these studies require at least two groups of subjects or repeated measures from one group of subjects. When data analysis is begun, the data must be organized and summarized for each group of subjects, usually in the form of means, standard deviations, variances, medians, or simply frequency distributions. (See Appendix C-1.)

In the paragraphs that follow, analysis of variance, one of the most commonly used tests of significance for difference studies, is discussed. Many other statistical tests are closely related to analysis of variance. Some of these are also described briefly, along with the kind of data that each test uses, the descriptive statistics needed, and the situations in which the test is appropriate. Remember, these short descriptions are intended more for your reference than for thorough understanding. We have not given you all the information you will ever need about statistical tests, nor have we described all the tests you may read about. If you find a test that is not mentioned in this section, try to apply the information you have about tests in general and the context of the particular test to figure out what was done. Also, read about the test in one of the recommended references.

Analysis of variance (ANOVA). This parametric test is a very popular choice for analyses of data in difference studies. **Analysis of variance** can be a simple one-way analysis in which the effects of one independent variable on one dependent variable are examined. Some variations of ANOVA can be highly complex, as you will see later in this section. The null hypothesis tested through ANOVA is that any difference between groups is a product of chance variation in the population and is not the result of treatment. The outcome of the statistical analysis is an F-ratio (also called an F-value). A nonsignificant F-ratio means the null hypothesis should be retained and any differences found must be attributed to chance or sampling fluctuations. A significant F-ratio, however, suggests that the differences between means or variances may be due to different levels of the independent variable. (Appendix C-3 provides a rationale for ANOVA.)

Two-way (factorial) analysis of variance works on the same principles as one-way ANOVA. Used in factorial designs, this test allows analysis of the possible interaction between two or more different independent variables, yielding what is known as "effects of interaction." In addition, researchers find out whether there are differences brought about separately by each independent variable, much as in one-way ANOVA. These results are called "main effects." Information about these tests and other related tests for difference studies is summarized in Table 6.1.

Related analyses. Several statistical procedures related to ANOVA are *t*-tests, comparison tests, multiple regression, and analysis of covariance (ANCOVA). A *t*-test is used when the means of two groups are compared or when a sample mean is compared with a known population mean. If researchers have two groups, either one-way ANOVA or a *t*-test can be used to check for significant differences. The *F*-value obtained from using ANOVA in this case would be equal to the square of the *t*-test result. In association studies, the *t*-test can be used to determine the significance of correlation coefficients.

/ Analysis of variance in its general form tells researchers whether or not results as a whole are statistically significant. Comparison tests may determine the precise sources of possible statistical significance in the data. There are two categories of comparison tests. Those planned and conducted without the use of any overall significance testing are called planned comparisons or *a priori* (before the fact) comparisons. A second category, called posterior, *post hoc* (after the fact), or simply multiple comparisons, is used only after a significant *F*-value has been found. From a mathematical perspective, comparison tests involve computing a *t*-test or an *F*-ratio on subsets of the data.

Planned comparisons are used in situations where researchers have so carefully thought through their problem that they can decide in advance just which sets or pairs of group means will be tested. This task is done with great care, because the rules permit only a certain number of comparisons to be made. Even so, planned comparisons are the most powerful comparison tests available.

Post hoc comparisons must always follow the finding of a significant overall *F*-value. Commonly used *post hoc* tests are Scheffé, Tukey H.S.D.,* Duncan, and Newman-Keuls. They enable researchers to pinpoint just which effects, alone or in interaction, were responsible for the overall *F*-value. There are no limits to the number of combinations that can be tested *post hoc*, but none of these procedures has the power of planned comparison tests for detecting statistical significance.

Multiple regression, previously mentioned as a statistical technique for association studies, can also be used to analyze data from difference studies. Multiple regression in this situation involves correlating the different levels

* Tukey Honestly Significant Difference.

of the independent variable with the dependent variable. The R^2 values from the regression analysis are combined to form an F-ratio, identical to the outcome of analysis of variance with the same data. The advantage of using multiple regression over ANOVA shows when, for some reason, the number of subjects in each group in the design is not equal. Then the usual conditions for ANOVA are not met, but it is perfectly possible to analyze the data and obtain an F-ratio by using multiple regression.

Table 6.1
TESTS OF SIGNIFICANCE FOR
STUDIES WITH ONE DEPENDENT VARIABLE

Test	Symbol for test outcome	What is tested	Level of measurement
Analysis of variance (ANOVA)			
• One-way (simple)	F	Two or more means or variances	Interval
• Two-way (factorial)	F	Two or more means or variances and interaction	Interval
Related tests			
• t-test	t	One or two means, a correlation coefficient	Interval
• Planned comparisons	F	Means, interaction	Interval
• Post hoc comparisons	F	Means, interaction	Interval
• Multiple regression	F	Means	
• Analysis of covariance (ANCOVA)	F	Two or more means with a covariate	Interval
Nonparametric tests			
• Chi-square	χ^2	Frequency counts	Nominal
• Mann-Whitney	U	Two or more sets of ranks	Ordinal
• Median	χ^2	Two or more medians	Ordinal
• Sign		Pairs of measurements	Ordinal
• Wilcoxon		Pairs of measurements	Ordinal
• Kruskal-Wallis ANOVA	χ^2	Three or more sets of ranks	Ordinal
• Friedman ANOVA	χ^2	Three or more sets of ranks	Ordinal

In some circumstances researchers may want to statistically equate groups in terms of some important variable, called the covariate. **Analysis of covariance** (ANCOVA) allows the influence of the covariate to be removed from the data. This enables the results to be interpreted correctly by minimizing the effect of initial group differences on the results of the study. Quite often the subjects will have pretreatment scores that the researchers put into the analysis of data to make the groups more statistically comparable. ANCOVA is typically used in true and quasi-experiments that have two or more groups.

Nonparametric tests.   There are many nonparametric tests for nominal and ordinal data (Siegel, 1956). The following discussions describe briefly some of the more popular tests—chi-square, Mann-Whitney, median, sign, Wilcoxon, Kruskal-Wallis, and Friedman.

Chi-square (χ^2) tests are used when data are in the form of frequency counts or distributions. This test tells whether the frequencies observed are different from the frequencies that would be expected by chance.

The Mann-Whitney U is a nonparametric test that is roughly comparable to the parametric t-test. Two sets of ranks are analyzed to see if they differ by chance or because of the influence of an independent variable.

The median test compares two or more medians from ordinal data. This test is commonly used when the number of subjects is between 20 and 40, and it uses the chi-square formula. The sign test and the Wilcoxon matched pairs signed-rank test compare pairs of measurements of ordinal level. Whereas the sign test does not use the magnitude of the differences between the pairs, the Wilcoxon test does. These two tests may be part of the data analysis for repeated measures studies involving quasi- or preexperimental designs.

Kruskal-Wallis and Friedman analyses of variance are the nonparametric versions of parametric ANOVA. These tests work on the same principle as ANOVA except that ranks rather than interval level data are used. The Friedman test is selected when the measurements are repeated from the same group; the Kruskal-Wallis test is used when there are separate comparison groups.

Multivariate data analyses.   All the tests for difference studies described so far have been designed for research in which there is a single dependent variable. However, sometimes more than one dependent variable is of interest, so multivariate data analyses must be available. If researchers are interested in the effects of a treatment on both achievement and attitude, for example, both these variables will be measured. These data should be analyzed simultaneously rather than separately because there is a strong possibility of a correlation between achievement and attitude. To analyze the data separately is to run the risk of getting statistically significant results by error. This situation is comparable to doing a long series of t-tests with the result that some t-tests are significant *just by chance*. Performing more tests on the same set of data increases the probability that a result will appear to be significant because of chance variation.

There are comparable multivariate analyses for most of the analyses of variance and related tests described in this section. Multivariate analysis of variance, or MANOVA, is comparable to one-way ANOVA and can be extended to factorial designs as factorial MANOVA. In each instance variances representing two or more dependent variables are tested and if a factorial design is used, the variances are tested for interaction. When significant F-ratios are obtained, follow-up tests similar to *post hoc* comparison tests are used to determine the variables on which the groups differ. These follow-up tests are simultaneous confidence intervals and discriminant function analysis. The tests do not isolate the source of variance as specifically as *post hoc* comparison tests do, because the variables in a multivariate analysis are correlated. Table 6.2 summarizes information about tests of significance for difference studies that have two or more dependent variables.

Hotelling's T^2-test is similar in function to a t-test. It can test for differences between the means for two groups on two dependent measures. If a significant F-ratio is found, one of the follow-up tests will be used to locate the variables on which the groups differ. Finally, multivariate analysis of covariance (MANCOVA) tests hypotheses in which a covariate is considered. The influence of the covariate is removed from the combined dependent variables. This test is comparable to the univariate ANCOVA.

Table 6.2
TESTS OF SIGNIFICANCE FOR DIFFERENCE STUDIES
THAT HAVE TWO OR MORE DEPENDENT VARIABLES

Test	Symbol for test outcome	What is tested	Level of measurement
Multivariate analysis of variance (MANOVA)	F	Two or more means	Interval
Factorial MANOVA	F	Two or more means in interaction	Interval
Related tests			
• Hotelling's T^2	F (usually)	Two means	Interval
• Simultaneous confidence intervals		Variables on which groups differ	Interval
• Multivariate analysis of covariance (MANCOVA)	F	Two or more variances with a covariate	Interval
• Discriminant function analysis		Variables on which groups differ	Interval

Statistical Tests and Significance

Power of statistical tests. How much faith should you place in the results of a statistical test? That depends on how much you know about the factors that directly influence the test outcome. There are four aspects of the statistical analysis that contribute to the test outcome. These are the level of significance, power of the statistical test, number in the sample, and effect size. The relative magnitude of each of these factors works together in a particular statistical analysis to determine what the critical value must be to achieve statistical significance (Cohen, 1977).

The level of significance, you will remember, is the risk that researchers are willing to bear of erroneously concluding that the null hypothesis should be rejected. **Power of a statistical test** refers to the ability of a test to identify the presence of the hypothesized association or difference when it actually exists. Test power is expressed as a decimal; for example, .80 or .95. These power figures indicate that in 80 out of 100 times, or 95 out of 100 times, the statistical test will correctly detect the presence of a relationship if it occurs. The power statement also indicates how often researchers will incorrectly retain the null hypothesis when an actual relationship exists. In the first example, researchers would err 20 out of 100 times (100 − 80); in the second, only 5 out of 100 times (100 − 95).

Effect size is the magnitude of the association or difference. In association studies, correlation coefficients provide an index of effect size. Difference studies, however, require the translation of differences between means into standard units (such as units of one standard deviation) as indexes of effect size.

You can check your understanding of the purposes of some of these data analysis procedures by performing Checkpoint 6.1.

CHECKPOINT 6.1

Refer to the situations described in Checkpoint 5.1. Use the additional information provided here and identify a statistical test that is appropriate for each situation.

1. Suppose that progress in speech therapy is measured by counting the number of stages (operationally defined by changes in speech patterns) through which students pass in a given time period.
2. Suppose that listening ability is determined as "satisfactory" or "unsatisfactory" based on a test administered under standard conditions by a hearing specialist. Scores on the shorthand test are marked as percentages of accurately transcribed words.
3. Suppose that the end-of-semester achievement test uses objectively scored items such as multiple-choice and matching questions.

ANSWERS: 1. analysis of variance (measurement level of data is interval, probably a normal distribution considering size of sample)   2. correlation coefficient tested for statistical significance, probably by a t-test (measurement level of data: listening ability data is nominal, shorthand test data is interval)   3. analysis of variance or t-test (measurement level of data is interval)

Researchers want to get the right combination of these four factors in order to minimize both the risk of deciding that a relationship exists when it does not, or deciding that it doesn't exist when it actually does. Direct control over the first risk is possible through the choice of significance level; however, minimizing the second risk by increasing test power is more complicated.

In general, the power of a test decreases as the level of significance is made more stringent. Power also decreases with smaller sample sizes and smaller effect sizes. Power can be increased by selecting a less restrictive significance level, including more subjects in the sample, or having a larger effect size. It is also true that parametric tests are more powerful than non-parametric tests. The simplest way for researchers to increase power is to make the sample size larger.

. In research reports, it is relatively rare to see power or effect size discussed. Occasionally researchers formally determine the significance level and sample size necessary to achieve statistical significance with a particular degree of power, given the presence of a hypothesized effect of a specified minimal size. This procedure is known as a **statistical power analysis** and may be mentioned in the method section of a report.

Interpreting probability statements.   The most commonly reported aspect of a statistical analysis is the level of significance, stated as p values within probability statements. These statements usually contain a test outcome, such as an F- or t-ratio or chi-square value (χ^2), along with other information needed for interpretation. Here are some examples:

1. $F(1,43) = 13.01$, $p < .001$
2. $U(17,20) = 98$, $p < .025$
3. $\chi^2 = 8.1$, critical value is 9.5 at $p = .05$ level, df $= 4$
4. $R^2 = .73$, $p < .01$

In some cases a pair of numbers follows the outcome (see examples 1 and 2). Those numbers indicate degrees of freedom (sometimes written df) and are necessary for determining whether an outcome is significant. Degrees of freedom are based on how many items of the particular design can vary. For example, the F-ratio in example 1 may have come from a study in which there were two treatments, or one treatment and a control group, with a total sample of 44 subjects. There is only one group that can vary as soon as one group has been assigned. Therefore, the number of groups minus one gives the first figure in the df statement. When persons are placed in one of the two groups, 43 individuals can be assigned freely to one group or the other, but the last person's assignment is fixed after the other 43 are in place. Subtracting one subject from the total number of subjects gives the second figure in the df statement. In general, the greater the number of degrees of freedom, the easier it is to get statistically significant results.

Notice that the values of F (13.01), U (98), and χ^2 (8.1) are relatively unimportant for interpretation. They're included in case a reader wishes to check the researchers' claim for significance. What is important is the information in the "$p <$" (probability) positions. The F-ratio in example 1 is significant in that the probability or likelihood of an F of that magnitude occurring by chance alone is only 1 in 1,000. You can check this statement by referring to Appendix C-4, Critical Values of F. Look for one degree of freedom in the horizontal row and 40 degrees of freedom in the vertical column under $p = .001$. Where the row and column cross, you will find that the critical value of F is 12.61. Since the calculated F-value exceeds the critical value, the result is statistically significant at $p < .001$.

The U-value in example 2 is also significant, at $p < .025$. Only 2.5 times in 100 would a U-value of that size happen by chance alone. If you check this information by looking in a table of critical values for U, be sure to note that the U table is read in an opposite way to the other tables. If the test statistic is equal to the tabled value or is less than the value, then it is statistically significant.

The χ^2 value of 8.1 in example 3 is not statistically significant at $p < .05$. For this result to be significant, it would have to equal or exceed 9.5. Appendix C-4, Critical Values of χ^2, shows that 9.5 is the critical value at $p < .05$ with four degrees of freedom.

Finally the R^2 in example 4 is from a multiple regression procedure. This R^2, by the size of its value, shows that a relatively large amount of variance, 73%, is explained by the joint variation of the variables. The probability statement indicates that an R^2 of this magnitude would be likely to occur by chance only 1 time in 100.

Educational and statistical significance. What association (or difference) is important enough to be considered significant by the educational community? **Educational significance** is determined by the answer to this question. **Statistical significance,** however, is concerned with the answer to this question: What is the probability that a particular association (or difference) will occur by chance?

Let's apply these definitions to a practical situation. An experiment is planned and carried out. The treatment involves massive amounts of money for training, supplies, visits, testing subjects, and other needs. At the end of the experiment, subjects are tested and the results show a very small but statistically significant difference in achievement between treatment and control groups. The researchers can legitimately say that the results are statistically significant, but what can be said about educational significance? Is the treatment used in this experiment going to be applied in other educational settings? Are school systems going to spend the money that would be necessary to come up with other small differences in student achievement? We think this is unlikely. The statistically significant results from this study would not make much impact on educational practice.

There is also the opposite situation, where educational significance is lost because there is no evidence of statistical significance. On occasion researchers find results with potential educational significance that fail to meet the predetermined level of statistical significance. They are likely to discard the results and report that there was no significant difference, meaning that there was no *statistically* significant difference. Such results usually are not published and are therefore lost to the educational community. As this example shows, educational significance is often equated with statistical significance. Unless there is statistical significance, results are not commonly believed to have educational significance.

As early as 1931 Ralph W. Tyler questioned the meaning of statistical significance (Tyler, 1931). He suggested that differences that are statistically significant are not always educationally significant, and noted the other issue of losing educational significance due to lack of statistical significance. Despite Tyler's concern, the practice of inferring educational significance from statistically significant results has continued and is widely accepted. Of course, researchers want their work to be educationally important, however significance is demonstrated.

READING AND ANALYZING RESULTS SECTIONS

Content and Form

There's no way to describe a typical results section because they can vary greatly in content and form. However, you will usually find descriptions of data analysis procedures and descriptive statistics in this section unless these were discussed in the procedures subsection. In all cases you will read the results of significance tests and some mention of their importance to the problem or hypothesis.

Results sections may be long or short depending on the guidelines the authors followed. Usually in longer results sections, researchers relate details of data analysis and descriptive statistics, which are then followed by results of the significance tests. Results sections are often organized around the presentation of findings for each hypothesis in the study. Following this presentation are statements telling whether or not each hypothesis was rejected by the data. This rather straightforward organization makes reading the results easy.

Other results sections may be short because some information on data analysis is in the method section as mentioned previously. They also may be short because the authors simply choose to give scant attention to descriptive statistics and a minimum of detail about the significance tests. When this is the case, the results section is concentrated on communicating the outcomes of the test.

Descriptive statistics. If you find descriptive statistics in the report, note that their content generally depends on the kind of study. For example, in a difference study you should expect to see measures of central tendency and variation, since these are needed in significance testing. Since most researchers consider their data as interval, the measures will usually be means and standard deviations. However, there may be a few correlation coefficients in the results sections of difference studies. If you're reading an association study, you should expect to see correlation coefficients of one kind or another.

Frequently descriptive statistics are reported in tables. For example, in studies that use several instruments for data collection, tables may report descriptive statistics on the data from each instrument. The abbreviations in the title of Table 6.3 are well explained in the report as follows: GASC = General Anxiety Scale for Children, TASC = Test Anxiety Scale for Children, and MASC = Mathematics Anxiety Scale for Children. Notice how succinctly the table communicates the number of subjects by the notation "N =," and the means and standard deviations for each group.

No matter how well constructed a table is, however, the researchers must highlight the information in narrative form. Sepie and Keeling (1978) explain their table by saying that it "sets out the means and standard deviations of the groups on all three anxiety measures. It will be noted that under-achievers scored highest in every case, followed by achievers and over-achievers" (p. 18).

✓ **Inferential statistics.** At the heart of any results section is information from which the researchers will ultimately draw conclusions about answers to the research problem. Some mention of either the test(s) of statistical significance or the results of certain tests will be included along with statements of probability or significance.

Highlights of data analyses are spelled out in the text of the results section. The narration may include the name of the test and the specific purpose for which it was used. Often this statement is followed by an indication of

Table 6.3

MEANS AND STANDARD DEVIATIONS OF SCORES ON GASC, TASC, AND MASC OBTAINED BY OVER-ACHIEVERS AND UNDER-ACHIEVERS

Group		GASC		TASC		MASC	
		Mean	SD	Mean	SD	Mean	SD
Over-achievers	(N = 38)	13.79	5.53	6.58	4.97	5.82	4.40
Achievers	(N = 171)	14.95	6.84	7.66	5.67	7.68	4.70
Under-achievers	(N = 37)	15.68	6.51	7.89	4.63	9.16	4.62
TOTAL	(N = 246)	14.88	6.63	7.52	5.44	7.61	4.74

From A. C. Sepie & B. Keeling, The relationship between types of anxiety and under-achievement in mathematics, *Journal of Educational Research*, 1978, *72*, 18. Used by permission.

whether or not the hypothesis was rejected. In many cases, researchers include the level of probability at which the null hypothesis was rejected.

Here is an illustration. Meissner (1978) studied the ability of kindergarteners and second grade children to judge verbal clues. Students were given both their own concept verbalizations and some standard verbalizations of the concepts as the basis for selecting a target object. In the results section, Meissner gives all the information in narrative form as shown in Exhibit 6.1.

In other situations researchers communicate the results of their analyses without identifying the tests. You can figure out which tests were used, however, by reading the tables that are included to support the statements. For example, Dailey (1978) studied the relationship between locus of control, perceived group cohesiveness, and satisfaction with coworkers. The results section contains the following narrative statement:

> The results indicate that both hypotheses are supported. Locus of control had a significant main effect, e.g., externally oriented subjects were more satisfied with coworkers than were internally oriented respondents (Hypothesis 1) [pp. 313–314].

The basis for his statement is shown in Table 6.4. Notice that some of the sources of variance are indicated under the heading of that name. An additional source of variance, labeled error, is not reported in this table. The next two columns display the mean sum of squares (MS) and the calculated F-ratios. The final column with the probability values may be of the greatest interest to you, however, for this is where the authors indicate the significance or lack of it for the results.

This table represents one kind of standard table you will often see in results sections for studies where factorial analysis of variance has been used. On some occasions there may be additional columns reporting the sums of squares and the degrees of freedom (df) for each source of variance. When all this information is provided, it is easy for you to check the results for yourself.

Table 6.4
SUMMARY OF ANALYSIS OF VARIANCE FOR LOCUS OF CONTROL AND COHESIVENESS AS RELATED TO SATISFACTION WITH COWORKERS

Source	MS	F	p
Locus of control (A)	13.54	9.20	≤ .01
Cohesiveness (B)	43.34	29.44	≤ .01
A × B	4.31	2.93	≤ .08

From R. C. Dailey, Relationship between locus of control, perceived group cohesiveness, and satisfaction with coworkers, *Psychological Reports*, 1978, *42*, 311–316, Table 1. Reprinted with permission of the author and publisher.

A 2 (Order of Administration) $\times$ 2 (Grade) analysis of variance was performed on the number of correct concepts verbalized and also on the total number of own clues and standard clues appraised correctly. The analyses revealed no significant effects of task form on concept verbalization, $F(1,52) = 1.7$, $p > .05$, or order of administration of the own-clue condition, $F(1,52) = .03$, $p > .05$, or standard-clue condition, $F(1,52) = .04$, $p > .05$, on number of clues assessed accurately.

EXHIBIT 6.1.   Results section from J. A. Meissner, Judgment of clue adequacy by kindergarten and second-grade children, *Developmental Psychology*, 1978, *14*(1), 20.

Suggestions for Reading and Analysis

We suggest that you be very familiar with the problem statement before you read the results section. This may require rereading the problem after you've completed your analysis of the method section. As you read the results, look for definite answers to the problem. We mentioned that the discussion of results is sometimes combined with the findings. If you read a report that has this characteristic, search through the discussion section for answers to the research question.

As you read the results, try to understand exactly what the descriptive statistics mean in the context of the study. If you see a table that mentions means and standard deviations of scores on certain tests, look at the range of scores for the different groups that were involved. There should be a clear relationship between the information in the results section and the instruments used. To illustrate, if some type of rating scale is mentioned in the instrumentation section, you are very likely to find a summary of results from that rating scale in the results section.

You should also try to understand why particular test(s) of significance were used. Refer to Tables 6.2 and 6.3 if you need help in remembering particular statistical tests. Look back at the section on interpreting probability statements if you've forgotten how to interpret the results of the tests. When you read about analysis of variance, for example, see if you can figure out which characteristic of the data, variances, frequency distributions, and so on, were used in the test. Then interpret the probability statements accurately. Remember that if the result was significant at $p < .05$, the correct interpretation is that a difference (or association) of this size would occur less than 5 times in 100 if the null hypothesis were true. Therefore, the statistical conclusion is that the population characteristics (means, variance, etc.) do indeed differ. When this type of statement is made in a typical study, the researchers probably conclude that the independent variable or treatment brought about the difference.

A few pitfalls should be avoided in reading results sections. One of these is overlooking the possibility that a statistical test of inference is *not* in order even though the report carries information about the test. When the researchers have not sampled a population to get subjects, there is often no reason to report inferential statistics. When these results are given under such circumstances, you should search for their rationale.

When no information is given about sampling from a population, researchers can perhaps establish a historical population to which the results can be applied. A historical population exists over a period of time and works this way: Suppose a teacher continues to teach a certain subject and grade in the same location for several years. He or she observes that the students are very much alike from one semester or year to the next. Doing a research project on one semester's or year's group of students could conceivably be applied to like groups of students that the teacher sees in subsequent semesters or years.

Another pitfall concerns the possibility that an inappropriate test was used with the results. For example, doing an analysis of variance on pretest scores and a second ANOVA on the posttest scores is not the most appropriate way to see changes in the dependent variable. As indicated previously in this chapter, it might be preferable to use analysis of covariance with the pretest score as a covariate.

A third pitfall is accepting statistically significant results as being highly important without considering just how much of a difference or association they represent. For example, it is relatively easy to find tiny but statistically significant differences or associations when sample sizes are quite large.

The results section of a report contains the answers to the research question. Therefore, it is important that the answers be communicated very clearly. Here are some criteria for evaluating results sections:

1. *Data analysis procedures should be appropriate for the problem and should be clearly described.* The kind of study and sampling procedures dictates the descriptive statistics and statistical tests used. Correlation coefficients are typically found in association studies; and means, standard deviations, and variances are found in difference studies. Statistical tests need to be appropriate for the kind of study.

2. *Results or findings should clearly answer the problem/hypothesis.* Researcher-authors are obligated to give findings concerning the problem with a certain amount of definiteness. If hypotheses are mentioned, there should be statements about whether each was retained or rejected.

SUMMARY

Data analysis procedures include organizing and summarizing data from subjects, applying appropriate statistical tests, and interpreting their results. These procedures are applied in studies in which the findings from a sample can be generalized to a population.

There are several steps in the analysis of data. First the null hypothesis is considered, and an appropriate inferential test and level of significance are selected. Data from the subjects are used in the mathematical formula for the test, and the results are compared with critical values of that test. On the basis of this comparison, the researchers decide whether to retain or reject the null hypothesis. If the null hypothesis is rejected, the research hypothesis is usually accepted as an explanation for the results.

Statistical procedures for two-variable association studies include several simple correlation techniques and simple regression analysis. To assess the significance of correlation coefficients, t-tests may be used. If more than two variables are involved, multiple regression, discriminant analysis, canonical correlation, or factor analysis may be used.

Statistical tests for difference studies with a single dependent variable include analysis of variance, t-tests, comparison tests, multiple regression, analysis of covariance, and several nonparametric tests. If there are two or more dependent variables, multivariate analyses are appropriate

The outcome of a statistical test depends on four factors: the level of significance, power of the statistical test, sample size, and effect size. The power of a statistical test is its probability of detecting the presence of an actual relationship between variables. Effect size is the magnitude of an association or difference. Researchers try to balance these factors in order to minimize their chances of making incorrect decisions about their hypotheses. A statistical power analysis is a formal way of seeking appropriate outcomes from statistical tests.

Probability statements that result from statistical tests are interpreted with reference to a table of critical values for the particular test in question. To use these tables researchers must know the degrees of freedom afforded by the particular circumstances of the study. In most cases a test outcome that is as great or greater than the value shown in the tables is considered statistically significant at the predetermined significance level.

Results sections of research reports communicate the findings of a project both with words and with tables and graphs. Many reports begin by presenting summary data in descriptive statistics. Next there may be information on the results from the inferential statistical tests. Details of these results may be given in tables, and highlights are presented in the narrative portion of the report.

As you begin to read results sections, we suggest that you be very familiar with the problem statement. This will help you understand the results. Note particularly whether an inferential test can be used appropriately. When no population is mentioned, the use of such a test may be questioned. You should also determine whether the selected inferential test is appropriate for answering the problem of the study. If results are statistically significant, consider how well they provide answers to the problem.

EXERCISES

Read the results sections of "Effects of Peer Presence on Sex-Typing of Children's Play Behavior" and "Perceptions of Social Control Among Black

College Students," which are included immediately after the questions. Write answers to the following questions. Compare your answers with those in the feedback for exercises at the end of this chapter.

1. Name each of the statistical tests used. For what purpose was each test used? How appropriate is each test for achieving its purpose?
2. Select and interpret two probability statements.
3. How appropriate are the results or findings for answering the problem or for testing the hypothesis of the study? Explain.

Serbin et al., *Effects of Peer Presence on Sex-Typing of Children's Play Behavior*

RESULTS

Effects of Peer Presence

Proportion of time spent in play with opposite-sex-typed toys in the three conditions is given in Table 1. Proportions are based on 36 observations per subject taken every 5 sec during each 3-min experimental trial. As seen in Table 1, proportion of play with opposite-sex-typed toys is higher for both boys and girls in the solitary condition (mean = 27.1%), and lowest in the opposite-sex peer condition (mean = 17.1%), with the same-sex peer condition intermediate (mean = 21.9%). Planned comparisons showed (Keppel, 1973) that the solitary and the opposite-sex peer conditions differed significantly, $F(1,60)$ = 4.68, $p < .05$. The same-sex peer condition did not differ significantly from either the solitary or opposite-sex peer condition.

Sex Differences

A 2 × 3 repeated measures ANOVA, using unweighted means, was performed to examine the effects of sex of subject and the interaction of sex with experimental condition. Average proportion of play with opposite-sex-typed toys was 29.2% for females, 14.5% for males. The main effect of sex was statistically significant, $F(1,60)$ = 6.13, $p < .025$. The effects of peer presence were similar for boys and girls, as indicated by the lack of a significant interaction between sex of child and experimental condition.

Table 1
PROPORTION OF TIME SPENT IN PLAY WITH OPPOSITE-SEX-TYPED
TOYS AS A FUNCTION OF PEER PRESENCE[a]

	Time (%)			
	Solitary	Same-sex peer	Opposite-sex peer	Average
Girls	33.5	30.7	24.1	29.2
Boys	20.6	13.0	10.0	14.5
Average	27.1	21.9	17.1	

[a] Proportions are based on 36 observations per subject taken every 5 sec during each 3-min experimental trial.

Order Effects

There appeared to be an increase in proportion of time spent playing with opposite-sex-typed toys over the three exposures to the testing situation that each child received (see Table 2). A second two-way repeated measure ANOVA, orthogonal to the preceding analysis, was performed to examine the significance of this effect and the interaction between order and sex of child. This analysis revealed a significant effect of order, $F(2,120) = 6.00$, $p < .005$. This pattern did not differ as a function of sex, as indicated by the lack of a significant interaction between order and sex of child.

Finally, there was no evidence of an interaction between experimental condition and the order in which the child received these conditions. This was evaluated by comparing the nine order $\times$ condition means after removing the variability due to the main effects of order and conditions. This interaction was not significant, $F(4,120) < 1$.

Talking between Subjects and Peers

No significant differences in amount of talking were found as a function of either sex or condition. Comments relating to the toys or play activities were occasionally noted, but were relatively rare (less than 5% of peer trials). Peers had been instructed to "pay attention" to their drawing, which may have reduced the frequency of interaction.

Table 2

PROPORTION OF TIME SPENT IN PLAY WITH OPPOSITE-SEX-TYPED TOYS AS A FUNCTION OF ORDER OF TRIAL AVERAGED OVER THE THREE PEER PRESENCE CONDITIONS[a]

	Time (%)			
	First trial	Second trial	Third trial	Average
Girls	21.6	26.5	40.2	29.2
Boys	9.7	12.8	21.2	14.5
Average	15.7	19.7	30.7	

[a] Proportions are based on 36 observations per subject taken every 5 sec during each 3-min experimental trial.

Babbit and Burbach, *Perceptions of Social Control Among Black College Students*

FINDINGS AND DISCUSSIONS

An examination of the data presented in Tables I, II, and III reveals a similar pattern across all three indexes of social control.

In all comparisons involving university and college Blacks with their urban

Table I
MEANS, STANDARD DEVIATIONS, AND *t*-RATIOS FOR
BLACK STUDENTS ON SOCIAL CONTROL (ADMINISTRATIVE CONTROL)

| Educational setting | Social control score | | | Comparisons | Value of *t* |
	Number	Mean	S.D.		
Urban center	49	21.78	4.13	College and urban center	8.83*
College	55	29.14	4.37	University and college	4.28*
University	56	32.54	3.95	University and urban center	13.57*

*Level of significance = .001

Table II
MEANS, STANDARD DEVIATIONS, AND *t*-RATIOS FOR
BLACK STUDENTS ON SOCIAL CONTROL (FACULTY CONTROL)

| Educational setting | Social control score | | | Comparisons | Value of *t* |
	Number	Mean	S.D.		
Urban center	49	20.40	3.75	College and urban center	12.09*
College	55	30.76	4.95	University and college	4.24*
University	56	34.84	5.18	University and urban center	16.47*

*Level of significance = .001

Table III
MEANS, STANDARD DEVIATIONS, AND *t*-RATIOS FOR
BLACK STUDENTS ON SOCIAL CONTROL (PEER CONTROL)

| Educational setting | Social control score | | | Comparisons | Value of *t* |
	Number	Mean	S.D.		
Urban center	49	23.00	4.64	College and urban center	12.80*
College	55	35.67	5.45	University and college	.39
University	56	36.05	4.63	University and urban center	14.39*

*Level of significance = .001

center counterparts, the latter group was found to perceive their school's authority structure in a significantly more positive light than the former. Fur- ther, students representative of the university setting were significantly more negative in their attitudes toward administrative and faculty authority than were those from the college. However, the comparison between these two groups on perceptions of peer control did not produce a significant difference.

Although our central concern in discussing these findings is with group differences, the level of social control at which the differences were found is also of interest. For purposes of discussion, let us use the arithmetic midpoint of each scale (administrative control = 25; faculty control = 30; peer control = 32.5) as the points of division between the positive and negative halves of hypothetical control continua. Viewed in this way, it can be seen that the mean scores for the college and university groups are all located on the negative side of the three continua. The means produced by the urban center sub-sample, on the other hand, all point toward the extreme positive end. Thus, it is not only that these groups were found to differ on social control in a comparative sense, it is that their means are representative of theoretically different areas along hypothetical continua, one set signifying generally positive and the other two more negative perceptions of social control.

The fact that these findings show that Black students can differ in their perceptions of social control across three institutional structures in higher education is of primary importance. This, of course, raises the question of what factors might be contributing to these differences. Although the limited scope of the present investigation precludes any kind of empirical answer at this time, a speculative probing of the question suggests the possibility that student perceptions of social control are based on (1) size of organization, (2) racial composition of administrators, and (3) span of control.

Complicating the discussion of a subject as complex as student perceptions of social control is the probability that there is a multiplicity of factors involved. Among these are several which we were unable to explore in the present study, but which should be considered by future researchers. For example, it may be that in addition to race, the sex, age, values, attitudes, personality, and leadership style of key authorities figure prominently in the formation of student perceptions of social control. Also, it seems reasonable to assume that social factors such as organizational climate, friendship cliques, living arrangements, communication patterns, and the like, influence the way in which a student perceives the authority structure of an institution. What is needed from this point is a line of additive research designed to search out the role that these and other variables play in the development of student perceptions of social control in educational settings. Hopefully, the evidence acruing from this research will help college and university personnel develop more supportive learning environments for their students.

FEEDBACK FOR EXERCISES

"Effects of Peer Presence on Sex-Typing of Children's Play Behavior"

1. Planned comparisons were applied to the data for testing the effects of peer presence on the choice of toys. The proportions of time spent in play with opposite-sex-typed toys were compared for each of the three experimental conditions. Two analyses of variance were used in this study. A two-way ANOVA was run to see whether

there was statistically significant interaction between the sex of the subject and the experimental conditions. A second two-way AN-OVA was used to determine whether there was a significant interaction between the order of the treatments and the sex of the child. Each of these tests of statistical significance is appropriate for the analysis in which it was used. Unnamed tests of statistical significance were used to see whether there were significant differences between the amount of talking and sex and the amount of talking and order of treatments.

2. We counted the following statements that involved probability or significance testing. (You need only *two* of these.)

    Under "Effects of Peer Presence":

    Planned comparisons showed that the solitary and the opposite-sex peer conditions differed significantly, $F(1,60) = 4.68$, $p < .05$.

    Interpretation: The average proportions of all the children under the solitary conditions differed significantly from the average proportion of children under the opposite-sex condition. The difference was so great that it would have happened by chance only 5 times in 100.

    The same-sex peer condition did not differ significantly from either the solitary or opposite-sex peer condition.

    Interpretation: Whatever differences existed between the children in the same-sex peer condition compared with the solitary or opposite-sex peer condition could have happened by chance. They were probably due to variations within the sample.

    Under "Sex Differences":

    The main effect of sex was statistically significant, $F(1,60) = 6.13$, $p < .025$.

    Interpretation: Proportions of play with opposite-sex-typed toys were compared for girls and boys. The difference was great enough that it could have happened by chance only 2.5 times out of 100. The girls therefore represent a different population than the boys.

    The effects of peer presence were similar for boys and girls, as indicated by the lack of a significant interaction between sex of child and experimental condition.

    Interpretation: The experimental condition produced similar effects in both boys and girls; it did not bring out a statistically stronger or weaker response for either sex group.

Under "Order Effects":

This analysis revealed a significant effect of order, $F(2,120) = 6.00$, $p < .005$.

Interpretation: A second ANOVA was done, which was independent of the first analysis. The differences that were observed indicated that the order of the conditions did have an effect on the children in terms of the proportion of time spent playing with opposite-sex-typed toys. The difference was so great that it could have happened by chance only 5 times in 1,000.

This pattern did not differ as a function of sex, as indicated by the lack of a significant interaction between order and sex of child.

Interpretation: The sex of the child did not interact with order to produce a statistically significant difference. Order affected girls and boys in the same way.

Finally, there was no evidence of an interaction between experimental condition and the order in which the child received these conditions. . . . This interaction was not significant, $F(4,120) < 1$.

Interpretation: Comparison of proportions of time spent with opposite-sex-typed toys in terms of interaction between condition and order showed no statistically significant differences.

Under "Talking between Subjects and Peers":

No significant differences in amount of talking were found as a function of either sex or condition.

Interpretation: Boys and girls talked about the same amount regardless of the experimental condition.

3. The results are appropriate for answering the problem of the study. From the number of analyses, it appears that the authors exhausted the possibilities for analyzing the data. The results do give evidence that peers function directly as discriminative stimuli for preschoolers' sex-typed play behavior.

"Perceptions of Social Control Among Black College Students"

1. In this study *t*-tests were used to compare means between pairs of schools (see "Comparisons" in each table). Some type of analysis of variance would have been a more appropriate statistical test since three means/variances are being compared. If there had been

a significant F-value, then one or more multiple comparison tests could have been used to locate significant differences.

2. In each table two or more t-values are noted as significant at $p < .001$. There are no other statements related to probability or results of significance testing. In Table I, the t-ratio of 8.83 is interpreted as follows: The difference between the means of the college and the urban center was of such size that it would have happened by chance only 1 time in a 1,000. Therefore, the means probably represent different populations. Each of the other t-ratios can be interpreted similarly.

3. It's difficult to say that the results are appropriate for answering the problem of the study because t-tests were used instead of analysis of variance. Because of the large number of t-tests that were computed, there's a strong possibility that some of the significant t-values were the result of chance.

RECOMMENDED REFERENCES

Ary, D., & Jacobs, L. C. Introduction to statistics: Purposes and procedures. New York: Holt, Rinehart and Winston, 1976. This book lives up to its name. The fog level is low making the information readily understandable.

Bartz, A. E. Basic descriptive statistics for education and the behavioral sciences (4th ed.). Minneapolis: Burgess, 1971. This book contains information about the meaning and the calculations of all the descriptive statistics. If you read it now, concentrate on understanding terms.

Cohen, J. Some statistical issues in psychological research. In B. B. Wolman (Ed.). Handbook of clinical psychology. New York: McGraw-Hill, 1965. Cohen presents a practical and highly readable discussion of statistical power, significance, and parametric versus nonparametric statistics.

Elzey, F. E. A first reader in statistics (2nd ed.). Monterey, Calif.: Brooks/Cole, 1974. Elzey does an excellent job of explaining basic statistical concepts without unnecessary jargon. If you prefer to learn about statistics without having to read formulas, this book is for you.

Huck, S. W., Cormier, W. H., & Bounds, W. G., Jr. Reading statistics and research. New York: Harper & Row, 1974. Part II provides a well-written, fairly easy to understand explanation of the statistical tests discussed in this chapter. Excerpts from reports illustrate the text material.

Keppel, G. Design and analysis: A researcher's handbook. Englewood Cliffs, N.J.: Prentice-Hall, 1973. If you've had some background in statistics, this book is a very helpful source for data analysis procedures in experimental designs.

Kimball, G. A. How to use and misuse statistics. Englewood Cliffs, N.J.: Prentice-Hall, 1978. Everyday examples and humor make reading this book a delight. Kimball does a good job of making statistics understandable.

Mendenhall, W., McClave, J. T., & Ramey, M. Statistics for psychology (2nd ed.). North Scituate, Mass.: Duxbury, 1977. Numerous examples of statistical concepts are present in this text. The approach is to make statistics understandable to beginning students. Because of these features, this book is one of the more readable statistics texts.

Roscoe, J. T. *Fundamental research statistics for the behavorial sciences* (2nd ed.). New York: Holt, Rinehart and Winston, 1975. This text explains the rationale for statistical concepts very lucidly. It merits careful reading.

Runyon, R. P., & Haber, A. *Fundamentals of behavioral statistics* (4th ed.). Reading, Mass.: Addison-Wesley, 1980. Most of the concepts that we've mentioned about statistics are treated in this popular text. The content of the exercises and the physical format of the book make it easy to read.

Siegel, S. *Nonparametric statistics for the behavioral sciences.* New York: McGraw-Hill, 1956. Siegel's book is a classic on nonparametric statistical tests. All the tests we've described and many others are discussed in his book. Also there are tables of critical values for the nonparametric tests in the appendices.

7

Reading
Discussion
Sections

When you've completed this chapter, we believe you will be able to read almost any research report with understanding. You have previously read about all parts of a report except the final discussion section, which is the subject of this chapter. Dissussion sections contain conclusions, interpretations of results, and recommendations. The material in this chapter will help you understand some of the things that researchers must consider in order to make conclusions, interpretations, and recommendations about their results.

Chapter objective.   After you complete this chapter, you should be able to assess the appropriateness of *conclusions* of the study, *interpretations of results*, and *recommendations* in selected research reports.

BACKGROUND FOR READING DISCUSSION SECTIONS

Definition of Conclusions

Most people read the discussion section of a report to learn the outcomes of a project. It is important to understand that the outcomes are more than the results from the analysis of data. Researchers must judge whether or not their results shed light on answers to the research problem. **Conclusions** are the researchers' statements of what the results say about the problem. Usually they spell out answers to the problem or subproblems, and tell if the research hypothesis was supported. Still other conclusions indicate how well a theory or part of a theory stood the test of an empirical investigation.

Processes in Drawing Conclusions

Drawing conclusions involves examining the results of the project in terms of the problem statement. A researcher must first decide how plausibly the results answer the problem. If the results are confusing, the project will have to be repeated before conclusions can be drawn. If, on repetition, there is still no definite pattern in the findings, the design may either be modified and tried a third time or the researchers may decide that the variables are not related and scrap the project. On the other hand, results may turn out just as expected on the first try, which would enable the researchers to draw conclusions.

In difference studies, conclusions allow readers to draw inferences about cause-and-effect relationships among variables. The following are illustrative conclusions for difference studies mentioned in Chapter 2:

1a.   First-graders learn about the same number of new words whether the teacher uses a multisensory approach or an auditory-visual approach to reading instruction.

Conclusion 1a is logical if results of the study were statistically nonsignificant. This suggests that the research hypothesis should not be accepted. If results had been statistically significant, the conclusion could be stated this way:

1b. First-graders learn more words when taught with a multisensory approach to reading than they do when an auditory-visual approach is used.

These two conclusions are typical of those possible from the results of a simple research design where the effect of only one independent variable (reading instruction method) in two forms (multisensory approach and auditory-visual approach) was analyzed. The conclusions are apparent based on a test result such as a statistically significant t- or F-ratio.

In studies that use more complex designs, conclusions must be based on more than just an overall test result that is statistically significant. These designs include those with more than two levels of treatment. The test result may indicate that the systematic variance is different from what would be expected by chance, but the precise reason for this difference may not be revealed. To pinpoint the source of the unusual variation, researchers do *post hoc* analyses of their data. This enables them to draw conclusions about which forms of the independent variables, alone or in interaction, were the source of differences. Here is such an example, based on another research problem:

2. Counterconditioning procedures for improving spelling performance are more effective with elementary grade children of low-average performance than they are with children of high-average performance.

In this situation researchers found a significant F-ratio in a factorial design that used three methods of spelling instruction and two levels of student academic performance as independent variables. The overall F-ratio did not enable them to state which forms of spelling instruction were more effective with the two kinds of students. *Post hoc* analyses indicated that a specific conclusion could be made about the effectiveness of the counterconditioning method with students of low-average performance.

In association studies, results indicate the degree and direction of the relationship between variables. This allows rather definite conclusions to be drawn. Here are some hypothetical conclusions for studies mentioned in Chapter 2:

3. Prealgebra aptitude can be used to predict success in Algebra I.
4. Self-concept has a positive correlation with public-speaking abilities among high school students.

Association studies usually yield correlation coefficients, which, if squared, tell the percentage of variance that is shared by the variables (see Appendix C-2). This information can be very valuable, although no cause-and-effect relationship can be stated about the variables.

Although conclusions are usually based on the results of inferential tests, researchers do weigh alternative explanations of the results. In experimental studies, for example, finding a statistically significant difference between groups is supposed to mean that the independent variable (treatment) made a difference. Did it? Researchers must review the procedures of the project and satisfy themselves that manipulation of the independent variable is the most probable explanation of the results. Variables that were not controlled must be ruled out as major contributors to changes in the dependent variable. Having decided this issue, researchers are in a position to state conclusions.

READING AND ANALYZING DISCUSSION SECTIONS

Content and Form

The discussion section of most research reports does not follow a prescribed format, nor is the content as standard as that in other sections of the report. The discussion reflects the author's individuality by both the things that are mentioned and those that are omitted. Other section of reports have very definite items that must be included, sometimes in a particular order. Discussion sections do not require this structure. As Chapter 6 indicated, authors sometimes combine results and discussion. This seems true particularly when researchers decide to make several *post hoc* analyses of data or when they gradually introduce the "statistics" of the study.

There are some common threads of content running through most discussion sections. Researchers draw conclusions about the study, interpret or discuss the results, and make recommendations based on the findings. The paragraphs that follow describe these functions in detail.

Conclusions.   Researchers answer the problem of the study in the conclusions based on their implementation of a research design. Conclusions are sometimes numbered and listed at the beginning of the discussion section. In other reports, authors present some or all of their discussion of the results before drawing conclusions.

Here are two problem statements and the conclusions from published reports. As you read them notice how conclusions answer problems.

1. Daniels and Hewitt (1978) investigated the effects of different levels of test anxiety on actual classroom test performance over the course of an entire semester. They tried to find out whether the effects of

anxiety interacted with the difficulty and type of exam questions, and sex and intelligence of subjects. These are their conclusions:

> The effect of anxiety seemed to be a highly consistent one across a variety of conditions. The results were the same for men and women. The results were the same when intelligence was held constant and regardless of the type of exam question asked. . . . Overall, there seemed to be an extremely strong relationship between anxiety and performance. . . . (pp. 344–45).

2. Messé, Crano, Messé, and Rice (1979) examined the relationship between scores on tests of mental ability and classroom performance in a large sample of British elementary school students. Results from their study led to these conclusions:

    > . . . standardized tests of mental ability can be reasonable predictors of young children's classroom performance in traditional academic topics. . . . the predictions derived from mental ability tests are not biased against lower SES [socioeconomic status] children (p. 240).

Interpretations of results.   Researchers almost always offer an **interpretation** of their results, which refers to the body of related research and theory as well as to the circumstances of the study. These statements reveal at least part of the deliberations they went through in drawing conclusions. Commonly there are two frames of references for interpretations: those that are internal to the design components and those that are external to the problem context.

Interpretations in terms of research design.   Interpretations may be made in relation to any one or all of the components of research design: subjects, instruments, treatment administration, data collection, and data analysis. When results are discussed in terms of these components, researchers are often able to show how alternative hypotheses were ruled out in experiments, and explain why the results happened as they did. The paragraphs that follow illustrate these kinds of interpretive statements.

1. *Subjects.* Sepie and Keeling (1978) studied the relationship between three types of anxiety and under-achievement in mathematics in elementary students. Girls scored higher than boys on measures of general anxiety, test anxiety, and mathematics anxiety, but differences were large and statistically significant only for general anxiety scores. The authors indicated two possible reasons for this pattern of results: Boys may defend against their anxiety to a lesser degree in testing or mathematics than they do in other circumstances. Since girls are reportedly more acculturated to schooling, their anxiety may be less evident in academic situations. Both of

these reasons could explain why girls and boys scored similarly on measures of test anxiety and mathematics anxiety. In this case the researchers are interpreting their findings in light of generally accepted beliefs about boys and girls.

2. *Instruments.* The relationship between locus of control, group cohesiveness, and job satisfaction was the focus of a study by Dailey (1978). One of the findings showed a weak interaction between locus of control and cohesiveness with respect to workers' satisfaction with their coworkers. Dailey interpreted the weakness of the interaction as a defect in instrumentation for locus of control. He said that the instrument used in his study was not specifically designed to measure that variable in a work setting. Hence, the measurement was not specific enough for the problem and could be responsible for the weak interaction.

3. *Treatment administration.* Westervelt and McKinney (1980) compared the aspirations and interests of nonhandicapped children with those of able-bodied and handicapped peers. Results of a multivariate ANOVA showed that able-bodied girls who viewed the film (the treatment) showed an increased similarity of interests with handicapped peers but only in physical education activity. The researchers interpreted this result with reference to the treatment by saying that the physical education area had the greatest potential for change, and the majority of activities in the film were in physical education. The specifics of the treatment, therefore, could be expected to have an effect on the dependent variable.

4. *Data collection.* Teacher comments were related to student achievement in a study by Fredrick, Walberg, and Rasher (1979). The authors explained that the number of evaluation statements by teachers to students was "surprisingly low and this needs further checking. The observers may have missed the subtle evaluative statements" (p. 65). In this interpretation the researchers suggested that possible errors in data collection may have been responsible for incorrect or incomplete data.

5. *Data analysis.* Interpretations involving data analysis can include *post hoc* analyses or explanation of difficulties with the data. A study to see whether learning and retention were facilitated by advance and post organizers in orally presented instruction was done by Alexander, Frankiewicz, and Williams (1979). There were several treatments and measurements, which meant that a multivariate data analysis was necessary. A global null hypothesis of treatments interacting with learning and retention was rejected. The authors pointed out that *post hoc* multivariate techniques— namely, discriminant function analyses—were used to determine the particular sources of variation between groups but that the results of these analyses did not lead to conclusions about which treatment was most advantageous.

Daniels and Hewitt (1978) suggested the second type of interpretation with respect to data analysis. In their study of effects of anxiety, they found that the only variable to interact with anxiety was item difficulty, which was measured at two levels. They attempted to do *post hoc* analyses to examine this interaction further, but they were unable to do so because there were too few items in some of the categories in the new analysis. Therefore, they felt there could be no reliable analysis.

Interpretations in terms of context.   Interpretations of findings are also made in terms of the context for the problem of the study. Chapter 2 indicated that researchers review literature related to their problem and often report summaries and evaluation statements about the most pertinent studies. Based on the literature review, researchers usually state the need for their study as a replication of previous studies, an exploration of a new field, or a study of problems of long standing. At the end of a study, researchers look back at the events of the project and try to tie results from their current study with those mentioned in the review. They should show evidence to support their justification for the study; in a sense they may try to "prove" the significance of their project.

Interpretations based on the context show that results of the current study either support, partially support, or contradict previous research. The following examples illustrate the extremes of these possibilities.

1. Messé and associates (1979) reviewed a number of studies concerning mental ability tests and classroom performance measures, pointing out possible reasons for inconsistent results. Their stated justification was to analyze data from three years of longitudinal information on the relationship of socioeconomic status, classroom performance, and mental ability scores of a large sample (about 5,200 children). They hoped to "provide the means by which the critical IQ-classroom performance issue can be investigated in a reasonably definitive manner" (p. 336). After completing their data analyses, the researchers explained that the results clearly supported the general correlational findings of two studies mentioned in their review of literature.

2. Meissner (1978) found that boys performed significantly better than girls in describing concepts. She pointed out that this finding contradicts the results of other studies of general verbal fluency.

Recommendations.   Suggestions that researchers make on the completion of a project are called **recommendations.** We have commented several times about differences among research reports and readerships of various journals. Because of these differences, you are likely to see recommendations meant primarily for other researchers as well as those for practitioners, sometimes within the same report.

When authors recommend ideas to other researchers, suggestions typically take the form "if we had it to do over, we would. . . ." These statements are finished by suggested changes in design that the researchers believe might bring about more favorable results, or that might add to the body of knowledge about the topic. Suggestions could include designing a project that uses experimental rather than descriptive methodology, using subjects from other populations, lengthening the treatment period, or using alternative instruments better suited to measuring the variables.

Here are some examples of recommendations addressed primarily to other researchers:

1. Lawton and Fowell (1978) tested Ausubel's subsumption theory of learning in a study with preschool children. Although the researchers found that treatment produced significant differences in learning on a short-term basis (seven weeks), they recommended doing similar preschool studies involving long-term assessment to give further information about the treatment.
2. Having studied locus of control and group cohesiveness, Dailey (1978) found a weak interaction between these variables with respect to satisfaction with coworkers. He recommended research with other aspects of perceived group processes and characteristics as a condition for making practical applications of the findings of his study.

Occasionally researchers simply state that additional research needs to be done without specifying how or why. Unless there is reason for doing new research in the problem area, blanket-type recommendations are wasted. The more clearly researchers communicate suggested alterations in research design, the easier and more productive the next project in that area is likely to be.

Researchers also address recommendations to practitioners. This is particularly true when the research setting was in schools or when the findings are relatively easy to translate into actual practice. These are some examples of recommendations for practitioners:

1. Spiegel and Bryant (1978) found that mean response time for processing information correlated well with results on standardized intelligence tests. Based on this finding, they suggested substituting a response time measure where conventional intelligence tests cannot be used.
2. Mangieri and Baldwin (1979), on finding a high correlation between word meaning and spelling, recommended integrating meaning into spelling instruction by combining spelling and vocabulary study.
3. Based on a study of the amount of time students actually spend on school work, Fredrick, Walberg, and Rasher (1979) recommended

bringing in absent students and increasing the quality of classroom interaction to improve student learning.

These examples document how some research findings are applicable in schools. Although the recommendations are not usually cast as specific suggestions, reading them in the context of their respective reports should add to your confidence that they are appropriate and applicable.

Suggestions for Reading and Analysis

When you begin reading a discussion section, it's a good idea to have a very clear understanding of both the problem and the results or findings. Both sets of information are critical for understanding the discussion. We suggest that you read the discussion through just to get a general idea of what the author is saying. Then reread the section to determine what the conclusions of the study are. You should determine whether there is a conclusion for *each* question or hypothesis. Then decide whether the results point to the conclusions; for example, have the authors drawn conclusions that are warranted on the basis of results? Are the conclusions limited to the population to which they can legitimately be generalized? If your answer to any of these questions is uncertain, reread the discussion, trying to see whether you may have missed some information.

We further suggest that you try to figure out whether any unusual results are explained. If the researchers predicted that one result would take place and another actually happened, you are entitled to know the probable reasons for the unexpected outcome. The researchers need to explain these unanticipated results. Even if the outcomes weren't unusual, there should be a few details about the actual execution of the project.

At some point in the discussion, the authors should refer to the context of the problem. Try to determine whether their justification for doing the study was well-founded. Did research that was done as a replication yield similar results? Has the new research shed new light on long-unresolved issues? Did the research break ground in a new area in a fruitful way? The authors should indicate how well the study has met their justification. To do this, they will usually compare their work to previous studies.

Finally, look for recommendations that the authors make. As you read them, decide whether the findings and interpretations really support such suggestions. Beware of global statements suggesting additional research. Recommendations should give specific directions for additional research efforts. The conclusions of the study need to clearly support recommendations to practitioners.

Occasionally readers may make mistakes in analyzing discussion sections. One of these is failing to assess the viability of the conclusions. The results and the setting for data collection should clearly support the conclusions. Unless they do, the conclusions may be unwarranted. Conclusions should also point toward the goal of science suggested by the problem of the study.

A descriptive study, for example, should not have cause-and-effect relationships mentioned in the conclusions.

These are criteria for judging discussion sections:

1. *Conclusions should state clear answers to the research problem(s).* You should have no trouble locating straightforward answers to each research problem or subproblem mentioned in the introduction to the study. Conclusions should be generalized to the appropriate population.

2. *Interpretations of findings should be insightful.* Results are often influenced by imperfections in the research design, which can be explained in the discussion. Also, results of the current study need to be interpreted in terms of previous research in the problem area. Suitable explanations of contradictory results should be made. The interpretation should support the stated justification for the study.

3. *Appropriate recommendations should be made.* If modification of the design is likely to produce more definitive results, recommendations should state which design components should be changed. Wholesale recommendations for replicating the study are not suggested. Recommendations should also be made when conclusions can be appropriately applied in practical situations.

SUMMARY

Conclusions are the answers to research problems. In difference studies conclusions affirm the cause-and-effect relationship between the independent and dependent variables. In association studies conclusions indicate the degree and direction of the relationship among variables. Drawing conclusions involves the researchers' judgments about the results of the study as answers to the problem. Even armed with statistical significance, researchers still have to rule out alternative explanations for the findings of the study before drawing conclusions.

The discussion section is the most informal part of a research report. Though loosely organized, this section has conclusions and usually contains interpretations and recommendations. Interpretations may be in terms of the design components and/or the literature review or context of the study. Ideally both kinds of interpretations are presented. Recommendations may be made to other researchers doing studies in the problem area. These recommendations suggest modifications in the design such as altering the instruments, using subjects from a different population, or using a different methodology. Recommendations may also be made to practitioners when the results can be applied in educational settings.

We suggest that you first read the discussion section quickly to get an overview of its organization. Then reread the section to figure out what the conclusions are, keeping in mind how well the results support the conclusions. Look also for any statements explaining unusual results. If the researchers' results are not what were expected, some explanation should be included. As you read the discussion, see whether the justification for the study is supported and look for the recommendations. Note whether the recommendations are specific enough to be helpful to other researchers or to practitioners.

In discussion sections, conclusions should state clear answers to the research problem. Interpretations of findings may reflect consideration of the actual execution of the research design components. Finally, appropriate recommendations may be made, both to other researchers investigating variables in the problem area and to practitioners, where suitable.

EXERCISES

Read the discussion sections of "Effects of Peer Presence on Sex-Typing of Children's Play Behavior" and "Perceptions of Social Control Among Black College Students," which appear immediately following the questions. The introductory sections of these reports are at the end of Chapter 2. Write your answers to the following questions and compare them with the feedback for exercises at the end of this chapter.

1. Identify the conclusions of the study. How well do the statements answer the problem of the study? Explain.
2. Are there statements that interpret the findings in terms of one or more components of research design? If so, cite at least one. How appropriate is this interpretation?
3. Are there any interpretations of findings or results related to the context of the problem statement? If so, cite at least one. How appropriate is this interpretation?
4. Cite at least one recommendation. Does this recommendation seem warranted in view of the results of the study? Explain.

Serbin et al., *Effects of Peer Presence on Sex-Typing of Children's Play Behavior*

DISCUSSION

Results of the present study indicate that peer presence, specifically the presence of opposite-sex peers, reduces the probability that children will play with opposite-sex-typed toys. These results are consistent with those of Bem and Lenny (1976) using college students. With the present paradigm, in which children had to choose between masculine and feminine toys and no "neutral" toys were available, it is impossible to specify whether peer presence increased avoidance of sex-inappropriate toys or approach toward sex-appropriate toys. If the effect of peer presence was primarily inhibitory, the specific mechanism for the peer inhibition effect is unclear. Glances by the peer and in some cases negative remarks may have discouraged exploration. In many instances, though, a subject child who picked up an inappropriate toy merely looked over at the peer who was busily engaged in drawing and then switched back to an "appropriate" activity. This suggests that simply the presence of a peer, without unfriendly glances or remarks, is a sufficient stimulus to discourage participation in activities which are culturally labeled as sex inappropriate.

The alternative hypothesis is that peer presence, especially the presence of an opposite-sex peer, increased childrens' approach behavior toward sex-appropriate toys. Opposite-sex peers may have served to "remind" the subjects of the cultural sex-typing of the toys and thus to enhance the probability of conformity to their own sex role. Of course, it is possible, and even likely, that peer presence can serve to either increase sex-appropriate play or decrease sex-inappropriate play, depending on the specific play materials available. Further studies in which nonsex-typed toys are made available in addition to sex-appropriate or -inappropriate toys will be necessary to clarify this issue. However, regardless of the specific function of the peer effect, the fact that peer presence already affects the probability of sex-typed play in these preschool age subjects suggests that children have had a learning history which has established peers, especially those of the opposite sex, as discriminative stimuli for sex role conformity.

The sex difference in overall rates of play with sex-inappropriate toys confirms many reports in the literature that boys' sex-typing of play behavior is more firmly established and pervasive than girls' during the preschool period (Hartup, Moore, & Sager, 1963; Maccoby & Jacklin, 1974, pp. 283–284). The finding that play with opposite-sex-typed toys increased gradually over trials with increased exposure to the toys and playroom may have simply reflected satiation with the sex-appropriate toys available. Alternatively, this finding may indicate that children will begin to explore toys initially considered "inappropriate," if allowed the time to do so. This finding has implications for the assessment of sex-typing of toy choices in laboratory situations, since initial toy choices may be more stereotypic than later choices.

In conclusion, the results of the study support the hypothesis that peers function as discriminative stimuli for conformity to sex-typed play patterns during the preschool period. Further research is needed on the development of this phenomenon and on the specific function of peers as discriminative stimuli in classroom and other play environments.

Babbit and Burbach, *Perceptions of Social Control Among Black College Students*

FINDINGS AND DISCUSSIONS

An examination of the data presented in Tables I, II, and III reveals a similar pattern across all three indexes of social control. In all comparisons involving university and college Blacks with their urban center counterparts, the latter group was found to perceive their school's authority structure in a significantly more positive light than the former. Further, students representative of the university setting were significantly more negative in their attitudes toward administrative and faculty authority than were those from the college. However, the comparison between these two groups on perceptions of peer control did not produce a significant difference.

Although our central concern in discussing these findings is with group differences, the level of social control at which the differences were found is also of interest. For purposes of discussion, let us use the arithmetic midpoint of each scale (administrative control = 25; faculty control = 30; peer control = 32.5) as the points of division between the positive and negative halves of hypothetical control continua. Viewed in this way, it can be seen that the mean scores for the college and university groups are all located on the negative side of the three continua. The means produced by the urban center sub-sample, on the other hand, all point toward the extreme positive end. Thus, it is not only that these groups were found to differ on social control in a comparative sense, it is that their means are representative of theoretically different areas along hypothetical continua, one set signifying generally positive and the other two more negative perceptions of social control.

The fact that these findings show that Black students can differ in their perceptions of social control across three institutional structures in higher education is of primary importance. This, of course, raises the question of what factors might be contributing to these differences. Although the limited scope of the present investigation precludes any kind of empirical answer at this time, a speculative probing of the question suggests the possibility that student perceptions of social control are based on (1) size of organization, (2) racial composition of administrators, and (3) span of control.

Complicating the discussion of a subject as complex as student perceptions of social control is the probability that there is a multiplicity of factors involved. Among these are several which we were unable to explore in the present study, but which should be considered by future researchers. For example, it may be that in addition to race, the sex, age, values, attitudes, personality, and leadership style of key authorities figure prominently in the formation of student perceptions of social control. Also, it seems reasonable to assume that social factors such as organizational climate, friendship cliques, living arrangements, communication patterns, and the like, influence the way in which a student perceives the authority structure of an institution. What is needed from this point is a line of additive research designed to search out the role that these and other variables play in the development of student perceptions of social control in educational settings. Hopefully, the evidence accruing from this research will help college and university personnel develop more supportive learning environments for their students.

Table I

MEANS, STANDARD DEVIATIONS, AND *t*-RATIOS FOR BLACK STUDENTS
ON SOCIAL CONTROL (ADMINISTRATIVE CONTROL)

Educational setting	Social Control Score			Comparisons	Value of *t*
	Number	Mean	S.D.		
Urban Center	49	21.78	4.13	College and Urban Center	8.83*
College	55	29.14	4.37	University and College	4.28*
University	56	32.54	3.95	University and Urban Center	13.57*

*Level of significance = .001

Table II

MEANS, STANDARD DEVIATIONS, AND *t*-RATIOS FOR BLACK STUDENTS
ON SOCIAL CONTROL (FACULTY CONTROL)

Educational Setting	Social Control Score				Value of *t*
	Number	Mean	S.D.	Comparisons	
Urban Center	49	20.40	3.75	College and Urban Center	12.09*
College	55	30.76	4.95	University and College	4.24*
University	56	34.84	5.18	University and Urban Center	16.47*

*Level of significance = .001

Table III

MEANS, STANDARD DEVIATIONS, AND *t*-RATIOS FOR BLACK STUDENTS
ON SOCIAL CONTROL (PEER CONTROL)

Educational Setting	Social Control Score				Value of *t*
	Number	Mean	S.D.	Comparisons	
Urban Center	49	23.00	4.64	College and Urban Center	12.80*
College	55	35.67	5.45	University and College	.39
University	56	36.05	4.63	University and Urban Center	14.39*

*Level of significance = .001

FEEDBACK FOR EXERCISES

This section is intended to let you know how well you answered the questions in the exercises. Your wording may differ, but the meaning should be the same. Write answers to one or more of the reports in Appendix A for additional practice.

"Effects of Peer Presence on Sex-Typing of Children's Play Behavior"

1. The conclusion of the study is stated in the final paragraph as follows: "In conclusion, the results of the study support the hypothesis that peers function as discriminative stimuli for conformity to sex-typed play patterns during the preschool period." That this statement directly answers the problem of the study is shown by the fact that the authors simply restated the hypothesis, adding the words concerning support. The conclusion provides a very clear statement of the answer to the problem.

2. Two sets of statements clearly seem to interpret findings in terms of research design. You should have discussed at least one of these.

   a. Beginning in the first paragraph is this statement: "With the present paradigm, in which children had to choose between masculine and feminine toys and no 'neutral' toys were available, it is impossible to specify whether peer presence increased avoidance of sex-inappropriate toys or approach toward sex-appropriate toys. If the effect of peer presence . . . culturally labeled as sex inappropriate." The researchers indicate that because their design did not call for any neutral toys, it was really impossible to be sure whether there was avoidance behavior (as the hypothesis suggests) or approach behavior. Observations of the subjects indicate that either avoidance or approach behavior could account for differences in the choice of toys.

b.   Near the end of the discussion are these phrases, which seem to interpret the findings in terms of the research design: "The finding that play with opposite-sex-typed toys increased gradually over trials with increased exposure to the toys and playroom . . . if allowed the time to do so." The design used in this study involved repeated measures; for example, the *same* children were observed under three different conditions. The researchers are saying that the sameness of toy choices on the three occasions seems to have an effect on what the children did. They are pointing out that perhaps the repeated exposure to the same set of toys may have provoked children to explore toys initially considered "inappropriate."

3.   Two sets of statements clearly seem to interpret the findings in terms of the context for the problem. You should have discussed one of these.

a.   Beginning in the first paragraph are these words: "Results of the present study. . . . These results are consistent with those of Bem and Lenny (1976) using college students." The authors are indicating that the results of their study with preschoolers are very much like those that Bem and Lenny found in a group of college students.

b.   In the next to the last paragraph are these words: "The sex difference in overall rates of play . . . . pp. 283-284." Again, what Serbin and associates found in their study confirms what two other research efforts in this area found.

4.   We were able to find two recommendations in the discussion section. You should have discussed *one* of these.

a.   Midway in the discussion are these words: "Further studies in which non-sex-typed toys are made available in addition to sex-appropriate or -inappropriate toys will be necessary to clarify this issue." In view of the authors' interpretation of the findings (see 2), this recommendation seems highly appropriate.

b.   The last sentence is: "Further research is needed on the development of this phenomenon and on the specific function of peers as discriminative stimuli in classroom and other play environments." This recommendation seems to be a general one, and we believe it is unnecessary. Research in the present study combined with that in the studies cited in the introduction supports the fact that peers *do* function as discriminative stimuli.

"Perceptions of Social Control Among Black College Students"

1. The conclusion to this study is located in the next to the last paragraph, as follows: "The fact that these findings show that Black students can differ in their perceptions of social control across three institutional structures in higher education is of primary importance." This statement answers the problem of the study directly.
2. The researchers interpreted the findings by comparing the mean scores for the college and university groups with the arithmetic midpoints on each of the scales. This comparison showed "one set [the urban center group] signifying generally positive and the other two [the college and university groups] more negative perceptions of social control." The appropriateness of this interpretation is difficult to judge. If these interpretations had been made from *post hoc* tests following analysis of variance, they would be stronger statements about the results.
3. There are no interpretations of the findings in terms of the context.*
4. In the final paragraph, the authors recommend additional research involving personal-social characteristics and organizational social factors with social control. The recommendation seems warranted based on the results of the study. A more specific recommendation would be of greater help to other researchers who investigate this topic.

* Several interpretations of the findings were made in terms of the context in the original version of this article. These were omitted in the published version to save space, according to Burbach. (Personal communication, February 4, 1980.)

RECOMMENDED REFERENCES

Kerlinger, F. N. *Foundations of behavioral research* (2nd ed.). New York: Holt, Rinehart and Winston, 1973. The subsection, "The Interpretation of Research Data," in Chapter 9 clarifies the meanings of some concepts involved in interpreting data. It is well written.

Stephens, J. M. Making dependable use of published research. *Journal of Educational Research*, 1967, *61*, 99–104. The checklist and flow chart are helpful for critical readers of experimental research reports. By going through the set of questions to be answered, the reader moves quickly toward drawing his or her own conclusions for a study.

Tukey, J. W. Conclusions vs. decisions. In R. O. Collier, Jr. & T. J. Hummel (Eds.), *Experimental design and interpretation*. Berkeley, Calif.: McCutchan, 1977. Tukey discusses, in a very practical way, some considerations that researchers need to take in drawing conclusions. The information relates very closely to what we've described as judgments about the results as answers to the researcher's questions.

8

Consuming Research: Ethics and Other Issues

Now that you know how to read and analyze research reports, we would like for you to consider some broader topics related to research. This chapter starts with a discussion of important issues that you need to think about as you read research, even though they may not be directly mentioned in reports that you read. These include ethical constraints on research and limitations that arise from doing research in educational settings. The chapter ends with a review of the merits and problems of consuming research.

ETHICS OF RESEARCH

In any situation, research requires the collection of information about subjects and often includes participation by subjects in some kind of treatment as well. These actions imply that researchers will learn information about subjects that was previously unknown or private. In experimental studies, they will have not only information but also some degree of control and influence over the subjects through the manipulation of treatment.

Is this always fair, even in the name of scientific inquiry? What happens when researchers use "captive" subjects, such as school students who may not be in a position to say whether they wish to participate in a research project? Suppose the target population from which subjects are drawn lacks the competence to understand and give consent to participation. How should they be treated? Are there limits to the kinds of variables researchers can investigate through methodology that requires experimental manipulation? What are the ethical limitations and responsibilities of a researcher?

These questions and others related to the same issues arise whenever you realize that research, especially in education, involves dealing with people. Every researcher must have a basic respect for humankind, knowing that the process of investigation brings with it the responsibility to tend carefully to the participants. The procedures of research should be designed to ensure that every part of a research effort is ethical and protects as strongly as possible the rights of individual subjects. The concern for proper ethical conduct has led to the development of certain widely accepted guidelines for researchers. In many situations, researchers must have their activities approved in advance and monitored by a review board whose purpose is to maintain high ethical standards. All federally funded research has this requirement as a part of governmental ethical regulations. The suggestions that we discuss in the following paragraphs are adapted from ethical standards developed by the Committee on Scientific and Professional Ethics and Conduct of the American Psychological Association (1977). For further information, consult the recommended references.

Scientific Purpose for Project

From the very outset of a study, the purpose must involve more than the researchers' personal gain or curiosity. There must be a scientific justification for the research, or else it should not be attempted. There may be variables of vital interest that cannot be manipulated if the rights of the subjects are considered. For example, researchers might want to know how academic performance is influenced by drug addiction, racial prejudice, or cultural deprivation. Yet it would not be appropriate to induce these undesirable conditions in subjects. In these cases, researchers are limited to using designs that seek the goals of explanation or prediction, but control is not ethically available.

Consent of Subjects

Researchers must carefully maintain the rights of subjects. Ideally the exact requirements and responsibilities of subjects are outlined before selection procedures begin and are strictly adhered to throughout the project. Subjects should be informed precisely about the extent of their responsibilities and should be asked for their consent. In all cases, researchers are to tell subjects about anything in the project that might influence their willingness to participate. Everyone has the right not to participate in the experiment and to withdraw at any time if they so desire. This is true even after subjects or employees are chosen. Furthermore, parental approval and understanding must be secured for minors. As you can see, there are stiff requirements for research involving school students.

If potential subjects have questions about the project, researchers are supposed to answer them whenever possible. In some cases, it is in the best interest of the project to defer such answers until data are collected. Nevertheless, researchers must offer the requested information afterward, along with an explanation of why the information was withheld originally.

This brings up the topic of deception. Frequently researchers do not want to reveal the true nature of their project for fear of contaminating the results. If subjects know that researchers are looking for improvements in self-concept, for example, they may be inclined to modify their behavior or to respond differently to treatment. It would be nice to fully inform every subject, but this ideal must be weighed against the desire to have accurate, unbiased results. To overcome this difficulty, researchers may tell subjects all that they can without jeopardizing the project and fully inform subjects afterward. Sometimes subjects can be told an initial purpose that seems plausible but incomplete, an explanation that will satisfy their immediate need to know without prejudicing the results. This course of action must always be followed by an accurate discussion of the full nature of the project.

Another technique researchers occasionally use is called *assumed consent*. In this case, persons similar to the subjects, ideally from the same population, are told about the experiment and its treatment and measurement conditions. They are then asked whether they would be willing to participate in such an experiment. If a very high percentage agrees to serve as subjects, researchers assume that the actual subjects would probably consent also.

Such a procedure does not relieve researchers of the obligation to completely explain the project to the subjects at the conclusion of the study. Subjects would still be permitted the freedom to participate or not participate as they chose.

Safety of Subjects

Throughout a project, researchers are responsible for the safety of the subjects, as well as the protection of their rights. If other persons are involved in dealing with subjects through administration of treatment or collection and analysis of data, their ethical conduct is also the researchers' responsibility as the creators of the project. The actions of everyone involved must serve to protect the subjects. After the project is completed, the subjects must be thoroughly debriefed. All procedures must be explained well enough that no subjects have any ill effects, physical or psychological, following their participation in the project.

Confidentiality of Results

The data and results of the project should also be handled and communicated with great care. The confidentiality of the results for each subject should be respected. Often researchers are able to use a form of coding to prevent the association of any piece of data with a particular person.

As you read research reports, consider whether the procedures appear to be ethical. Frequently reports do not include details of all the procedures related to guarding the rights of the subjects. Therefore, you will have to use your own judgment to determine how carefully the project was executed in this respect.

LIMITATIONS OF EDUCATIONAL RESEARCH

Research Settings

In addition to ethical considerations, there are limitations on research in education that result from the situations in which research is usually done. To begin with, the whole arena of education is highly complex. Even a study limited to one or two classrooms, investigating only a few variables, is affected by an almost infinite number of factors because of the many relationships within the setting. There are different ways of dealing with this complexity, none of which provides a perfect solution.

One approach is to look at only a few variables. In these cases, it is easy to overlook other variables that may be contaminating the results, even if efforts are carefully designed to control unwanted variance. The results may oversimplify the actual relationships in the setting because the influence of related variables is not known. Certainly, moving the study from a classroom to some kind of laboratory may minimize the complexity, but the results of such a study may bear little resemblance to results found in natural settings. Nevertheless, well-done research in controlled laboratory settings may provide a direction for actual practices (Hilgard, 1964). The benefits of being able to study the variables with a minimum of complication must be weighed against the need to apply the results to situations removed from the highly controlled setting.

Another way researchers handle the complexity of the educational setting is to select designs that permit them to look at several variables at the same time. Factorial designs and multivariate data analyses are now available and permit this kind of research. Even with such analyses, however, variables may be overlooked, misinterpreted, or poorly measured, thus limiting the conclusions of a study.

Measurement of Variables

As we discussed previously, the measurement of variables is crucial to a research study. Often devices are simply not available to adequately measure variables in highly complex settings. Sometimes so little is known about a variable or there is so much controversy about it that measurement is at best imprecise. To cite one instance, the measurement of intelligence continues to be the subject of much disagreement after decades of study. Dozens of instruments exist, each representing a different way to measure mental ability according to the variety of ways intelligence is defined.

Institutional and Community Concerns

Other limitations involve the political and legal constraints of institutions in which educational research is conducted. In keeping with the goal of providing equal opportunity within educational systems, formal policies and laws at many local, state, and federal levels prohibit bias in the distribution of resources and services. If researchers plan some form of treatment using public school subjects, their study may be construed as unfair to those potential subjects not placed in treatment programs. To make up for this possible deficit, it is common for subjects receiving no treatment to be given some form of compensatory assistance (Cook & Campbell, 1979). As you can see, this might affect any comparisons that are made, destroying the ability to make generalizations about treatment versus no treatment.

Similar situations can also occur less formally when research involves subjects or variables that are of interest to pressure groups such as parents, political organizations, religious groups, and local power structures within a school system. If researchers plan to use new curriculum materials in a treatment, for instance, they may find their work being monitored and publicized by concerned critics. Furthermore, if a project appears to give special attention to certain schools or classrooms, researchers may find that some administrators and teachers—particularly among control groups receiving no treatment—become resentful and may be motivated to put forth extra effort to avoid unfavorable comparisons.

There are no clear-cut ways to avoid all these constraints in education. Therefore, researchers attempt to put together the best combination of procedures they can given their situations.

CONSUMING RESEARCH

Continuing with Research

If you have never done research, it may be a little hard to understand why people are motivated to complicate their lives by carrying out experimental or descriptive projects. Perhaps the most important reason that people do research is to satisfy their own thirst for knowledge. The excitement of finding out information that is unknown to others is a rare occurrence for most people, but is a real possibility for researchers.

Many educators who become involved in research do so first because of a graduate study requirement. Some of these people get hooked on the process and continue to make research contributions throughout their professional lives. Although a majority of educational researchers may work in college or university settings, many people in the field—teachers, administrators, counselors—find research to be a valuable tool. We encourage you to extend your research skills by becoming a producer of research.

However, the most common result of developing a strong interest in research is to become an active consumer of research. The knowledge gleaned from research must be communicated and translated into practice. Consuming research provides a strong foundation for the decision making that you must do in your professional role.

Final Considerations

In this text you have learned to analyze research reports section by section. Although this is a convenient and systematic way to read articles, keep in mind how all the sections fit together. It is easy to be so interested in one aspect of a study that you neglect to check the overall quality of the research. Reports can describe appealing teaching techniques or amazing results with subjects just like the people you work with. If you look no further, you can make inaccurate assumptions about the nature and generalizability of results.

Recently a department of education in a southwestern state published an attractive report about a large-scale pilot study concerning the effectiveness of a special instructional technique. The report included glowing testimonials from many teachers who had field-tested the new method. Several persons who saw the positive statements failed to notice that the results showed almost no difference between subjects in the treatment and control groups.

Some of the readers even decided to use the new method. As this example illustrates, it is particularly important to be thorough in your analysis of research if you plan to apply the results to your own setting.

As you analyze a report, prepare to think carefully and alter your original thoughts about one component of the project design when you read about the other components. Each part of the design should fit well with the remaining design features. Are the instruments suitable to measure the effects of treatment? Do the data collection procedures seem appropriate for the subjects and compatible with the treatment and instrumentation? Do the subjects possess the necessary characteristics to provide data for the problem variables? If there is a question about the quality of the instrumentation, for example, the merits of the other design components are seriously affected. In a sense, a research study is only as strong as the weakest element of the design.

For difference studies, all the design components shown in Figure 8.1 should be considered. For association studies, of course, treatment administration procedures are not used. After you read a report through, it may help to begin with any of the components and work your way through the diagram to see how well the design is constructed.

Perhaps the biggest limitation on research from the consumer's perspective is having to make judgments about research based on a written report. No matter how important or well-done a research project is, the findings will be meaningful in direct relation to the clarity and detail with which they are

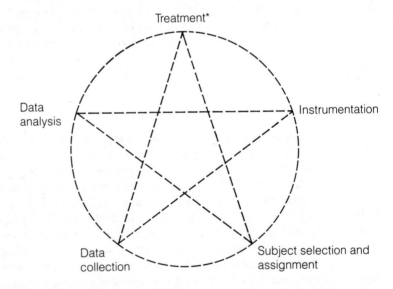

* In *ex post facto* designs, the independent variable is not manipulated as a treatment but is selected as it already exists within the subjects. In association studies, there is no treatment.

FIGURE 8.1 Interrelationships among design components.

reported. For this reason, some of the criteria included in this book sound more like literary criteria than research criteria. This is true to a degree. Unless the research is carefully reported, the merits of the study are difficult to judge. Lest we sound too critical of research articles, we hasten to say that there is a difference between research that is not as well reported as it might be and research that is not well done. Judging the quality of the reports is usually easier than judging the quality of the research. In particular, the space limitations of journal articles may make an analysis of the research findings in a complex study difficult at best. When a study is especially appealing to you, don't hesitate to contact the authors to find out more details about the project. Researchers are usually willing to provide additional information to persons who are interested in their work.

SUMMARY

Researchers must maintain the highest ethical standards, carefully preserving the rights of subjects in all situations. Any project must have a sound scientific purpose. Subjects must be given free choice to participate or not participate in research. As much as possible, subjects should be informed about the purpose of the study in advance; otherwise they are told soon after the project's conclusion. Data from individual subjects are carefully guarded to respect their privacy and released only with their informed consent.

Educational settings may limit the use of research processes. Many situations are so complex that research may tend to be oversimplified or very complicated. Variables can be difficult to measure precisely. In public institutions, political and legal pressures may prevent researchers from conducting research in the way they would like to.

Maintaining an interest in research can be of benefit to you in any professional role in education. Although most producers of research work in higher education, many educational practitioners are involved in producing and consuming research. Research results need to be translated into practice as a way of improving the quality of education.

Although you may initially read research reports section by section, you will learn to tie various parts of the design together. Otherwise, you could make incorrect inferences about the study. While you are reading a report, keep in mind that it may not contain all the information about the actual research processes. Therefore, judge the report of the project rather than the project itself.

RECOMMENDED REFERENCES

Committee on Scientific and Professional Ethics and Conduct. Ethical standards of psychologists. *APA Monitor*, 1977, 8(3), 22–23. This is an authoritative statement of ethical standards for research in all the behavioral sciences. It's essential reading for anyone who is planning to do research.

Cook, T. D., & Campbell, D. T. *Quasi-experimentation: Design and analysis issues for field settings.* Chicago: Rand McNally, 1979. Chapter 2 contains one of the better discussions of limitations that arise when researchers conduct research in field settings.

U.S. Department of Health, Education, and Welfare. Part 46—Protection of human rights. *Code of Federal Regulations, Title 45, Public Welfare.* [OPRR Reports, NIH PHS DHEW, 45 CFR 46]. Washington, D.C.: Author, 1975. This booklet contains federal guidelines for research using human subjects. Revisions since the 1975 publication date are not available from the U.S. Government Printing Office but have been published in the *Federal Register.*

Appendices

Appendices

Appendix A

Sample Research Reports

The Relationship Between Type of Teacher Reinforcement and Student Inquiry Behavior in Science

CLIFFORD H. EDWARDS, *Brigham Young University*

MICHAEL SURMA, *Illinois State University*

INTRODUCTION

It has long been assumed and demonstrated in numerous studies that reinforcers which are associated with particular behaviors produce an increased frequency of these behaviors. Recognition of the power of reinforcers to influence and shape behavior has persuaded many teacher educators to encourage trainees to develop patterns of praise as a simple means of eliciting appropriate behavior from their students. In addition, to be sure, parents use the same patterns of praise to encourage desirable responses from their children. It is assumed that this is the basic reason why Rowe (1974) found in her study that praise and mimicry (mimicry is a pattern of reinforcement where student verbal responses are parroted

back by the teacher) seem to be habituated in the speech of many teachers.

In Rowe's research, it was discovered that verbal praise and mimicry were associated with a decrease in the frequency of inquiry behavior in science by elementary school children. Such a finding obviously has enormous implications for teachers in many areas, but particularly for teachers of science, where inquiry constitutes a substantial part of the curriculum effort. Rowe states that it may be more advantageous to allow intrinsic rewards to drive inquiry, especially since verbal praise apparently does not and since intrinsic rewards are more likely to be suited to the intentions of the learner. Rowe goes on to explain how Pritchard (1969) has shown that overpayment in terms of rewards decreases attention to task. Rowe concluded that extrinsic rewards draw attention away from the task and encourage focus on competition for rewards and concern for equity.

From Journal of Research in Science Teaching, *1980, 17 (4), 337–41. Copyright © 1980 by the National Association for Research in Science Teaching. Reprinted by permission of John Wiley & Sons, Inc.*

This analysis tends to distort somewhat the potential use that can be made of extrinsic reinforcers. The findings of Rowe seem reasonable if extrinsic rewards are limited to short verbal statements of praise and mimicry. However, there is a whole range of reinforcers with demonstrated potency that needs to be explored in relation to inquiry. Reinforcement theory generally indicates that if a particular stimulus is genuinely reinforcing, it will increase the incidence of the behavior it is associated with (Bijou & Baer, 1961). In the case of short verbal statements of praise and mimicry, these reinforcers are given as rewards for short student responses, thus encouraging these responses to occur. In other words, verbal praise and mimicry encourage the display of short student responses and discourage inquiry because they are given as contingencies for the short responses and not inquiry. The problem is whether a reinforcement system designed to make inquiry truly dependent upon appropriate contingencies of reinforcement can increase the frequency of inquiry or if reinforcement *per se* limits the incidence of inquiry.

The purpose of this study was to determine the effect on inquiry of two different contingencies of reinforcement. The first of these was using the ideas and input by students in the inquiry process by integrating them into the lesson and referring to them again periodically as appropriate. This is called "using student ideas" and is the first of two independent variables. The second reinforcement approach was to reward inquiry behavior with tokens being used as generalized reinforcers with a variety of backup reinforcers. This is a second independent variable. It was hypothesized that tokens as well as the practice of using student ideas in the inquiry process would increase the frequency of inquiry responses by students. Student inquiry responses constituted the dependent variable.

METHOD

Subjects

Subjects (Ss) for the study were four intact groups (25–30 per class) of biology students primarily at the sophomore level in high school. Ss self-selected themselves into various classes based on normal scheduling constraints and thus were assumed to be in somewhat random placements, with all groups essentially equal. The school was a laboratory school where a deliberate effort is made to insure that the total student population is a true cross section of the community. The same teacher taught all four classes and altered his behavior to correspond to the appropriate treatment.

Experimental Design

The design was a posttest-only design with a control group and involved the use of intact groups. However, all groups were essentially equivalent on the criterion measure prior to treatment in that almost no student inquiry behaviors could be noted in any of the groups. It was assumed that this was likely due to the pretreatment behavior of the teacher, which consisted primarily of using mimicry and verbal praise as reinforcement.

Each of the four groups was randomly assigned to one of four treatments. Group 1 received verbal reinforcement and mimicry exclusively as a treatment. Verbal reinforcement consisted of praise given verbally by the teacher for student responses which he deemed appropriate to the class discussion. Mimicry is defined as the teacher parroting back the correct response of the student immediately following the response.

Group 2 received the treatment of extending and using student ideas as a reinforcing function. In this instance, the teacher attempted to incorporate the student's response into the lesson by allowing these ideas to help provide direction for the lesson. Student ideas were explored in more depth and referred to subsequently by the teacher when they appeared to have relevance to the subject being discussed. Particularly, student inquiry responses were used and explored by the class.

Group 3 was exposed to a token reinforcement system using special privileges as backup reinforcers. Tokens were dispensed when students engaged in inquiry behavior.

Group 4 was the control group and the treatment consisted of the teacher providing no verbal reinforcement and carefully avoiding reinforcing students in the form of extending and using their ideas.

Statistical analysis included an *F*-test followed up by Scheffé procedures to determine the significance of the differences of means between the control group and the various treatments and between treatments.

PROCEDURE

No special instructions were given to Group 1. In this treatment the teacher provided verbal reinforcement and mimicry at an average rate per class period of 12.88 instances of verbal reinforcement and 54.94 instances of mimicry. Five days were allowed for applying this procedure to insure a stable rate of student response to this treatment.

Again, no special instructions were given to Group 2. Here, the teacher provided reinforcement by extending and using the ideas of students in the inquiry process. This was accomplished by his focusing attention on the student responses that were central to the inquiry

process. To do this, the teacher explained to the class how the student response fit into subject consideration. These ideas were then used as points for discussion and served as the basis for direction in the inquiry process. The average instance of verbal reinforcement and mimicry during data collection was 3.91 per class period.

The treatment given to Group 3 was a token reinforcement system. Students were told that they would be given tokens as a consequence of making inquiry responses and that these tokens could be exchanged for a number of backup reinforcers. These backup reinforcers consisted of special privileges suggested by the teacher as well as additional reinforcers suggested by the students themselves. This list included (1) being able to play a game during the subsequent period, (2) being excused from class early, (3) adding points to a grade, (4) being the teacher's lab assistant, (5) being given free time, and (6) being able to run projectors. There was an average of 4.05 instances of mimicry and verbal reinforcement per class period during data collection.

Group 4, the control group, received no special instructions. The teacher was instructed to eliminate the use of verbal reinforcement and mimicry, which was part of his verbal pattern. A period of about 10 days was required to reduce the instance of verbal reinforcement and mimicry to below 10 for a full class period. An additional 5 days were allowed for applying this procedure before data were collected. During data collection the average instance of verbal reinforcement and mimicry was 1.87 per class period.

Data Collection

The dependent variable consisted of the measure of inquiry responses made by students. These included (1) questions by students of an inquiry nature, (2) alternative explanations, (3) suggestions for new experiments, and (4) sharing ideas between students and between students and teacher. In addition, the length of the student response was considered to be associated with inquiry, but was treated separately because it by itself could not be considered to be an inquiry response. These categories of inquiry are consistent with those utilized by Rowe (1974), with the exception of inflected speech, which again was considered by the authors to accompany inquiry but not be an inquiry behavior *per se.* The categories were thus considered to have construct validity.

All classroom sessions were recorded on audiotape. Student and teacher responses were coded and recorded in 3-second intervals for the entire class period during tape analysis. All different responses occurring during a 3-second interval were recorded. If a response lasted longer than 3 seconds, it was recorded for each 3-second interval that it lasted. The 3-second interval was used based on the experience of Flanders (1970) in his Interaction Analysis System, where similar types of behavior were coded and recorded. The following categories of behavior were observed and recorded: mimicry (M), verbal reinforcement (V), using student ideas (U), student inquiry responses (I), questions by the teacher (Q), structuring and conveying information by the teacher (S), student response to a question by the teacher (R), teacher responses to student inquiry (R-t), silence or confusion (Si), and controlling responses by the teacher (C).

One-fourth of the tapes were checked for interrater reliability. Scores ranged from .79 to .93. Average reliability was .84.

RESULTS

The research question was to determine if reinforcement *per se* reduces the frequency of inquiry behaviors of high school biology students or if various reinforcers differentially affect inquiry responses. Three different types of reinforcers were used. The first was verbal reinforcement and mimicry (1); the second, using student ideas (2); and the third was a token reinforcement system (3). Group 4 was the control group, where there was an absence of reinforcement. The analysis of variance was the statistical technique used. This was followed up by Scheffé *post hoc* procedures.

The results of the analysis of variance for the different treatments are shown in Table I. The *F* ratio of 25.15 is significant beyond the .001 level.

The Scheffé values were as follows: The value for treatment 1 (mimicry and verbal reinforcement), as compared to treatment 2 (using student ideas), was 37.95. Treatment 1, as compared to treatment 3 (token reinforcement), produced a value of 65.45. Treatment 1 versus 4 (control group) had a Scheffé value of 24.9. The Scheffé value for treatment 2 compared to treatment 3 was 3.76; treatment 2 versus 4 was 9.61; and treatment 3 contrasted with treatment 4 was 9.30. The critical value at the .05 level of confidence is 9.30, at the .01 level is 14.82 and at the .001 level is 24.3. Thus two contrasts exceeded the .05 level while another three exceeded the .001 level of confidence. Only the contrast between treatments 2 and 3 was not significant.

The length of student response was also studied for each of the four groups. Group 1 had a mean response length of 3.34 seconds. For Groups 2, 3, and 4 it was 6.12, 6.11, and 7.43, respectively. For Group 1 only 5 student responses exceeded 3 seconds in length. None exceeded 12 seconds. Group 2 had 39 student responses exceeding 3 seconds while Group 3 had 24 and Group 4 had 20.

DISCUSSION

The results of the study help to verify the outcome of Rowe's (1974) study, which indicated that verbal reinforcement and mimicry are related to a reduced frequency of inquiry in science. In fact, the results show that less inquiry results from the use of mimicry and short verbal reinforcers than from no reinforcement at all. However, as hypothesized, the same relationship does not hold for other contingencies of reinforcement. It cannot, therefore, be concluded that reinforcement has a negative effect on student inquiry behavior, but rather that it is a function of the nature of the reinforcement. The results of this study indicate that inquiry behavior can be significantly increased through reinforcement based on the utilization of student ideas in the instructional process as well as through reinforcement in the form of tokens with appropriate backup reinforcers.

These findings have important implications for the science teacher. As pointed out by Rowe, a good deal of teaching is accompanied by verbal reinforcement and mimicry. Such behavior on the part of the teacher is counter-productive in terms of inquiry by students, having the opposite effect to the one intended. Because mimicry appears to be habitual rather than deliberate, teacher training efforts in science and other areas which foster inquiry need to insure that teachers undergoing training learn to bring their behavior under conscious control. That means that in addition to breaking the mimicry habit, teachers need to learn patterns of reinforcement that do encourage inquiry. Using student ideas as defined in this study is one of these patterns. Abandoning mimicry and supplanting it with skills in using student ideas will likely be a difficult training task if the experience in this study is any indication. Yet such alterations in teaching patterns will be required to bring about increased student inquiry.

REFERENCES

Bijou, S. W., & Baer, D. M. *Child development 1: A systematic and empirical theory.* New York: Appleton-Century-Crofts, 1961.
Flanders, N. A. *Analyzing teaching behavior.* Reading, Mass.: Addison-Wesley, 1970.
Pritchard, R. D. Equity theory: A review and critique. *Organizational Behavior and Human Performance,* 1969, **4**, 197–211.
Rowe, M. B. Relation of wait-time and rewards to the development of language, logic and fate control: Part II—rewards. *Journal of Research in Science Teaching,* 1974, **2**, 291–308.

Manuscript accepted October 29, 1979.

Table I
ANALYSIS OF VARIANCE FOR REINFORCEMENT TREATMENTS

Source of Variation	Sum of Squares	Degrees of Freedom	Mean Square	F
Between groups	12,106.80	3	4035.60	25.15*
Within groups	3,690.16	20	160.44	
Total	15,796.96	23		

* p < .001.

Teacher Attitudes Toward Administration in Low and High Suspension Schools

FRANK BICKEL, *University of Kentucky*

ROBERT QUALLS, *Jefferson County (Ky.) Education Consortium*

The hypothesis that administrative behavior would affect school suspension rates, and that teachers' perceptions of administration in schools identified as having low or high suspension rates would be different, is tested.

INTRODUCTION

The principal's behavior has a direct effect on school climate, and ultimately, student behavior. Tjosvold and Kastelic[1] studied the effects of student motivation and principals' attitudes toward student control on teacher directiveness and found that the values held by the principals concerning student control definitely influenced the manner in which teachers interacted with their unmotivated students.

Valentine, Tate, Seagren, and Lammel[2] found correlations between the directness of the principal's verbal interactions and positive attitudes among the school community. Their findings indicated a "domino effect" within the school, and that the quality of the principal's interactions with the faculty is the critical point in this chain, inasmuch as the teacher has the most direct contact with students.

The principal's functions as a leader and mediator are suggested in the following statement by Ackerly and Gluckman, focusing on the centrality of the principal's position in the school:

From American Secondary Education, *1980, 10 (2), 19–26. Reprinted by permission.*

Because the principal of a secondary school is a highly visible and influential figure in the administration structure of the school, he characteristically finds himself at the point where the often conflicting wishes and ambitions of students, teachers, and parents collide with overall school administration policy. It is the principal above all others who must undertake to make these divergent interests compatible so that the school can be what it is intended to be, a place where learning can occur.[3]

The roles of manager, change agent, and disciplinarian could also be implicit in their description.

A part of the management function involves the direct managing of discipline problems, a legitimate function of a principal according to several writers.[4] The general consensus among them is that the teacher has a right to expect assistance and support from the principal in discipline cases when the teacher has exhausted all other resources in dealing with the problematic situation.

It is obvious that the principal exerts a considerable influence over all aspects of school operations. The current study is an attempt to assess the reactions of teachers to differing principal styles and attitudes in two distinct sets of schools, those with high and low suspension rates. The criterion of suspension rate was selected as an indicator of discipline problems within a school.

METHODOLOGY

a) Sample

A sample of teachers was drawn from eight secondary schools, four with high and four with low suspension rates. The high/low criterion was based on a rank-order of the suspension rates of the system's 25 secondary schools. All teachers were selected on the basis of a ninth-grade assignment in science, English, or mathematics. Random samples were drawn from the roster of each school, so that 10 teachers were selected in each school. The final sample was N = 70, with 38 from low and 32 from high suspension schools.

b) Instrument

A 55-item questionnaire was constructed to assess teacher attitudes toward the following administrative characteristics; (1) leadership, (2) mediation, (3) discipline, (4) decision-making, and (5) school climate. A Likert-type scale was utilized for subjects' responses. The instrument was reviewed for construct validity and item appropriateness by a panel of administrators.

c) Statistical Analysis

Factor analysis (varimax rotation) was utilized to identify commonalities of scales. Low and high suspension classifications of teacher responses were done with discriminant analysis. The variables of suspension rate, race, and sex were utilized in ANOVA procedures. A series of t-tests was done on individual item means using the suspension rate, race, and sex variables.

RESULTS

The factor analysis over all items yielded eight factors. Scales were reduced to single factors in three cases. Subscales derived from the original five scales are in Table 1.

A discriminant analysis was done for low/high suspension classification utilizing the eight factors yielded from the factor analysis. Results of the discriminant analysis are displayed in Table 2. The results of the discriminant analysis indicate that teachers in low and high suspension schools responded very differently to the survey. They were accurately classified into low and high suspension categories based on the eight factors. Accuracy of classification was greater for those teachers in low suspension schools, with their responses being more homogenous.

In order to clarify apparent differences in the responses of teachers, analysis of variance was utilized with individual item means as dependent variables. High/low suspension rate, black/white, and male/female were the independent variables.

The results of subsequent t-testing of item means between high and low suspension schools confirmed the ANOVA results. Teachers in high suspension schools responded more positively on three of the 11 items, while those in low suspension schools were more positive on the remaining eight items (p < .05). Climate items comprised six of the 11 items on which significant differences were found, with teachers in low suspension schools responding more positively on all six climate items. Items 12, 23, and 25 (see Table 3, below) elicited a more positive response from teachers in high suspension schools, while items 8, 34, and 50–55 were more positively responded to by teachers in low suspension schools.

There was a total of 13 items on which High/Low × Sex interactions were significant (p < .05). These are displayed in Table 4.

A series of t-tests was done with these item means. Females in low suspension schools responded more positively on 11 of the 13 items, (14–55), while males in high suspension schools responded more positively on items 12 and 13 (p $<$ .05). The results of the ANOVA and t-tests were consistent over all items.

Items 12, 13, 14, 16, and 17 (see Table 4, below) were from the Leadership scale; items 21, 25, 26, and 27 were components of the Mediator-Facilitator scale; and items 47, 48, 50, and 55 represent the Climate scale. Females in low suspension schools responded more positively on all items except 12 and 13, on which males in high suspension schools were the most positive.

Comparison of item means revealed interesting findings between and within the low/high $\times$ sex variables. T-tests of individual item means resulted in significantly more positive responses by females than males in low suspension schools on 15 items. Items from the Leadership and Mediator-Facilitator scales comprised 13 of the 15 items. There apparently were wide differences in male and female attitudes toward

Table 1
TEACHER SUBSCALES DERIVED FROM
FACTOR ANALYSIS OF 55 ITEMS

Leadership

Factor I-A Style of leadership
Factor I-B Role of principal in planning school structure
Factor I-C Style of management

Mediation-Facilitation

Factor II Principal's role as mediator-facilitator

Discipline

Factor III-A Student as the focus of the school
Factor III-B Rule enforcement

Decision-making

Factor IV Principal's style of decision making

Climate

Factor V Climate

Table 2
DISCRIMINANT ANALYSIS FOR TEACHERS
IN LOW AND HIGH SUSPENSION SCHOOLS

	Low	High
Low	* 93.10	6.90
High	30.43	69.57
	**(55.47)	(44.23)

*Underlined indicates percent of correct classification
**Prior probabilities

Table 3
SIGNIFICANT ITEMS (P .05) FOR HIGH/LOW MAIN EFFECT

ITEM#

8   The prinicpal is seen in the halls and cafeteria interacting with students and staff. p = .008

12   The principal is the driving force in this school. p = .007

23   The principal attempts to deal with potential problem situations before a major problem develops. p = .05

25   The principal is sympathetic to the needs of teachers. p = .05

34   The principal is supportive of the teacher in discipline situations. p = .05

50   In this school students have respect for the teachers. p = .02

51   People are honest and sincere in this school. p = .01

52   Students find this school to be an enjoyable experience. p = .04

53   In this school students are not afraid of other students. p = .05

54   Students feel welcomed and accepted at this school. p = .01

55   The school provides a good learning environment. p = .04

Table 4
SIGNIFICANT ITEMS (P .05) FOR HIGH/LOW × SEX INTERACTION

ITEM #

12   The principal is the driving force in this school. p = .05

13   The school's goals and objectives are clear. p = .007

14   The school moves toward accomplishments of its goals and objectives. p = .001

16   The principal encourages new ideas from students. p = .01

17   The principal elicits output and production from school personnel. p = .05

21   The principal waits to hear the facts in a case before making a decision. p = .05

25   The principal is sympathetic to the needs of teachers. p = .05

26   The principal makes every effort to understand concerns of the student. p = .05

27   The principal is receptive to constructive criticism concerning his/her performance as an administrator. p = .03

47   When a student has a problem, it is easy to find help. p = .002

48   In this school, teachers respect the students. p = .05

50   In this school, students have respect for the teachers. p = .05

55   The school provides a good learning environment. p = .02

administration within the set of low suspension schools on these two factors.

Differences in male and female attitudes were less evident within the set of high suspension schools. Significance was reached on three items on the sex variable, with males responding more positively than females on the three items, which were all from the Climate scale. Male and female attitudes toward school administration in high suspension schools appear to be only slightly different in contrast to low suspension schools.

T-tests on the sex and low/high variables by individual item means resulted in significant differences in female responses between low/high suspension schools on 12 items; significance was reached on three items for males.

CONCLUSIONS AND DISCUSSION

The assumption that the administrative behavior of the principals would influence the suspension rates of their respective schools was the basis for including the two distinct sets of schools in the sample. Further, it was hypothesized that teachers' perceptions of school administration would be significantly different in low and high suspension-rate schools. This hypothesis was confirmed by the results of the discriminant analysis with all factors (Table 2). The classification of teachers into the low/high suspension categories was very accurate, indicating widely divergent teacher perceptions.

Results of subsequent ANOVAs and t-tests provided some clarification of the nature of the divergence. Teachers in low suspension schools responded more positively than their counterparts in high suspension schools on eight of 11 items which were significant at $p = .05$. The school climate scale accounted for six of the eight items, with teachers in low suspension schools in-

dicating a more favorable attitude toward climate on all six items.

The 11 items covered aspects of administrative behavior including the visibility of the principal, support for teachers, and a range of interpersonal relationships. Teachers in high suspension schools were more positive toward principals who could be characterized as "strong" leaders; e.g., the driving forces in the school and those able to anticipate potential problem situations. (This assertion is supported by data from the larger study. Responses of administrators and teachers in high suspension schools indicated that those principals were more authoritarian than their counterparts in low suspension schools.)

The attitudes of teachers in low and high suspension schools toward the administration can be summed up as follows:

1. Teachers in low suspension schools appeared to be positive toward principals who attend to interpersonal relationships that result in a favorable school climate.
2. Teachers in high suspension schools seemed to prefer principals who are authoritarian in their approach to leadership.

The within-school analysis for the sex variable yielded unexpected findings. Responses of males and females in low-suspension schools were significantly different on 15 items, with males responding more negatively on all items. Significance on approximately one-fourth of the total items indicates substantial differences in male and female perceptions of administrators in low suspension schools. It is possible that males in low suspension schools would prefer a greater degree of authoritarianism from the principals, as suggested by the large number of Leadership and Mediator scale items on which their responses were more negative. An alternate hypothesis might be that males may have ambitions to attain an administrative position and tended to compare current administrators' behaviors with those projected for themselves.

On the other hand, males' and females' responses in high suspension schools differed significantly on only three items, all from the Climate scale. This would suggest that there was little difference in the perceptions of male and female teachers within the set of high suspension schools. The more positive responses of males on the three climate items lend some support to the notion that males preferred a more structured, authoritarian approach to administration.

The t-testing of item means on the sex variable between high and low suspension schools suggests little variation in male responses, irrespective of the high/low variable. Significance was reached on only three of the 55 items.

However, the responses of females were significantly different on 12 of 55 items, seven of which were from the climate scale. There was a marked difference in female attitudes toward administration between low and high suspension schools. Females in low suspension schools were more positive than those in high suspension schools on all twelve items.

The following conclusions are offered:

1. Male teachers' attitudes toward administrations were similar in both low and high suspension schools.
2. Female teachers in low and high suspension schools had very different attitudes toward the administration in their respective schools.

Teacher attitudes toward school administration appeared to vary as a function of the sex variable within low suspension schools, but not in high suspension schools. The most apparent differences in teacher attitudes occurred with females as a function of the low/high variable, while there were little differences for males on the same variable.

While these findings may not safely be generalized beyond the study sample, they raise questions that might be explored further. Does the notion that administrators in high suspension schools seem to be more authoritarian have implications for selection of staff? Perhaps if staff preferences for authoritarian vs. permissive or supportive administrative styles were known, staff selection would enhance compatibility of administration and faculty.

The apparent differences in teacher attitudes as a function of the sex variable suggests further research to determine whether administrative styles within a single school might be modified to accommodate varying teacher attitudes on the basis of the sex variable.

NOTES

1. Tjosvold, D. and Kastelic, T. Effects of Student Motivation and the Principal's Values on Teacher Directiveness, *Journal of Educational Psychology* 68 (1975): 768–773.
2. Vacca, R. S. The Principal as a Disciplinarian: Some Thoughts and Suggestions for the 70's, *High School Journal* 54 (1971): 405–409.
3. Valentine, J. W.; Tate, B. L.; Seagren, A. T.; and Lammel, J. A. Administrative Verbal Behavior: What You Say Does Make a Difference, *National Association of Secondary School Principals Bulletin* 59 (1975): 67–74.

4. Wolcott, H. F. *The Man in the Principal's Office: An Ethnography* (New York: Holt, Rinehart and Winston, 1973).

5. Vacca, R. S. The Principal as a Disciplinarian: Some Thoughts and Suggestions for the 70's, *High School Journal* 54 (1971): 405-409.

6. Zanella, R. E. Looking at Corporal Punishment: Can Principals Still Discipline? *National Association of Secondary School Principals Bulletin* (1976) 67-70.

7. Ackerly, R. L. and Gluckman, I. B. *The Reasonable Exercise of Authority, II* (Reston, Va.: NASSP, 1976).

8. Wolcott, H. F. *The Man in the Principal's Office: An Ethnography* (New York: Holt, Rinehart and Winston, 1973).

Does Socioeconomic Status Bias the Assignment of Elementary School Students to Reading Groups?

EMIL J. HALLER, *Cornell University*

SHARON A. DAVIS, *General Research Corporation*

This study examined the standardized reading test scores, family socioeconomic status (SES), and teacher-assigned reading groups of pupils in 37 midelementary classrooms from four school districts. The analysis assessed: (1) the relative relationship of SES and reading test measurements with assignments to reading groups; (2) the relative degree of socioeconomic segregation resulting from grouping based on teacher judgments and reading tests; (3) the relationship of teachers' own SES background to the extent of socioeconomic segregation in their classrooms. Little support was found for the conjecture that either pupil or teacher social class plays a major role in reading grouping in elementary schools.

It is often argued that high school tracking is one mechanism by which the social status of parents is passed on to their children. In its skeletal form this argument is structured as follows: parental socioeconomic status (SES) is an important determinant of enrollment in a high school's "college track;" placement in a college track strongly influences actual attendance and, thus the

This study was supported in part by Hatch Grant (#6418). Thanks are due to David Goold and Deborah Cohen for their help at earlier stages of the project and to Christopher Moacdieh for his assistance with the statistical analysis.

From American Educational Research Journal, *Winter 1980, 17 (4), 409–18. Copyright 1980, American Educational Research Association, Washington, D.C. Reprinted by permission.*

probability of college graduation; college graduation conditions the possibility of entering high status occupations (Jencks, 1972; Rosenbaum, 1976; Schafer & Olexa, 1971; Warner, Havighurst, & Loeb, 1944).

Recently, considerable controversy has emerged over these assertions. Much of this controversy has turned on the relative influence of pupil achievement and parental SES on track placement. While some writers (often termed "revisionists," see Ravitch, 1978) have argued that family background is critical (Bowles & Gintis, 1976; Katz, 1971), others have asserted that its influence is weak and indirect and that ability or achievement is most important (Alexander, Cook, & McDill, 1978; Heyns, 1974; Rehberg & Rosenthal, 1978). However, much of the evidence adduced in support of either position may be peripheral to the debate. It is quite possible for family SES to be the more important determinant of track assignment, though ability and achievement correlate more highly with those assignments. This would occur if family background exerted its principal influence much earlier in a student's educational career.

Suppose that elementary school pupils from different social classes were differentially educated in such a way as to create class-related differences in intellectual development and achievement. These differences, compounded over time, could later serve as the basis for meritocratic–appearing selection processes in the high school. That is, the secondary school could assign pupils to vocational, general, or college curricula on the basis of real and substantial differences in measured achievement; hence, appear to operate on meritocratic principles, when, in fact, it was operating as a straightforward extension of class-biased elementary schooling.

This conjecture is supported by the literature indicating that elementary teachers' perceptions of students are related to the students' social class, and teachers' treatment of students based on these perceptions is similarly differentiated (Becker, 1952; Brophy & Good, 1974; Goodacre, 1968; Rist, 1970). Of particular note here is Rist's work. From an ethnographic study of a single class of children over a 3-year period, Rist describes how home background differences among kindergarten pupils can be transformed into achievement differences among third graders. He suggests that kindergarten teachers initially divide pupils into instructional groups on the basis of social, class-related criteria and then give more instructional time to the "faster" groups. Soon real differences in achievement emerge, affecting children's capacity to learn new material and influencing subsequent teachers' judgments and expectations. Hence, Rist argues, lower-class students emerge from their elementary schooling less academically able than their classmates. This suggests the potential importance of grouping practices in the elementary school for understanding the consequences of high school tracking.

Of all instructional grouping practices in the elementary grades, intraclassroom reading grouping is the most likely to be important in establishing an SES-achievement link. The practice is the most prevalent form of differentiated instruction in U.S. elementary education, touching the lives of most pupils. Further, reading achievement is central to most definitions of school success and influences achievement in other subjects. In addition, learning to read is perceived by parents and students as one of the most important outcomes of schooling; thus, perceptions of their own reading ability may have an important influence on students' motivation and self-concepts. Finally, in elementary schools, the reading group to which a child is assigned is primarily a matter of a single teacher's judgment, providing latitude for the conjectured class bias to operate relatively unchecked.

The first purpose of this paper, then, is to assess the role of SES and measured reading achievement as determinants of elementary children's reading group assignment. If Rist and other critics are correct, we would expect the reading group-SES correlation to be substantial and to equal or exceed the correlation between group assignment and measured reading ability. Also, if children's early group assignments are primarily on the basis of SES, the differences in measured reading ability between reading groups should be smaller in the lower grades than in the upper grades.

A second purpose of the paper is to investigate the degree of SES segregation resulting from grouping based on teacher judgments compared with the segregation which would result if standardized tests alone were used. Because achievement tests correlate positively with SES, some degree of socioeconomic segregation in classrooms would occur were test scores to be the sole criterion in grouping decisions. However, tests are seldom the only—or even the most important—criterion. Instead, school districts frequently encourage teachers to use their own judgment and to consider criteria other than tests (Findley & Bryan, 1970). These additional criteria might be more closely correlated with SES than reading ability. Rist (1970) implies this in stating that dress and cleanliness are major grouping criteria; and in England, Barker Lunn (1970) found that when teacher judgments were solicited in making grouping decisions, the result was a greater degree of segregation than would have been the case were tests alone used. Thus, it is important to know the relative consequence for classroom segregation following from decisions derived from teachers and tests. This is particularly so because standardized tests are commonly held to be biased against low-SES children. It is possible, however, that substituting teacher judgment for these presumably biased tests may result in greater, not lesser, segregation.

Finally, for a considerable time some researchers (e.g., Brookover, 1953; Schafer & Olexa, 1971; Warner, Havighurst, & Loeb, 1944) have argued that teachers' own social backgrounds influence their judgments in the classroom. When standards derived from a middle-class upbringing are applied in the school, it is asserted, pupils from lower-class homes may be discriminated against. (See Charters, 1963 for an incisive evaluation of this argument.) One form such discrimination may take is a failure to recognize academic talent among low-SES children, assigning them instead to slower groups. Hence, we asked whether teachers whose classrooms evidenced greater SES segregation were more likely to have come from middle-class homes.

METHOD

Data were collected in 37 fourth-, fifth- and sixth-grade classrooms in five schools located in four separate school districts in central New York. These schools and districts serve communities with considerable socioeconomic variation. One, for example, serves both an upper-middle-class business and professional suburb and a relatively-poor, rural community nearby. (While socioeconomic variation is great, racial variation is virtually nonexistent. Black children constituted less than 1 percent of the districts' populations. Thus, while we avoided the potential confounding of class and race effects, we limited the external validity of our results.)

In our initial contact with school administrators, it was ascertained that intraclass reading grouping was practiced in each school; each teacher involved in the study grouped students into three reading groups. In all, 963 students were included in the study.

Students' percentile scores on the reading comprehension portion of the *Iowa Test of Basic Skills* were collected. In addition, a measure of family SES was collected from the children, using an abbreviated version of *The Home Index* (Gough, 1949, 1971).

In an interviewing situation, teachers were given a set of index cards, each one of which had the name of a pupil in the class. They were asked to sort the cards into three groups as if they were recommending the children's reading-placement to next-year's teacher. Teachers were free to form groups of whatever size they deemed desirable. After the sorting, an interview with the teacher was conducted during which data regarding the educational level and occupation of each teacher's parents were collected. For the teachers, parental education was coded on a 5-point scale and occupation was coded on the Duncan decile index (Reiss, Duncan, Hatt, & North, 1961).

Using the Iowa test data and the pupils' SES scores, two hypothetical groupings were formed for each classroom to parallel the teacher-assigned groups. Students were ranked within their classroom according to their scores on each measure. Cuts were then made in these rankings corresponding to the size of the reading groups the teacher had established. Where cuts fell between students with identical scores, the ties were broken randomly.

RESULTS

Table I presents a classification of pupils according to teacher judgment and student SES group. Evidently, the commonly observed association between SES and virtually all educational outcomes also holds in the case of reading grouping. However, the association is far from perfect; $\tau_b = .32$. In slightly less than 50 percent of these cases do reading group and SES group correspond. If assignment was random, we would expect the percentage to be .33.

The revisionists' argument suggests that SES would have as strong a relationship to teachers' reading group assignments as would test scores. In testing this hypothesis we first paired the reading groups in each classroom (i.e., the top with the middle group and the middle with the lower group). This

was done because the relative effect of SES and reading ability might differ according to the group under study. For example, relatively good ability may be sufficient to overcome relatively low SES and secure a student a place in the top group, while average ability may be insufficient to offset low SES and prevent assignment to a bottom group. Next, we computed the zero-order correlations between SES and group assignment and between reading ability and group assignment within each classroom. This analysis, shown in Figure 1, allowed us to assess the variation among classrooms in these correlations.

Eight of the 74 correlations fell on or above the diagonal, indicating an instance in which the association between SES and group was stronger than that between reading ability and group, while 68 fell below the diagonal. It is also interesting to note that in 17 cases the SES-group correlation was negative. These patterns, and the generally weak association between SES and group assignment do not seem to support the revisionists' position.

We summarized these effects and directly tested the hypothesis by regressing the dichotomous variable,

Table I
TEACHER-ASSIGNED READING GROUP BY
STUDENT SOCIOECONOMIC STATUS (SES)

		SES Group			
		High	Middle	Low	N
	High	197	107	36	340
		(57.9)	(31.5)	(10.6)	(100%)
	Middle	101	170	90	361
Teacher-Assigned		(27.9)	(47.0)	(25.1)	(100%)
Reading Group	Low	42	84	83	209
		(20.1)	(40.2)	(39.7)	(100%)
	N	340	361	209	911

$$\chi^2 = 123.4 \quad p < .001$$
$$\tau_b = .318 \quad p < .001$$

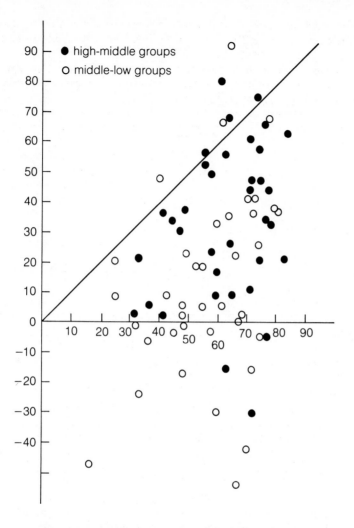

FIGURE 1 Scatterplot of Zero-order correlations between SES scores and group (vertical axis) and test scores and group (horizontal axis) by classroom.

group assignment, on students' SES and test scores (see Table II). The standardized regression weights indicate that the effect of measured reading ability is three times more powerful than home background in the case of the upper groups and over 10 times more powerful for the lower groups. In neither instance is there support for the proposition that SES has a greater effect on assignment than reading ability.

The revisionist argument posits that in the higher grades the difference between the mean test scores of the top and bottom groups will be greater than in the lower grades. To test this we computed the difference in Iowa means within each classroom, calculated the average of these differences for each grade level (four, five, and six) and

Table II
REGRESSION OF READING GROUP ASSIGNMENT ON READING TEST SCORES
AND PARENTAL SOCIOECONOMIC STATUS

	High-Middle Groups			Middle-Low Groups		
	Stan-dardized Weight	Unstan-dardized Weight	F	Stan-dardized Weight	Undstan-dardized Weight	F
Test Score	.529	.0099	358.6*	.538	.0087	340.0*
SES	.172	.0332	37.7*	.050	.0084	2.97 (n.s.)

$$R^2 = .368 \qquad R^2 = .310$$
$$F = 263.1^* \qquad F = 202.9^*$$
$$df = 2/698 \qquad df = 2/567$$

*$p < .01$.

Table III
MEAN DIFFERENCES IN TEST SCORES BETWEEN TOP AND BOTTOM GROUPS
AT THREE GRADE LEVELS

	Grade 4	Grade 5	Grade 6
Mean Difference	50.2	42.2	51.4
SD	11.9	19.3	20.6
N	12	12	13
ANOVA: $d_f = 2.34$	$F = .97$		

tested these differences for significance. Note that we are contrasting the extremes—top and bottom groups—where the effects of differentiated instruction should be greatest. Table III presents the relevant results, which do not support the hypothesis. In the fourth grade, the difference between the top and bottom reading groups averaged about 50 percentile points, in the fifth grade about 42 points, and in the sixth grade, 51 points.

Our second question concerned the relative segregating effects of teacher-judged ability as compared to standardized tests. To answer that question, we chose as a measure of socioeconomic segregation the τ_b correlation between SES and reading group placement. We computed this correlation twice for each classroom—once, for reading groups formed according to the

teacher's recommendations, and once for groups formed solely on the basis of Iowa scores. If teachers are more biased against lower-status children than are tests, we would expect that the first set of correlations would be greater than the second. To assess this possibility, the averages of the two sets were taken and a t-test for correlated means computed. This information is presented in Table IV.

If these classes had been divided solely on the basis of Iowa scores, some socioeconomic segregation would occur; $\tau_b = .222$. However, when teacher judgment is the basis of grouping, the resulting segregation is 20 percent higher. We conclude that, among this sample of schools, instructional grouping based on teacher-judged ability creates more, not less, socioeconomic segregation than would grouping

Table IV

MEANS LEVELS OF SES SEGREGATION:
TEACHER GROUPING VERSUS TEST GROUPING

N = 37

	Mean	SD	t	p
Teacher Grouping	.280	.215	2.68	<.01
Test Grouping	.222	.194		

Table V

REGRESSION OF INCREMENTAL CLASSROOM SES SEGREGATION
ON TEACHER SES

N = 37

Independent Variable	Unstandardized Weight	Standardized Weight	F	p
Mother's Educ.	.0429	.2884	2.28	ns
Father's Educ.	−.0241	−.1682	.54	ns
Father's Occup.	.1157	.1641	.66	ns

$$R^2 = .076 \quad F = .931 \text{ (ns)} \quad df = 3/33$$

based on achievement tests alone.

Table IV hides as much as it reveals, however. While on the average, teacher judgment increased social class segregation, the variation among teachers was considerable, as Figure 1 illustrates. Is this variation related to the teacher's own SES background?

Table V addresses this question. We regressed the difference between the two measures of segregation (teacher-test) for each class on three measures of teacher SES: father's occupation and the educational level of both mother and father. If teachers from middle-class homes were discriminating against lower SES children in forming reading groups, we would expect positive and significant regression coefficients for our three measures of teacher SES.

Table V indicates that the measures of teachers' backgrounds taken singly or together are not significantly related to increments in the amount of social class segregation in their classrooms. While the regression weight for

mother's education approaches statistical significance, those for father's education and occupation do not, and the former is opposite to the predicted sign. The entire regression, with an R^2 of only .076, is not statistically significant.

SUMMARY

The relationship between parental SES and teacher-assigned reading groups in this study was relatively small ($\tau_b = .32$), closely approximating the SES-high school track association found in other studies (see Rehberg & Rosenthal, 1978, for a recent review). Further, and also in line with the studies of high school tracking, measured ability was considerably more important as a determinant of curricular placement than was parental SES. Contrary to the self-fulfilling prophecy hypothesis advanced by Rist (1970), there was no evidence that any differential allocation of instructional time going on in these classrooms had resulted in increasing the gap in measured reading skill between top and bottom groups. Finally, the degree of socioeconomic segregation in these classrooms did not vary as a function of teachers' own social class backgrounds.

These findings incline us to the educational conclusion that neither pupil or teacher SES plays a major role in the grouping decisions of most teachers, and that grouping itself may not be an important mechanism for establishing the SES-high school track relationship.

REFERENCES

Alexander, K., Cook, M., & McDill, E. Curriculum tracking and educational stratification. *American Sociological Review*, 1978, *43*, 46-66.

Barker Lunn, J. *Streaming in the primary school*. London: National Foundation for Educational Research in England and Wales, 1970.

Becker, H. Social class variations in the teacher-pupil relationship. *Journal of Educational Sociology*, 1952, *25*, 451-465.

Bowles, S., & Gintis, H. *Schooling in capitalist America*. New York: Basic Books, 1976.

Brookover, W. Teachers and the stratification of American society. *Harvard Educational Review*, 1953, *23*, 257-267.

Brophy, J., & Good, T. *Teacher-student relationships: Causes and consequences*. New York: Holt, Rinehart, & Winston, 1974.

Charters, W. W. The social background of teaching. In N. L. Gage (Ed.), *Handbook of research on teaching*. Chicago: Rand McNally, 1963.

Findley, W., & Bryan, M. *Ability grouping: 1970*. Athens, Ga.: University of Georgia, Center for Educational Improvement, 1970.

Goodacre, E. *Teachers and their pupils' home background*. London: National Foundations for Educational Research in England and Wales, 1968.

Gough, H. A cluster analysis of home index status items. *Psychological Reports*, 1971, *28*, 923-929.

Gough, H. A short social status inventory. *Journal of Educational Psychology*, 1949, *40*, 52-56.

Heyns, B. Social selection and stratification within schools. *American Journal of Sociology*, 1974, *79*, 1434-1451.

Jencks, C. *Inequality*. New York: Basic Books, 1972.

Katz, M. *Class, bureaucracy and schools*. New York: Praeger, 1971.

Ravitch, D. *The revisionists revised: A critique of the radical attack on the schools*. New York: Basic Books, 1978.

Rehberg, R., & Rosenthal, E. *Class and merit in the American high school*. New York: Longman, 1978.

Reiss, A., Duncan, O., Hatt, P., & North, C. *Occupations and social status*. Glencoe, Ill.: The Free Press, 1961.

Rist, R. Student social class and teacher expectations: The self-fulfilling prophecy in ghetto education. *Harvard Educational Review*, 1970, *40*, 411-451.

Rosenbaum, J. *Making inequality*, New York: John Wiley, 1976.

Schafer, W., & Olexa, C. *Tracking and opportunity*. Scranton, Pa.: Chandler, 1971.

Warner, W., Havighurst, R., & Loeb, M. *Who shall be educated?* New York: Harper, 1944.

Differential Teacher Grading Behavior
Toward Female Students of Mathematics

CONCETTA M. DUVAL, *Brighton Central Schools, Rochester, New York*

Entry into many of today's careers is a function of the amount of mathematics studied in schools. In spite of the future relevance of mathematics to most careers, females in our society continue to self-select themselves out of mathematics courses in high school after such courses cease to be required (Fennema, Note 1). Encouraging females to continue their study of mathematics is therefore one of several vital steps that must be taken to overcome much of the occupational segregation that characterizes the American labor scene.

Fox (1976) has written, "If cultural biases have been operating which have led girls less than boys to consider the possibility of careers in mathematics and related areas, one must study to what extent and how these biases can be counteracted" (p. 186). By the expectations they hold, secondary teachers of mathematics, as one group of significant others, may play an important role in encouraging or discouraging female learners of mathematics.

Brophy and Good (1974) have conducted extensive research into the field of teacher expectations and student behavior. They assert that differential expectations toward students can function as self-fulfilling prophecies. They

From Journal for Research in Mathematics Education, *1980, 14, 202–13. Reprinted by permission.*

This article is based on the author's doctoral dissertation completed at the University of Rochester, 1978, under the direction of Norman Gunderson. Portions of this report were presented at the meeting of the Association of Mathematics Teachers of New York State, September, 1978.

further suggest that some teachers develop simplistic and rigid stereotypes and react more to the stereotypes than to the students themselves.

Teacher expectations have been said to be important determiners of student attitudes and achievements (Finn, 1972; Kehle, 1974; Palardy, 1969; Rist, 1970; Rosenthal & Jacobsen, 1968; Rowell, 1971; Zach & Price, 1973). Robert Coles (1971) has raised the question, "Can the child's performance in school be considered the result as much of what his teachers' attitudes are toward him as of his native intelligence or his attitude as a pupil?" (p. 76).

In mathematics, Fennema and Sherman (Note 2) found that teachers' expectations of students as learners of mathematics were significantly related to the students' decisions to take additional courses in mathematics. Casserly (Note 3) noted that girls who were enrolled in advanced placement mathematics and science courses reported having had teachers who had expected and encouraged high levels of achievement.

Yet, mathematics is considered by some to be a masculine domain. Ernest (1976) found that 41% of a small sample of elementary and secondary teachers believed that boys do better than girls in mathematics, whereas no one felt that girls do better than boys. Similarly, he reported that in a survey of 506 students, Grades 9 through 12, 32% believed that boys do better than girls in mathematics, whereas only 16% believed that girls do better.

Believing that the study of mathematics in inappropriate for girls, teachers may unwittingly reinforce and thus perpetuate cultural stereotypes. Fox (Note 4) has written, "It seems likely that most teachers are 'unconscious sexists' and should be made aware of the negative outcomes of their sex-role stereotyped attitudes and behaviors" (p. 15).

One way in which possible teacher bias against female learners of mathematics may be detected is in a study of teacher grading practices. As one form of teacher behavior, subtle differences in expectations of student performance may appear. If teachers hold differential expectations for females and males, might such expectations be reflected in evaluations of identical student performances?

Numerous studies have examined differences between grades assigned to boys and girls, at a variety of levels and in a number of different areas (Arnold, 1968; Bridgham, 1971; Carter, 1952; Day, 1938; Douglass, 1937; Edminston, 1943; Garner, 1935; Hadley, 1954; Lobaugh, 1942; Schinnerer, 1944; Swenson, 1942). The results of all these studies support Ross's contention, as cited by Hadley, that "it seems too bad that the marks received by certain individuals are conditioned more by the contours of the face than by the contents of the head" (p. 306).

The inherent subjectivity in grading, however, was the key to this experimental study. Patterned after similar disguised studies, a fictitious sample of an individual's performance was prepared (Finn, 1972; Goldberg, 1968; Kehle, 1974; Marshall & Powers, 1969; Scannell & Marshall, 1966; Walster, Cleary, & Clifford, 1970; Pheterson, Kiesler, & Goldberg, Note 5). While purporting to be an investigation of reliability in teacher grading practices in mathematics, the study was designed to determine if teacher subjectivity was exacerbated by knowledge of a student's sex and ability level.

METHOD

This study involved having a sample of secondary mathematics teachers grade a final examination paper consisting of four problems presumably written by a high school geometry student. Actually, the paper to be graded was prepared by the researcher using examples of student responses taken from the 1976 New York State Regents Examination in Geometry.

Geometry was chosen as the mathematical medium for two reasons. Starch and Elliott (1913) had demonstrated earlier that an "exact science" such as mathematics (geometry) was just as vulnerable to subjective ratings as essays in English and history. Secondly, geometry is often the last high school mathematics course elected by many females (Fennema & Sherman, 1976).

The four problems chosen to make up the experimental task had been originally written by three individuals and suffered from numerous errors of content and logic. The original errors were preserved, although each example was edited by the investigator for continuity. Every effort was made to convince the readers that the work was that of a single student.

The sex of the student was indicated by a name (Jeanne or Thomas) appearing at the top of the examination paper. A separate academic profile was prepared and the student's name rewritten for reinforcement. The three different ability levels (above average, average, and below average) were implied by a series of grades included in the profile of each *Jeanne* or *Tom*. These grades included the student's preceding final mark in elementary algebra, his/her final grade on the algebra Regents Exam, and four of his/her current marking period grades in geometry.

Teachers selected to participate in the experiment were to be randomly assigned to one of six treatment cells in a 2×3 factorial design. The independent variables were the indicated sex and the three ability levels of the *student* whose paper was to be graded. The dependent variable was the numerical grade assigned to the paper by the teacher. Each problem was worth 10 points for a maximum score of 40. A seventh cell was prepared to evaluate the neutral condition. Neither the sex nor the ability level of the student was conveyed to the reader. Teachers assigned to this control condition were simply asked to evaluate a nameless copy of the same exam being graded by the other graders, and no academic profile was included.

At the outset, the three research hypotheses to be tested were as follows: (a) There is no difference between the mean scores of the teacher-assigned grades of male and female students; (b) there is no difference between the mean scores of the teacher-assigned grades of the three ability levels of the students; (c) there is no difference between the mean scores of teacher-assigned grades of the sex-by-ability cells for males and females.

Sample of Teachers

To ensure that the research conclusions to be drawn would be statistically valid, a preliminary power analysis was performed to determine the necessary sample size (Cohen, 1977). Based on several parameters, including effect size and alpha level, the minimum sample size necessary to conduct a meaningful experiment was 32 responses per cell, or a total of 224 responses for the six experimental treatment conditions and the control condition.

The sample of teacher-graders was drawn from the State Education Department list of approximately 12,000 secondary mathematics teachers in New York State for the year 1976. A stratified sampling technique was used to divide New York State into 10 regions by county. In the investigator's view, these regions seemed to be both demographically and geographically homogeneous. This method of sampling ensured representation from the less populated regions within the state and prevented a disproportionate representation from the more populated downstate area. (Nearly 60% of the teachers were from the metropolitan New York City area.)

From each of the 10 regions, 102 teacher names were randomly selected, and within each region these names were randomly assigned to one of the seven experimental conditions. Each teacher selected to participate received a packet of materials that included the following: (a) a cover letter explaining the purpose of the exercise as an inquiry into the reliability of the State Regents Examination in geometry; (b) guidelines published by the State Education Department for the correction of state exams; (c) the examination paper and academic profile of the student (except for the control group); (d) a stamped postcard that the respondent could return with an address so that the results of the study could be provided; and (e) a 17-item teacher questionnaire to be answered anonymously that could provide information about the teacher's age, sex, and experience.

Of the 1020 packets mailed in October 1977, nearly 250 responses were received during the first three weeks. To generate as large a response as possible, a follow-up mailing was conducted one month after the original mailing. Eventually, 315 responses were received. Of these, 13 could not be used in the statistical analysis because either the examination paper had been returned ungraded or only the teacher questionnaire had been returned. Five responses received after the data analysis had been conducted were included in an analysis of late respondents. The 297 responses analyzed included 253 treatment papers and 44 control papers. Table 1 lists the number of responses received per cell and the calculated mean scores and standard deviations for each of the six experimental conditions. The corresponding data for the control group are noted with Table 1.

RESULTS

Two separate chi-square analyses were performed to determine if the unequal cell sizes obtained were statistically significant. The results of each analysis did not indicate that the unequal distribution of responses was significantly related to either the experimental design or the individual treatment conditions.

The experimental data, including the control group, were analyzed in an analysis of variance technique for unequal cell sizes (Winer, pp.468–472). The results of this analysis appear in Table 2.

According to Winer (p. 201), each treatment condition can also be compared with the control condition, regardless of the outcome of the overall F values. The calculated t values for the comparisons appear in Table 3.

With a critical t value (Winer, p. 873) approximately equal to ±2.3, none of the obtained values were statistically significant at the .05 level. Hence, there was insufficient evidence to conclude that the mean scores in the treatment conditions were statistically different from the mean score of the control condition.

Late Respondents

A survey that depends on a return mailing may not furnish results that are representative of the larger population. Thus, to judge whether or not the 297 responses accurately reflected the grading behaviors of the total number of secondary mathematics teachers in New York State, the data received from a group of individuals classified as late respondents were compared to the entire sample (Simon, 1969).

For this study, papers received one month or more after the original mailing and also after the follow-up mailing were designated late responses. This subsample of responses consisted of

Table 1

NUMBER OF RESPONSES, MEAN SCORE, AND STANDARD DEVIATION FOR EACH EXPERIMENTAL CONDITION

	Ability Level		
Group	Above average	Average	Below average
Males			
N	37.00	36.00	44.00
M	19.43	19.36	18.96
SD	6.07	3.32	5.29
Females			
N	41.00	39.00	56.00
M	19.12	19.87	18.70
SD	5.11	5.07	5.32

Note. Control: $N = 44$, $M = 18.66$, $SD = 4.54$

Table 2
ANALYSIS OF VARIANCE FOR CONTROL AND THE EXPERIMENT GROUPS

Source	SS	df	MS	F
Control vs. all others	11.214	1	11.214	$.0448_{ns}$
S (sex)	0.0003	1	0.0003	0.00001_{ns}
A (ability)	25.731	2	12.866	0.514_{ns}
S × A	8.584	2	4.293	0.172_{ns}
Within cell	6329.8	253	25.02	

Table 3
t VALUES OBTAINED FROM COMPARISON OF CONTROL GROUP
WITH EACH EXPERIMENTAL CONDITION

| Group | Ability Level | | |
	Above average	Average	Below average
Males	−0.693	−0.624	−0.278
Females	−0.426	−1.103	−0.037

38 papers (3 treatment and 6 control). These numbers were significantly below the power analysis demands per cell established earlier. Table 4 summarizes the distribution and mean scores of the late respondents.

As with the experimental data, an analysis of variance involving unequal cell sizes was performed on these data. None of the F statistics was significant.

DISCUSSION

An expectation that a student's sex or ability level influences the grade assigned to a paper was not supported by the results of this study. Although some teachers may indeed believe that boys are better than girls in mathematics (Ernest, 1976), their behavior on this experimental task appeared to be objective. The degree of variability in grading seemed to rest more on some abstract geometry criterion held by the individual teachers than to any normative standard for males and females of different abilities.

The calculated values for the F statistics in the source table deserve some comment. By definition, the F statistic is given as the ratio of two measures that reflect (a) variation due to intergroup treatment effects (MS between) and (b) intragroup variations due only to chance (MS within). This last factor is referred to as the *error* term. Theoretically, if there is no treatment effect, the F ratio should equal 1.

The analysis of variance technique is used to determine if differences between means are sufficiently large to consider them to be nonchance events. If the F statistic, under the sampling conditions for a study, exceeds the chance expectation of $F = 1.00$ by an amount associated with a predetermined significance level, then the difference in means is considered to be statistically significant. The F statistic may exhibit very low values in the range of 0 to 1. According to Hays (1973), finding an F ratio less than 1 can be due to chance or to some failure of the ex-

Table 4
NUMBER OF RESPONSES AND MEAN SCORES RECEIVED FROM LATE RESPONDENTS

Group	Ability Level		
	Above average	Average	Below average
Males			
N	6.0	2.0	3.0
M	19.7	17.0	20.0
Females			
N	5.0	9.0	7.0
M	16.0	21.3	17.4

Note. Control Group: $N = 6$, $M = 19$.

periment itself. Very low *F* ratios, therefore, can represent observed differences so small as to be unexpectedly free of chance variation.

In this experiment, the calculated value for *F* due to the main treatment effect, sex of student, was .00001. Similarly, the *F* ratios for the ability effect and the interaction effect were .514 and .172, respectively. Although these values may well be due to chance, another explanation may lie in the experimental design itself.

This was a disguised study. That is, the participants were told that the grading exercise was to determine how reliable teacher grading practices were in a subjective subject such as geometry. Actually, teacher variability in grading practices was accepted as a given. The major intent of the study was to detect a sex and/or ability bias. Accepting the naive assumption of the purpose of the task, teachers may have contributed to the failure to detect the very thing being sought. In an effort to be impartial, perhaps participants were extra careful in evaluating the paper. Thus, they may have masked their own personal idiosyncracies, producing instead a very large error term.

Similarly, the isolation of this experimental task may have provoked greater scrutiny than the correction of a set of different papers written by students that had been in class all year long. Except for the control group, each teacher in the study had been given some background information on the student whose paper was being graded. Such information may have been too clinical and too obvious. A student, male or female, does not exist as a series of mathematics grades alone. Comments made by individual teachers who returned the graded paper reflected this concern.

The differences in the grading behaviors of both the experimental group and the group of late respondents may be seen in Figure 1.

Although both groups tended to grade above-average-ability males and below-average-ability males slightly higher than or nearly equal to the neutral condition, there seems to be a difference in the mean score given to the average-ability male. For the group of late respondents, this may suggest that either the average male in mathematics is penalized for a less than adequate performance or that both his higher achieving and lower achieving peers are given the benefit of the doubt more often.

For the female students, the above-average-ability and below-average-ability females are graded differently by

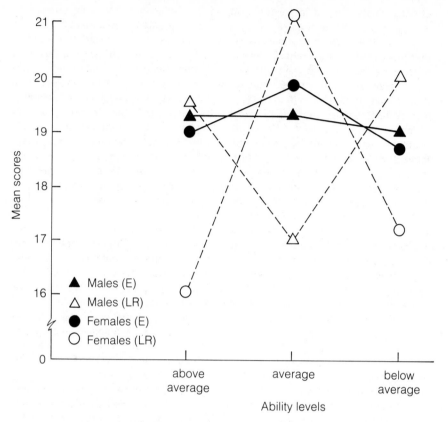

FIGURE 1 Mean ratings of examination papers by total experimental group and by late respondents. (E = total experimental group, *N* = 297; LR = late respondents, *N* = 38.)

each group. For the late respondents, this may suggest that there is less tolerance for poor performance from a female student believed to be above average in mathematics and little expected if she is below average in ability. Females of average ability achieved the highest mean scores from both groups of teachers, suggesting that they might be subject to different standards. Mediocre performance is rewarded more highly in this case perhaps because mediocrity is all that is expected.

Similarly, the low-ability female is not given the same benefit of the doubt as her male peer. Perhaps there is less tolerance for a poor performance on the part of the less talented female. This phenomenon, if it does exist in the larger population, could explain the differential drop-out rates in mathematics among males and females. Being given poorer grades than her male peer for the same mediocre performance may discourage a female from continued mathematics study.

Among the late respondents, there appear to be discrepancies between the scores assigned to males and females of comparable ability. Unfortunately, the suggested interaction effect, if it exists, could not be detected with such a small sample size.

Finally, the experimental conclusion that the variability in teachers' grades of students' performance is not affected significantly by certain student characteristics may be attributable to the subject itself. Geometry, as taught in most of the secondary schools in New York State, is clearly defined by a state syllabus and is presented as a formal axiomatic system. Teachers at this level may be highly content oriented. Data from the teacher questionnaire revealed that approximately 70% of the teachers responding had majored in mathematics as undergraduates. Unlike their elementary and perhaps junior high school colleagues, high school mathematics teachers may possess more rigorous mathematical standards and demand such from their students.

Implications

To determine whether or not secondary teachers of mathematics, as one group of significant others, are unconscious sexists requires further study. Although the differences were not statistically significant, there was some appearance of discrepant grading behavior. Having heard from only a small percentage of interested teachers, a generalization to the larger population is tenuous at best. Studies that investigate a larger, more representative sample of mathematics teachers are necessary. This includes additional experimental studies as well as classroom observations and case studies. Although many studies have been conducted dealing with the classroom behaviors of teachers, few, if any, have focused specifically on those behaviors that occur within classrooms and that result in discriminatory behavior against females. Conversely, no evidence is available that isolates and describes those behaviors that might be supportive of females in mathematics.

Studies that examine the additive effects of other student variables on teacher behavior are important. In addition to student ability and sex, such things as attractiveness, motivation, behavior, and attitude are important student variables that may differentially affect a teacher's behavior and expectations. Similarly, the ways in which teachers' characteristics themselves affect their perceptions of students— particularly females—are also of interest.

There appear to be four major areas of investigation with respect to secondary teachers of mathematics: (a) attitudes toward females as learners of mathematics; (b) behaviors toward females as learners of mathematics; (c) the effects of discriminatory attitudes or behaviors on females; and (d) the effects of teacher characteristics (sex, age, experience, etc.) on female learners of mathematics.

The existence of prejudicial attitudes among mathematics teachers may not adversely affect teacher behavior or the attitudes and achievement of their students. The presence of discriminatory behaviors against females well might. A measure of these, either separately or jointly, involves examining teacher-student interactions.

What may or may not be present either in a teacher's thoughts or actions may be secondary to what a student perceives is true. Any study of teachers, therefore, should involve their interactions with students. Using mathematics education as a focus, such interaction research should be actively pursued.

Although this study focused on secondary teachers, attention should be paid to differences that may exist between teachers of mathematics at the elementary and junior high school level.

Most high school mathematics teachers are certified in mathematics and have enjoyed success in its study. Elementary and junior high school teachers, however, may not share the same positive attitudes toward mathematics or even have been very successful in its study (Ernest, 1976). Possibly, their own apprehensions and insecurities about mathematics may be communicated to students, including the stereotyped belief that mathematics is predominantly a male domain.

The junior high school level is particularly crucial. Adolescence is a time when socialization is very important. Attitudes toward male and female roles in our society become further crystallized as both boys and girls become more conscious of acceptable sex roles. Investigating the ways in which teachers of mathematics at this level view their students and behave toward them in the classroom is of major interest.

Future efforts should also be directed toward working with classroom teachers at all levels to dispel conscious or unconscious stereotyped notions about females and mathematics. Clinging to old notions, many teachers may be unaware of the growing significance mathematics has come to play in our society. Mathematics has been described as a "critical filter" and has become an essential prerequisite for a great number of careers in today's world (Sells, Note 6).

In conclusion, however, the overall findings of this study do not support the contention that these secondary teachers, as one group of significant others, were guilty of discrimination against females in the grading of a set of mathematics papers. Indeed, this grading experiment supports the hypothesis that secondary teachers as a group appear to be neutral and assign grades on the basis of quality of performance.

One should, perhaps, recall Carl Sagan's advice in *The Dragons of Eden* that "absence of evidence is not evidence of absence" (p. 7). The analysis of the late respondents, although an admittedly small sample, is suggestive of the presence of some evidence. Thus, to assume on the basis of this study that the population of secondary teachers, as a group of significant others, does not evince a bias against females as learners of mathematics may be premature.

5. Pheterson, G., Kiesler, S., & Goldberg, P. *Evaluation of the performance of women as a function of their sex, achievement and personal history*. Unpublished manuscript, 1976.

6. Sells, L. *High school mathematics as the critical filter in the job market*. Unpublished manuscript, March 1973.

REFERENCES

Arnold, R. D. The achievement of boys and girls taught by men and women teachers. *Elementary School Journal*, 1968, *68*, 367-373.

Bridgham, R. G. *Severity of grading in the sciences and its relation to science enrollment*. Stanford, Calif.: Stanford University, 1971. (ERIC Document Reproduction Service No. ED 052064)

Carter, R. S. How invalid are marks assigned by teachers? *Journal of Educational Psychology*, 1952, *43*, 218-228.

Cohen, J. *Statistical power analysis for the behavioral sciences*. New York: Academic Press, 1977.

Coles, R. What can you expect? In J. D. Elashoff & R. E. Snow (Eds.), *Pygmalion reconsidered*. Worthington, Ohio: Charles A. Jones Publishing, 1971.

Day, L. C. Boys and girls and honor ranks. *School Review*, 1938, *46*, 288-299.

Douglass, H. R. Relation of high school marks to sex in four Minnesota senior high schools. *School Review*, 1937, *45*, 282-288.

Edminston, R. W. Do teachers show partiality? *Peabody Journal of Education*, 1943, *20*, 234-238.

Ernest, J. *Mathematics and sex*. Santa Barbara: University of California, April 1976.

Finn, J. Expectations and the educational environment. *Review of Educational Research*, 1972, *42*, 387-410.

Fox, L. H. Sex differences in mathematical precocity: Bridging the gap. In D. P. Keating (Ed.), *Intellectual talent: Research and development*. Baltimore: Johns Hopkins University Press, 1976.

Garner, C. E. Survey of teachers' marks. *School and Community*, 1935, *21*, 116-117.

Goldberg, P. Are women prejudiced against women? *Transaction, 1968, 5* (5), 28-31.

Hadley, T. S. A school mark—Fact or fancy? *Educational Administration and Supervision*, 1954, *40*, 305-312.

Hays, W. L. *Statistics for the social sciences* (2nd ed.). New York: Holt, Rinehart & Winston, 1973.

Kehle, T. J. Teachers' expectations: Ratings of student performance as biased by student characteristics. *Journal of Experimental Education*, 1974, *43*, 54-60.

Lobaugh, D. Girls, grades and IQ's. *Nations Schools*, 1942, *30*, 42-46.

Marshall, J. C., & Powers, J. M. Writing neatness, composition errors, and essay grades. *Journal of Educational Measurement*, 1969, *6*, 97-101.

Palardy, M. J. What teachers believe—What children achieve. *Elementary School Journal*, 1969, *69*, 370-374.

Rist, R. Student social class and teacher expectations: The self-fulfilling prophecy in ghetto education. *Harvard Educational Review*, 1970, *40*, 411-451.

Rosenthal, R., & Jacobsen, L. *Pygmalion in the classroom: Teacher expectation and pupils' intellectual development*. New York: Holt, Rinehart & Winston, 1968.

Rowell, A. J. Sex differences in achievement in science and the expectations of teachers. *Australian Journal of Education*, 1971, *15*, 16-29.

Sagan, C. *The dragons of eden*. New York: Random House, 1977.

Scannell, D., & Marshall, J. C. The effect of selected composition errors on the grades assigned to essay exams. *American Educational Research Journal*, 1966, *3*, 125-130.

Schinnerer, M. C. Failure ratio: Two boys to one girl. *Clearinghouse*, 1944, *18*, 262-270.

Simon, J. *Basic research methods in social science: The art of empirical investigation*. New York: Random House, 1969.

Starch, D., & Elliott, E. C. Reliability of grading work in mathematics. *School Review*, 1913, *21*, 255-259.

Swenson, C. Packing the honor society. *Clearinghouse*, 1942, *16*, 521-524.

Walster, E. T., Cleary, A., & Clifford, M. M. The effect of race and sex on college admission. *Sociology of Education*, 1970, *44*, 237-244.

Winer, B. J. *Statistical principles in experimental design* (2nd ed.). New York: McGraw-Hill, 1971.

Zach, L., & Price, M. *The teacher's part in sex role reinforcement*. (Source and date not given) (ERIC Document Reproduction Service No. ED 070 513)

Effects of Cooperative, Competitive, and Individualistic Conditions on Children's Problem-solving Performance

DAVID W. JOHNSON, LINDA SKON, and ROGER JOHNSON
University of Minnesota

The effects of interpersonal cooperation, competition, and individualistic efforts were compared on a categorization and retrieval, a spatial-reasoning, and a verbal problem-solving task. Forty-five first-grade children were randomly assigned to conditions stratified on the basis of sex and ability, so that an approximately equal percentage of males and females and high, medium, and low ability children were included in each condition. The results indicate that on all three tasks students in the cooperative condition achieved higher than did those in the individualistic condition, and on two of the three tasks students in the cooperative condition achieved higher than did those in the competitive condition. There were no significant differences between the competitive and individualistic condition. Students in the cooperative condition used higher quality strategies on the three tasks than did those in the other two conditions, and they perceived higher levels of peer support and encouragement for learning. High ability students in the cooperative condition generally achieved higher than did the high ability students in the competitive and individualistic conditions.

This study has three purposes. The first is to compare the relative effects of cooperative, competitive, and individualistic conditions on problem-solving performance. The second is to examine

From American Educational Research Journal, *Spring 1980, 17(1), 83–93. Copyright 1980, American Educational Research Association, Washington, D.C. Reprinted by permission.*

three possible influences on the problem-solving success of cooperative groups: (1) quality of strategy used, (2) medium and low ability students benefiting from their interaction with high ability group members, and (3) increased incentive to succeed resulting from peer support and encouragement for achievement. The third purpose is to provide further validation for a set of instructional strategies.

Three types of interpersonal goal structures can be implemented in instructional situations (Deutsch, 1962; Johnson & Johnson, 1975): cooperative, competitive, and individualistic. In a *cooperative* situation individuals' goal achievements are positively correlated; when one person achieves his or her goal, all others with whom he or she is cooperatively linked achieve their goals. In a *competitive* situation individuals' goal achievements are negatively correlated; when one person achieves his or her goal all others with whom he or she is competitively linked fail to achieve their goals. In an *individualistic* situation individuals' goal achievements are independent; the goal achievement of one person is unrelated to the goal achievement of others.

There is disagreement as to the relative effects of the three goal structures on achievement and productivity. Miller and Hamblin (1963) reviewed 24 studies and found that in 14 competition resulted in higher achievement than did cooperation, while in 10 the opposite effect was demonstrated. In their own study, cooperation promoted higher achievement on a task that required the exchange of information than did competition, but no difference was found on a task that did not require any exchange of information. In a subsequent review Johnson and Johnson (1975) found that on problem-solving tasks cooperation promoted higher achievement than did competition, while on simple motor tasks competition resulted in higher achievement that did cooperation. In a review of 10 studies, selected for including tasks in which others could not contribute additional resources. Michaels (1977) found that in seven competition promoted higher achievement than did cooperative or individualistic efforts. Slavin (1977) concludes from a review of the research that when individuals have important resources to share or withhold at their discretion, cooperation promotes higher achievement than does competitive or individualistic efforts, while the opposite is true when individuals do not have important resources to share or withhold. Davis, Laughlin, and Komorita (1976) conclude from their review that cooperation promotes higher achievement in concept attainment tasks than do competitive or individualistic efforts, and that the findings hold for a variety of conceptual rules, task difficulty conditions, and interaction formats. Johnson and Johnson (1979) and Johnson, Johnson, and Skon (1979) report a series of studies in which they found that on drill-review, conceptual learning, and problem-solving tasks, cooperation consistently promoted higher achievement than did competitive or individualistic efforts.

While the evidence concerning the relative efficacy of the three goal structures on achievement and productivity is inconsistent, there is general agreement that on conceptual, problem-solving tasks where others may provide needed information and resources, co-operation does promote higher achievement than the other two goal structures. There are at least three major problems, however, with this research literature. One is that the operationalizations of competitive and individualistic conditions were less than optimal. In many of the studies conducted in the schools care was taken to maximize the effectiveness of the cooperative condition, while little or no attention was paid to the effectiveness of the competitive or individualistic conditions. To find that a carefully structured instructional strategy is more effective than poorly structured instructional strategies does not confirm a theoretical proposition concerning the relative efficacy of cooperative, competitive, and individualistic goal structures, nor does it validate an instructional procedure. It is important to optimize all three goal structures in a comparative study. The second problem with the research literature in this area is that the processes mediating the effectiveness of cooperative learning experiences have not been illuminated by the previous research. It is not enough to simply demonstrate superiority; the dynamics of cooperative learning that lead to high performance in achievement situations must be delineated and understood. Finally, most of the previous research has been conducted within research laboratories rather than within actual classrooms.

The first purpose of this study is to compare the relative effects of cooperative, competitive, and individualistic conditions on problem-solving performance, while the operationalization of each is carefully structured. On the basis of the previous research, it is hypothesized that on all the problem-solving tasks included in this study, individuals in the cooperative condition will perform better than will individuals in the competitive and individualistic conditions.

If cooperation is, in fact, superior to competitive and individualistic efforts on conceptual, problem-solving tasks, the question remains as to what are the underlying dynamics that account for the superiority of cooperative groups. Three of the major variables that have been proposed as influences on the quality of cooperative problem-solving are: (1) the development of superior cognitive problem-solving strategies, (2) the medium and low ability students benefiting from their interaction with the high ability students without the opposite occurring and, (3) the incentive for achievement being increased by peer support and encouragement for learning. Each of these variables is examined in this study.

There is some evidence from research conducted in laboratory settings with college students, that the superiority of cooperative groups is not due to their having more information about the problem, but that the discussion process in cooperative groups enables members to evolve and use more effective cognitive strategies for learning and problem-solving (Laughlin, 1973). There is also evidence that high ability individuals perform at the same level regardless of whether they are in a cooperative, competitive, or individualistic condition (Laughlin, 1978; Wodarski, Hamblin, Buckholdt, & Ferritor, 1973; DeVries & Mescon, Note 1). This means that any superiority in performance found in the previous studies may be due to medium and low ability students benefiting from their interaction with high ability students in the cooperative condition; with students in the competitive and individualistic conditions being deprived of such stimulation. The third explanation for the superiority of cooperative groups on problem-solving tasks is that there is more peer support and encouragement for learning in the cooperative than in the competitive and

individualistic situations. There is some evidence that cooperative experiences promote perceptions of more peer support and encouragement than do the other two-goal structures (Cooper, Johnson, Johnson, & Wilderson, in press; Johnson, Johnson, & Tauer, 1979). On the basis of the current evidence, it may be hypothesized that in the cooperative condition, compared with the competitive and individualistic ones, students will use superior cognitive problem-solving strategies, the medium and low ability students will benefit from their interaction with the high ability students, and greater peer support and encouragement for learning will be perceived.

The operationalizations of cooperative, competitive, and individualistic instruction used in this study have been used in a series of 12 previous studies (Johnson & Johnson, 1978) and have been field tested extensively in regular classrooms throughout the United States (Johnson & Johnson, 1975). Any results found in this study, therefore, have direct practical application to classroom teaching.

It should be noted that there is a marked lack of studies that include cooperative, competitive, and individualistic conditions within the same study. This prevents a clear discussion of their relative merits. By including all three interpersonal goal structures, this study is aimed at providing direct evidence as to their relative efficacy in problem-solving situations. In addition, most of the previous research has included only one task per study. In this study three different types of problem-solving tasks are included: one requiring the categorization and retrieval of information, one requiring spatial-reasoning, and one requiring math operations to be logically structured from verbal material. It is expected that the inclusion of three different types of problem-solving tasks will more adequately test the above hypotheses than would the inclusion of only one such task.

METHOD

Sample

The sample consisted of two first-grade classes from a large, suburban elementary school in a large midwestern suburb. The 45 students, 27 males and 18 females, included in this study were from middle and working class backgrounds. A stratified random sampling procedure was used to assign students to conditions, so that an equal percentage of high, medium, and low students in reading and math ability were included in each condition, and so that an approximately equal percentage of males and females were included in each condition. Fifteen students were assigned to each of the three conditions.

Independent Variables

Two sets of independent variables were included in this study: (1) cooperative, competitive, and individualistic learning situations and (2) three different learning tasks. In the *cooperative* condition a stratified random sampling procedure was used, so that in each cooperative triad there was one high, one medium, and one low ability student and at least one female. Students were instructed to work together as a group, sharing materials and ideas, helping each other, and ensuring that each member was involved, agreed on the answers, and learned the material being studied. The teacher praised and rewarded the groups on the basis of each group's achievement.

The *competitive* condition was structured to maximize appropriate and effective use of competition. Students in this condition were assigned to triads

homogeneous in reading and math ability and instructed to compete for first, second, and third places. There were five triads. After each learning task was completed, students were informed of the results and were regrouped. Winners were moved up to a more challenging cluster and losers were moved to the next lower cluster. This was designed to maintain students' perceptions that each had a reasonable chance of winning. All clusters worked on the same learning tasks. Students were instructed to work alone, but to be aware of their competitors' progress by noticing when they raised their hands to signal completion of a task. Students were seated separately, but near the others in their cluster. The teacher praised and rewarded the winner in each cluster.

In the *individualistic* condition students were instructed to work alone, to ignore others, to work at their own pace, and to do their best work. Students were separated to minimize distractions. The teacher praised and rewarded each child individually on the basis of one's own work.

The second independent variable was type of learning task. The first task, adapted from the one used by Salatas and Flavell (1976), was a categorization and retrieval problem in which students were required to memorize 12 nouns during a study session and to complete several retrieval tasks during a subsequent testing session. The 12 nouns (apple, banana, peach, horse, pig, cow, hat, coat, belt, bike, ball, yo-yo) were on 3 inch by 3 inch cards accompanied by illustrations. The cards were placed in a random order, so that all sets of cards were in the same order, and so that the words were not grouped into categories. Students were instructed to put the cards in an order that made sense to them and that would aim at memorization, and then to memorize them. During the testing session the students were asked individually to name the words they had learned (free recall task) and the words were recorded in the order given by the subject. The responses were rated for the number of correct words given (0-12) and the degree of organizational strategy used (0-8, based on the extent to which the words were organized into the four categories of food, clothing, animals, and toys). Students were also asked individually which of these subjects were too big to fit in a box that was displayed (spontaneous retrieval task). These responses were rated in terms of the number of correct responses (0-6). Finally, students were asked individually whether they had arranged the words in any special order to help them remember the words (awareness of category structure and search strategy, scored 0-1).

The second task was a spatial-reasoning problem called the Rasmussen Triangle (Napier & Gershenfeld, 1973) and consisted of a diagram containing an ambiguous number of triangles. Students were given three pages, each containing nine copies of the diagram, and were instructed to color one triangle on each diagram until they had colored all of the possible triangles without repetition. The task included the learning of the concept "triangle," the reorientation of visual perception to include small, previously identified triangles within a large new triangle (combining of parts): the discrimination of triangles from nontriangles within the diagram; and the keeping track of triangles previously identified, so that the same triangle was not counted more than once. The strategy examined was the avoidance of errors and repetitions. Students practiced finding the triangles in a study session and were then tested individually on the task during a subsequent instructional session. There were 18 triangles in the diagram.

The third task was a verbal problem-solving task consisting of 10 math story problems given to the students and also read orally by the teacher. During the study session the students were allowed to use counters and number lines to practice solving the problems; thus, it was assured that the math required could be easily done by all students. The problems involved one-digit addition and subtraction; some of the problems involved two computations. Examples of these problems are: "Don needs nine pennies to buy a candy bar. He has four pennies now. How many more does he need?" and "Mom had ten plates. She broke four plates. Jan brought her two new plates. How many unbroken plates does Mom have now?" It was possible to assume (and verify) that any mistakes were due to failure to logically construct the correct math computations in order to solve them. During the testing session all students were individually given the same story problems, which again were read orally by the teacher.

Procedure

All students participated in six instructional sessions of 60 minutes each. Each instructional session was on a different day. In the first instructional session students studied the story problems, in the second session they were tested on the story problems. In the third instructional session students studied the Rasmussen diagram, and in the fourth session they were tested on their ability to identify the triangles in the diagram. In the fifth instructional session students arranged the words and tried to memorize them, and in the sixth session they were tested on their free recall, spontaneous retrieval, and awareness of category structure and search strategy.

Prior to the study all of the students had participated in cooperative, competitive, and individualistic learning situations. Thus, all students were familiar with the procedures of each condition. The three teachers who participated in the study included two first-grade teachers who had received 30 hours of training and had used cooperative, competitive, and individualistic goal structures in their classrooms prior to the study. The third teacher was a college professor with nine years of elementary school teaching experience and extensive experience in demonstrating the procedures for teaching cooperatively, competitively, and individualistically. The three teachers followed written directions for explaining the tasks and learning activities, so that the instructions given to the subjects were consistent among teachers. The three teachers were randomly assigned to conditions.

Dependent Measures and Analysis

The dependent measures were achievement on each of the tasks, quality of strategy used on each of the tasks, and perceptions of peer support for learning. Achievement scores were derived from the individual tests turned in at the end of the second, fourth, and sixth instructional sessions. On the seventh day of the study, students were individually asked three questions: (1) How much did other students care whether or not you learned? (2) How important was it to you that you did well? and (3) How much did you like the way you worked? The latter two questions were included to verify that students in all three conditions were motivated to do their best in the instructional sessions and that the conditions were all operationalized effectively. The teachers recorded the students' responses on 4-point scales. A 1 $\times$ 3 analysis of variance with Newman-Kuels post-hoc comparisons among means was used to analyze the data.

A multivariate F was first conducted, and when it proved to be significant, univariate analyses were conducted on the dependent variables.

RESULTS

To verify that the cooperative, competitive, and individualistic conditions had been appropriately and effectively implemented, students were asked how much they liked the condition they were working in and how important it was to them to do well on the learning tasks. As indicated in Table I, no significant differences were found among conditions on these two measures. It may be concluded, therefore, that students in all three conditions enjoyed the operationalization of the condition and took the learning tasks seriously.

Table I shows the patterns of results for the three conditions for the three dependent variables examined in the study: performance on problem-solving tasks, quality of strategy used, and perceptions of peer support for learning.

To determine whether the superior performance of the cooperative learning groups was due to the high ability members giving the answers to the medium and low ability students, the results were reanalyzed for the high ability students only. From Table II it can be seen that the high ability students in the cooperative condition consistently performed higher on the problem-solving tasks and used superior strategies for deriving their answers, than did the high ability subjects in the competitive and individualistic conditions.

DISCUSSION

On three of the four task measures, students in the cooperative condition outperformed students in the competitive condition, and on all four task measures students in the cooperative condition outperformed students in the individualistic condition. These findings are im-

Table I

MEAN SCORES ON ACHIEVEMENT, STRATEGIES, AND ATTITUDE MEASURES

Measure	Coopera-tive	Competi-tive	Individ-ualistic	F
Liking Condition	3.20	3.13	3.40	n.s.
Importance of Doing Well	3.33	3.20	3.27	n.s.
Categorization & Retrieval				
Free Recall Performance	10.87	7.33	5.87	23.28**
Spontaneous Retrieval Performance	3.33	1.87	1.80	4.25*
Categorization Strategy	6.13	2.00	1.13	46.15**
Awareness of Strategy	.27	.07	0	3.14*
Spatial-Reasoning				
Number Correct (Performance)	15.13	13.53	8.40	29.86**
Errors (Performance)	1.27	3.53	5.93	6.60**
Verbal Reasoning Performance	8.33	5.93	6.27	4.05*
Peer Support	2.53	1.67	1.73	4.07*

*$p < .05$.
**$p < .01$.

Note Newman-Kuels Post-Hoc Comparisons, Significance at .05 or Less

Free Recall: Coop > Comp; Coop > Ind
Spontaneous Retrieval: Coop > Comp; Coop > Ind
Categorization Strategy: Coop > Comp; Coop > Ind
Awareness of Strategy: Coop > Comp; Coop > Ind
Spatial-Reasoning. Number Correct: Coop > Ind; Comp > Ind
Spatial-Reasoning. Errors: Coop > Comp; Coop > Ind
Verbal Reasoning: Coop > Comp; Coop > Ind
Peer Support: Coop > Comp; Coop > Ind

portant, as many of the previous studies compared only two of the three interpersonal goal structures or compared cooperation with an unstructured "traditionally taught classroom" control. The inclusion of all three interpersonal structures, the care taken in operationalizing all three goal structures, the inclusion of three different types of problem-solving tasks, all strengthen the problem-solving performance results of this study.

The results also provide some insight into the processes mediating the superior performance of cooperative groups on conceptual and problem-solving tasks. It seems evident that the discussion process in cooperative groups results in the development of superior cognitive strategies for solving problems. On all three of the problem-solving tasks, subjects in the coopera-

tive condition used strategies superior to those used by the students in the competitive and individualistic conditions. The most marked difference among conditions was on the categorization and retrieval task, where four of the five cooperative groups discovered and used all four categories and no one in the competitive and individualistic conditions did so. These results support Laughlin's (1973) previous research with college students in the laboratory setting.

The superior performance of cooperative groups does not seem to be due to the medium and low ability students benefiting from the work of high ability students, although there is some previous evidence that this would be so (Laughlin, 1978; Wodarski, et al., 1973; DeVries & Mescon, Note 1). The results indicate that when the high ability stu-

Table II

MEAN SCORES OF HIGH ABILITY STUDENTS
ON ACHIEVEMENT AND STRATEGY MEASURES

Measure	Coopera-tive	Competi-tive	Individ-ualistic	F
Categorization & Retrieval				
Free Recall Performance	10.80	7.80	5.80	11.05*
Spontaneous Retrieval Performance	3.80	2.60	2.00	3.15**
Categorization Strategy	6.60	2.00	1.60	17.55*
Awareness of Strategy	.20	0	0	n.s.
Spatial-Reasoning				
Number Correct (Performance)	16.00	13.20	9.00	9.70*
Errors (Performance)	.20	4.00	2.40	2.48***
Verbal Reasoning Performance	8.60	6.40	7.60	1.41****

*$p < .01$.
**$p = .08$.
***$p = .12$.
****$p = .28$.

dents do not know the correct answer, the cooperative discussion provides new insights into the most effective strategy to be used and the correct answers. The high as well as the medium and low ability students benefited from the cooperative discussion. These results are all the more intriguing, as they are with first-grade students who are far more diverse in intellectual ability than were the college students participating in Laughlin's (1978) studies.

Cooperative interaction, furthermore, does seem to promote perceptions of more support and encouragement for achievement than do competitive and individualistic conditions.

There were no consistent differences between the competitive and individualistic conditions. While there has been much less theoretical speculation as to the differences between these two conditions, it appears that essentially they are the same in regard to promoting achievement on problem-solving tasks, discovering strategies to use in solving problems, and perceiving peer support and encouragement for learning.

The findings have implications for classroom instructional practices (see Johnson & Johnson, 1978). When high problem-solving performance based on the use of effective strategies and peer support and encouragement are desired, the instructional situation should be structured cooperatively rather than competitively or individualistically.

REFERENCE NOTE

1. DeVries, D., & Mescon, I. Using TGT at the Moses DeWitt elementary school: A preliminary report. Mimeographed Report, Center for Social Organization of Schools, Johns Hopkins University, 1974.

REFERENCES

Cooper, L., Johnson, D. W., Johnson, R., & Wilderson, F. The effects of cooperative, competitive, and individualistic condi-tions on cross-ethnic, cross-sex, and cross-ability friendships. *Journal of Social Psychology*, in press.

Davis, J., Laughlin, P., & Komorita, S. The social psychology of small groups: Cooperative and mixed-motive interaction. In M. Rosenzweig & L. Porter (Eds.), *Annual review of psychology*. Palo Alto, Calif.: 1976.

Deutsch, M. Cooperation and trust: Some theoretical notes. In M. Jones (Ed.), *Nebraska symposium on motivation*. Lincoln: University of Nebraska Press, 1962.

Johnson, D. W., & Johnson, R. *Learning together and alone: Cooperation, competition, and individualization*. Englewood Cliffs, N.J.: Prentice-Hall, 1975.

Johnson, D. W., & Johnson, R. Cooperative, competitive, and individualistic learning. *Journal of Research and Development in Education*, 1978, *12*(1), 3–15.

Johnson, D. W., Johnson, R., & Skon, L. The effects of cooperative, competitive, and individualistic conditions on student achievement on different types of tasks. *Contemporary Educational Psychology*, 1979, *4*, 99–106.

Johnson, R., & Johnson, D. W. Type of task and student achievement and attitudes in interpersonal cooperation, competition, and individualization. *Journal of Social Psychology*, 1979, *108*, 37–48.

Johnson, R., Johnson, D. W., & Tauer, M. Effects of cooperative, competitive, and individualistic goal structures on students' achievement and attitudes. *Journal of Psychology*, 1979, *102*, 191–198.

Laughlin, P. Selection strategies in concept attainment. In R. Solso (Ed.), *Contemporary issues in cognitive psychology*. Washington, D.C.: Winston/Wiley, 1973.

Laughlin, P. Ability and group problem-solving. *Journal of Research and Development in Education*, 1978, *12*, 114–120.

Michaels, J. Classroom reward structures and academic performance. *Review of Educational Research*, 1977, *47*, 87–99.

Miller, L., & Hamblin, R. Interdependence, differential rewarding, and productivity. *American Sociological Review*, 1963, *28*, 768–778.

Napier, R., & Gershenfeld, M. *Instructor's manual, groups: Theory and experience*. Boston: Houghton-Mifflin, 1973.

Salatas, H., & Flavell, J. Retrieval of recently learned information: Development of strategies and control skills. *Child Development*, 1976, *47*, 941–948.

Slavin, R. Classroom reward structure: An analytical and practical review. *Review of Educational Research*, 1977, *47*, 633–650.

Wodarski, J., Hamblin, R., Buckholdt, D., & Ferritor, D. Individual consequences versus different shared consequences contingent on the performance of low-achieving group members. *Journal of Applied Social Psychology*, 1973, *3*, 276–290.

Appendix B

Selected Commercial Instruments

This appendix contains brief descriptions of some commonly used commercial instruments. They are grouped according to these broad categories of variables: achievement, intelligence, aptitude, personal-social adjustment, and attitudes and interests. Additional information about these instruments and others is available in *Mental Measurements Yearbook* and *Personality Tests and Reviews*, both edited by O. K. Buros. (See the references at the end of Chapter 4.)

MEASURES OF ACHIEVEMENT

There are many standardized achievement tests for students of all ages. Sometimes these tests are called survey batteries, single-subject matter, or diagnostic tests. All share the purpose of assessing student knowledge and skills at a particular time. As the names imply, survey batteries include a range of subject matter, but the single-subject and diagnostic tests cover only one area. Single-subject matter tests measure the status of a student's knowledge in a certain area; diagnostic tests are constructed to point out particular strengths and weaknesses of individual students. Achievement tests can be administered to groups of students by teachers. Since most of these tests are scored objectively, teachers are often the ones who do the scoring.

Examples of survey batteries are the following: California Achievement Tests, Iowa Tests of Basic Skills, Metropolitan Achievement Tests, Stanford Achievement Tests, SRA Achievement Series, and Comprehensive Tests of Basic Skills.

Single-subject tests include the Gates-MacGinitie Reading Tests, the Nelson-Denny Reading Test, College Level Examination Program Subject Examination in Biology, College Board Achievement Test in Biology, College English Placement Test, and the Advanced Placement Examination in American History. The Stanford Diagnostic Mathematics Tests, Prescriptive Mathematics Inventory, and Prescriptive Reading Inventory are examples of diagnostic achievement tests.

MEASURES OF INTELLIGENCE

These instruments can be classified as those given to subjects in groups and those given to individuals. Group tests measure such things as inductive reasoning, verbal comprehension and fluency, spatial relations, numerical skills, and figure comprehension. These tests are scored according to the number of "correct" answers, and they can be administered and scored by regular classroom teachers. Several commonly used tests are the Short-Form Test of Academic Aptitude (SFTAA), the Otis-Lennon Mental Ability Test, the Cooperative School and College Ability Test (SCAT), and the Henmon-Nelson Tests of Mental Ability.

Some of the better-known individual intelligence tests are the Stanford-Binet Intelligence Test-Revised, the Peabody Picture Vocabulary Test, the Wechsler Intelligence Scale for Children-Revised, the Wechsler Adult Intelligence Scale and the Wechsler Preschool and Primary Scale of Intelligence. Each of these tests is administered to only one person at a time by examiners who have special training in test administration and interpretation. These tests are constructed so that easier items precede more difficult ones. The test administrator has detailed instructions about starting and stopping the student on the tasks required.

MEASURES OF APTITUDE

Metropolitan Readiness Tests

This two-level test is used with young children who are about to begin reading instruction. Level I may be given by classroom teachers to assess such things as auditory memory, rhyming, letter recognition, visual matching, school language, and listening. Additional but similar kinds of content are measured in Level II. Results of the test can help teachers arrange instructional conditions for learning.

Differential Aptitude Tests

Used with students in grades 8 and higher, these tests can provide information about verbal reasoning, numerical ability, abstract reasoning, clerical speed and accuracy, mechanical reasoning, space relations, spelling, and language usage. Results of the DAT are plotted on profile charts, which can be interpreted by teachers and counselors. Combined scores serve as a measure of general intelligence.

Torrance Tests of Creativity

Two major sections of this test are Thinking Creatively with Words (measuring verbal abilities) and Thinking Creatively with Pictures (measuring figural abilities). Tasks require students to ask questions about given pictures, suggest improvements in toys, construct and complete pictures, and name unusual uses for commonplace objects. The test can be used in any elementary grade K–8. The tests are scored for number of responses (fluency), variety of responses (flexibility), originality, and elaboration. Scoring is both difficult and time-consuming.

MEASURES OF PERSONAL-SOCIAL ADJUSTMENT

Thematic Apperception Test

This test is typically used to measure personality dynamics, but it can be modified to measure prejudice, need to achieve, and classroom morale. The test is given to individuals, and the task for the respondent is to construct stories about picture cards. Thirty cards can be used, ranging from highly structured to unstructured pictures including a blank card. Most of the time only 10 or so are selected. Because the administrator must note the respondent's behaviors during the test, it is administered by a psychologist or another person with special training.

Scoring systems vary, but most focus on the respondent's identification of the "hero" and information related to the hero.

Tennessee Self-Concept Scale

This instrument is designed to measure how people view themselves, including their physical self, moral-ethical self, personal self, family self, social self, self-criticism, identity, self-satisfaction, behavior, defensiveness, general maladjustment, psychosis, personality disorder, neurosis, and personality integration. Unlike the previously mentioned personality tests, the Tennessee Self-Concept Scale can be administered to groups of people by a teacher, counselor, or school psychologist. The results can be plotted on a profile sheet to portray a student's overall level of self-esteem.

Rokeach Dogmatism Scale

This scale is frequently used to measure general authoritarianism, although it was originally designed to measure the variable of closed-mindedness. Teachers can give the scale to groups of students, score, and then interpret the results.

Minnesota Multiphasic Personality Inventory

Probably the most widely used measure of personality adjustment, this inventory is used with late adolescents and adults. It can be given to groups of students when information is sought concerning hypochondriasis, depression, hysteria, psychopathic deviation, masculinity-femininity, paranoia, psychasthenia, schizophrenia, hypomania, and social introversion. Interpretation is difficult and is not to be undertaken lightly. A trained person must do these tasks.

Edwards Personal Preference Schedule

This instrument is used to measure a person's orientation to each of 15 personality variables or needs, which include achievement, deference, order, exhibition, autonomy, affiliation, intraception, succorance, dominance, abasement, nurturance, change, endurance, heterosexuality, and aggression. For every need, the respondent gets a raw score, which can be used to make a personality profile for that person. This instrument is useful for college students and adults, although it may be used with subjects as young as age 15.

MEASURES OF ATTITUDES AND INTERESTS

Strong-Campbell Interest Inventory

This instrument is suitable for older adolescents and adults who are planning careers in higher-level professional or skilled occupations. It may provide insight into the development of specific vocational interests as well as peripheral information about personality characteristics. In this particular inventory the seven content areas are occupations, school subjects, activities, amusements, types of people, preference between two activities, and individual characteristics.

Appendix C

Statistics

Section C-1: Basic Concepts

Frequently researchers must summarize data from subjects in their research projects. Data in "raw form" are rarely easy to interpret, so they must be assembled in ways that will permit them to be communicated and used, particularly in statistical tests. There are a variety of ways to put a collection of data into useful form. The meanings of some of these procedures will be discussed here, including frequency distributions, measures of central tendency, and measures of variation. Such procedures are collectively referred to as **descriptive statistics**. This will be followed by related information about the normal distribution, standard scores, sampling distributions, and one-tailed and two-tailed tests.

FREQUENCY DISTRIBUTIONS

If you've ever given a test to a class, you may have done the following actions afterward: You graded everybody's paper, recorded a numerical score, and to see how the class as a whole performed on the test, you tallied the scores like this:

Score intervals	Numbers of students making the scores	Total
90–100	‖‖	6
80–89	‖‖ ‖‖ |||	13
70–79	‖‖ ||	7
Less than 70	||	2

What you did was to make a kind of **frequency distribution**, a breakdown of the number of students whose scores belonged to certain categories. A frequency distribution is the result of a procedure in which a group of observations is arranged to show how many fall within specified intervals on the measurement scale. Perhaps you picked score intervals because they coincided with your grading scale; for example, 90–100 is A, 80–89 is B, and so on. The point is that you could have picked intervals of any size and you would still have a picture of how the class as a whole performed. Strictly speaking, it's recommended that you have between 10 and 25 scoring intervals in a frequency distribution, with 15 to 20 considered ideal. In our current example, however, we've used intervals more familiar to classroom situations. The score intervals are equal in size except for the highest and lowest intervals, which may differ to accommodate extreme scores.

Another way of looking at a frequency distribution is to turn it into a bar graph, called a "histogram," or a line graph, called a "frequency polygon." These two kinds of graphs transform the information into a display, which is very easy to interpret. In both cases the scores or measures are placed on the horizontal axis and the frequency of each score or measure is placed on the vertical axis. Figure C-1.1 shows a histogram and a frequency polygon for the frequency distribution in our example.

MEASURES OF CENTRAL TENDENCY

Examine any form of the frequency distribution again. Do you agree that a score between 80 and 89 would best describe how the class as a whole performed on the test? There were more students with scores in that interval than in any of the other intervals. If you had to pick a single number that would most nearly represent the scores of the group, you would pick a measure of central tendency. There are three different measures of central tendency: mode, median, and mean. Each gives you an idea of where the scores tend to bunch up.

Suppose you really want a more precise idea of the typical score. The best way is to make a frequency distribution with score intervals of one as follows:

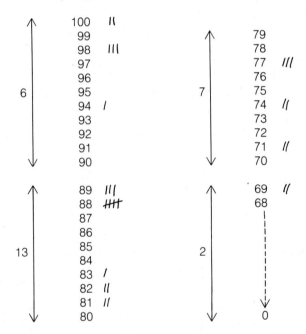

When you examine the distribution, you still find that most of the scores range from 80 to 89, but you can get a clearer idea of just where the bunching point is. One way of doing this is to look for the score that was made most frequently. You'll notice that five students made 88, making it the most numerous score in the distribution. This is the modal score or mode of the distribution. The **mode** is the measure that occurs most frequently in a set of measures. There could have been two or more modes if any five other people had made the same scores. Distributions with two modes are called *bimodal*.

A second way of looking for the bunching point is to find the middle score for the whole class. Since there are 28 students in the class, half that number is 14. Beginning at the lowest score, you can count to find the middle score, which is 83. This score is called the **median**, which is simply the midpoint of a distribution of scores. Actually, finding the median can be complicated, especially when you don't have a score that falls precisely in the middle of a distribution, or when the middle score isn't the only score at that particular point. You will need to consult an introductory statistics text if you plan to calculate medians.

A third and more familiar way of finding a measure of central tendency is to total the number of score points and divide the sum by the number of students to get an average. The total number of score points for this class of students is 2,363. Dividing this total by 28 gives an average score of 84.4. In statistical language you have calculated an arithmetic mean, usually called a *mean score*. The **mean** is the measure of central tendency obtained by summing a set of measures and dividing the sum by the number of measures.

So which of these ways is best for getting a measure of central tendency? The answer depends on the situation. If you just want a rough idea of the measure, a mode may do. If you need a very precise measure, the mean is the best choice, with a median being second best. Why is this true? Modes require the least amount of calculation, but they're also the least stable. In our illustration changes of two scores in some instances could have made three modes (98, 81, and 77). A median is more stable than a mode because the method of getting a median involves counting or finding the rank of the middle score. You might prefer this method of getting central tendency when there are extreme scores (either very high or very low), since scores at the end will have little influence on the median. Even if the score of 69 in the illustration had been 5, a very low score, the median

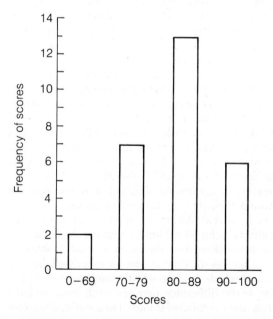
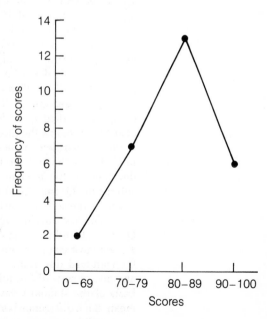

FIGURE C-1.1   Histogram and frequency polygon for the same frequency distribution.

would be exactly the same, 83. The mean, however, takes into account the value of every single score in the distribution and is subject to the influence of extreme scores. If the lowest score dropped from 69 to 5, the mean of the distribution would change from 84.4 to 82.1.

Let's put this information into the context of data analysis for research designs. When researchers have interval data (see the discussion of levels of measurement of data in Chapter 4), they will almost invariably calculate means as the preferred measure of central tendency. This gives them the most precise measure. Modes and medians can be used with interval data, but some precision is lost. When data are at the ordinal level, the most appropriate measure of central tendency is the median. If the data are nominal, only modes can be described.

But look again. Sometimes researchers give some kind of instrument to subjects and, based on the results, classify subjects as "high" or "low." This is a transformation of data (usually interval) to ranks. Typically, if there are two groups, a median is obtained and all subjects that have scores above the median are termed "high" and all those with scores below the median are called "low."

MEASURES OF VARIATION

For each measure of central tendency there is a corresponding measure of variation. This measure gives an index of the amount of dispersion among the scores. The smaller the variation, the closer the scores tend to cluster about the measure of central tendency.

The roughest measure of variation is the **range**, which is simply the difference between the top score and the bottom score. In our illustration of test scores, the range is 100 minus 69, or 31 points. The range can have some value in telling students about the relative position of their scores. If you were a student who scored 98, knowing the range of scores would tell you that you were near the top. On the other hand, if you made 74, you would know that you were near the bottom of the distribution. In research the range is rarely reported, but it is sometimes given if the researcher wants to communicate overall information; for example, the subjects ranged in age from 5.1 to 12.3 years.

The **quartile deviation** or *semi-interquartile range* is a measure of variation used with medians. This statistic is based on the division of the distribution into four equal-sized groups. The three points that separate the distribution into four groups are called *quartiles*. The first quartile equally divides the half of the distribution below the median, the second quartile is located at the median, and the third quartile separates the top two quarters of the distribution. Scores that fall between the first and third quartiles are considered to be within one quartile deviation of the median. The value of the quartile deviation is obtained by subtracting Q_1 from Q_3 and dividing by 2. From the distribution of scores in our example, the second quartile would coincide with the median, already identified as 83. The first quartile would be located at 76.8 and the third at 89.2. Subtracting Q_1 from Q_3 and dividing by 2 gives a value of 6.2 for the quartile deviation.

The most common measure of variation from the mean of a set of scores is the **standard deviation**. Calculating the standard deviation involves following any one of several formulas, all of which produce exactly the same result. The basis of the standard deviation is the difference between each score and the mean. Each difference is squared, and the squared differences are added together

Top

3rd quartile (Q_3)

Median — — 2nd quartile (Q_2)

1st quartile (Q_1)

Bottom

and divided by the number of scores. This preliminary result is called the *variance*, which is in itself a very important statistic (see section C-3). The square root of the variance is the standard deviation. The standard deviation or its square (variance) is found in some form in many statistical tests. The standard deviation gives you some idea of whether the scores were very spread out or rather close to the mean. If the standard deviation is small, the scores cluster around the mean. When the standard deviation is large, the scores are scattered farther from the mean.

In our example, the sum of the squared differences from the mean is 2,478.9. Dividing by 28 (the number of scores) gives us 88.5, which is the variance. The square root of the variance is the standard deviation for the set of scores, which is 9.4. Now let's find the standard deviation for the other situation we discussed previously, when the lowest score in the class is changed to only 5 points. In this case, we know that the mean is 82.1, which is not greatly different from our original mean of 84.4. However, the sum of the squared differences from the mean is now 8,465.5, and the variance therefore is 302.3. The square root of the variance is 17.4, which is the standard deviation. The original set of scores with a standard deviation of 9.4 is grouped more closely around the mean of the distribution than is the second group with its one very low score.

The standard deviation also provides a way to compare two or more scores in terms of their distance from the mean. This distance is measured in units of the standard deviation. The score of 94 in our example is about one standard deviation above the mean of 84.4, and the score of 71 is roughly one and a half standard deviations below the mean. We will return to this idea when standard scores are discussed later in this appendix.

NORMAL DISTRIBUTION

We can put some of these measures of central tendency and variation into another perspective by relating them to a special form of frequency distribution called a normal distribution or normal curve. A **normal distribution**, when graphed as a frequency polygon, is a bell-shaped curve. It results whenever most of the scores fall close to the mean and relatively fewer scores are higher or lower as you move toward the extreme values of the scores. The curve is symmetrical; that is, if you cut it out and folded it in half, both sides would appear to be the same. Figure C-1.2 illustrates graphs of two normal distributions. Notice that in a normal distribution the mean, median, and mode all have the same value. The extreme ends of the curve approach zero frequency, but they do not meet the baseline. In both graphs the curves are symmetrical, even though the two examples are not identical. In example B more scores are clustered around the mean than in example A. This is why the height of the curve in B is taller than that in A.

Figure C-1.3 shows the graphs of curves A and B again with the locations of standard deviations from the mean. Example B also shows the percentage of scores that fall under the portions of the curve separated by the standard deviations. As you can see, most scores fall within one standard deviation of the mean—about 68% of the total scores, to be more precise.

Many variables are considered to be normally distributed if there are enough cases. For example, a graph of the intelligence scores of all 17-year-olds in a town would probably be a normal curve unless the town were very tiny. In the same way, other characteristics such as height, achievement, and creativity are thought to be normally distributed throughout large populations.

A lot of statistical tests are based on the assumption that the measures used in the formulas approach a normal distribution. This helps to explain the necessity of including as many subjects as feasible when a researcher wishes to test data for statistical significance. The closer the measures come to approximating a normal distribution, the greater is the validity of the statistical analysis.

STANDARD SCORES

The characteristics of normal distributions and the standard deviation as a measure of variability bring us to the use of standard scores. As you can see in Figure C-1.3, the lines marking the standard deviations from the mean of each distribution are the same distance apart. The distance along the horizontal axis of the graph is the same for each standard deviation unit.

A **standard score** is a number that translates the value of a raw score into the distance of that raw score in standard deviation units from the mean of the distribution. For example, if the mean of some normally distributed group of measures is 60 and the standard deviation is 10, a score of 95 would be three and

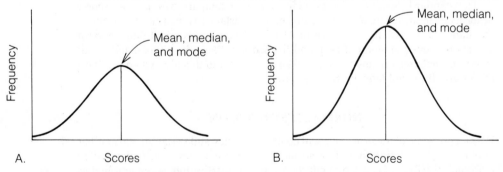

FIGURE C-1.2 Normal distributions.

a half standard deviation units above the mean. A score of 40 would be two standard deviation units below the mean. One kind of standard score, called the z-score, is written just that simply: For a mean score of 60 and a standard deviation of 10, a raw score of 95 gives z = +3.5, and a raw score of 40 gives z = −2. The minus sign indicates that the score is below the mean; the plus indicates distance above the mean. For z-scores, the mean is represented by 0, meaning zero standard deviation units. Sometimes it isn't convenient to use positive or negative numbers as standard scores. In this case the mean is represented by some selected number, such as 50 or 100, and the standard deviation is also given some fixed point value. One example of this is IQ scores, which are standard scores, with 100 being assigned to the mean of the distribution of all IQ scores, and the standard deviation commonly being 15 or 16. Therefore, an IQ score of 85 is about one standard deviation below the mean, and a score of 131 is approximately two standard deviations above the mean.

Standard scores allow you to compare two or more measurements in a better way than simply looking at the difference between the scores. In our previous example the two scores of 95 and 40 are 55 points apart, but the term *55 points* may not communicate very much about the nature of the difference between the scores. In some situations 55 points is a huge amount, but in other cases it doesn't represent very much difference at all. If we know the standard scores for 95 and 40—in this case the z-scores of 3.5 and −2, respectively—we can look at the z-scores to make a meaningful comparison. Subtracting −2 from +3.5, we see that the raw scores in this situation are five and one half standard deviation units apart. We could safely conclude that the difference between 95 and 40 is quite large in this case.

Standard scores also allow you to compare two different kinds of measures, such as an achievement measure in mathematics and achievement in science. Ordinarily, this would be like comparing apples and oranges, but standard scores simplify it. You have probably done this yourself if you took the Scholastic Aptitude Test or Graduate Record Examination. The SAT scores you might have received—say, for the Verbal and Quantitative subtests—came from measuring different areas of your performance. Nevertheless, you were able to compare your Verbal and Quantitative scores, since in both cases they were standard scores, with 500 being the mean and 100 the value of a standard deviation.

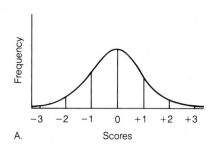

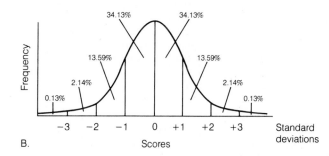

FIGURE C-1.3 Normal distributions with locations of standard deviations.

SAMPLING DISTRIBUTIONS

Frequency distributions form the basis for many of the analyses that are carried out when you use inferential statistical tests. One of these distributions is a **sampling distribution,** which is a frequency distribution constructed by repeatedly drawing a sample of a fixed size from a defined population, calculating and recording the mean of the sample, and then replacing the sample. The sample means are then plotted as a frequency distribution. This sampling distribution will be very close to a normal distribution. The mean of the distribution should be the same as the mean of the population, and the standard deviation of the sampling distribution will approximately equal the standard deviation of the population divided by the square root of the sample size.

As each sample is drawn, the best estimate for the value of the sample mean is the mean of the population, although the sample means will actually vary from the population mean. The degree of variation between sample means and the population mean is called the **sampling error** of the distribution. The important thing to remember about sampling error is that it decreases as larger and larger sample sizes are used. This is fairly easy to understand when you think of a real-life population such as a large high school. Suppose you draw samples and take the average IQ score of the samples. When you use a small sample size such as 5, it is highly likely that your sample mean will differ greatly from the mean IQ score for the entire student body. By increasing the sample size to 25, 50, or 100, you would be more and more likely to find a sample mean that is very close to the true mean of the population.

Why are sampling distributions important? If you use a sample in your research to represent a population, you will be making judgments about population characteristics or parameters based on the characteristic as you observe it in a sample. You will consider how probable it is that what you see in the sample occurs in the population by chance.

In the discussion above, we limited our sampling distribution to sample *means.* Other sampling distributions can also be made of differences between means, correlation coefficients, and other statistics. These sampling distributions have been constructed for many sample sizes and for many kinds of relationships (such as a variety of differences and associations) studied by researchers. When you use an inferential statistical test, such as the *t*-test for independent means, you will take the test result and compare it with the sampling distribution that was constructed for the *t*-statistic for your sample size. If your sample statistic is in the range of values in the sampling distribution that occurs in the population less than 95 out of 100 times (for an alpha level of $p = .05$), your result is said to be statistically significant. This means that the result of your *t*-test is so rare that you would find it in the sampling distribution no more than 5 times out of every 100 samples drawn.

ONE- AND TWO-TAILED TESTS

From the preceding discussion of sampling distributions, you can see that the result of a statistical test will be significant only when it is found with very low frequency in the population. Because such a result is so rare, it would be plotted on the ends of the distribution, which are called the "tails." (See Figure C-1.4.)

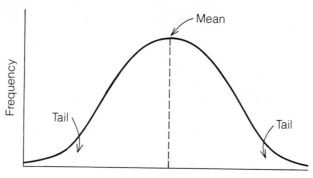

Distribution of some sample statistic

FIGURE C-1.4   Normal distribution showing tails.

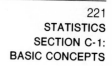

You will recall that when a research hypothesis is constructed, the researcher who plans to use inferential statistics to assess the results of the study also states the null hypothesis and sets a probability level such as $p = .01$ or $p = .05$. It is actually the null hypothesis that is tested. Unless the test result is so rare that it is found only 1 time (for $p = .01$) or 5 times (for $p = .05$) out of 100 samples within the sampling distribution, the researcher retains the null hypothesis. The null hypothesis states in effect that any relationship observed is likely to be the result of random variation within the population.

Considered graphically, if your probability level is set at $p = .05$, 95% of the area under the sampling distribution represents test values that will require you to support the null hypothesis. Only 5% of the area, located under one or both of the tails, represents test values that will enable you to reject the null hypothesis. In the same way, if $p = .01$, 99% of the area under the distribution curve represents values for retaining the null hypothesis, and only 1% represents values for rejecting it.

As a researcher, you have two choices about where to look for this small portion of test values that will enable you to reject the null hypothesis. You can look at the whole percentage available in one tail of the distribution, or split the percentage between the two tails. In the first choice you are making your statistical test a **one-tailed test;** in the second case it is a **two-tailed test.** In most situations you make this choice in advance. If you believe your test result will be statistically different from the sampling distribution, but you have no particular reason to believe that this difference will occur in one direction or the other, you will probably choose a two-tailed test. Figure C-1.5 shows the situation where $p = .05$ and a two-tailed test is used. Your test value must be found within the 2½% at either end of the frequency distribution, which are called the "regions of rejection" for the null hypothesis. Any test value within the 95% in the middle is within the region of retention for the null hypothesis.

If you have reason to believe that the test result would be found at one end of the distribution (maybe related research leads you to think so), you will make your statistical procedure a one-tailed test. Figure C-1.6 shows both a one-tailed test where only values at the lowest 5% of the distribution are in the region of rejection (a), and the opposite case (b) where the values in the top 5% of the distribution will be considered as evidence for rejecting the null hypothesis.

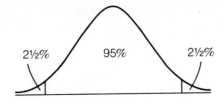

FIGURE C-1.5   Normal distribution showing areas of rejection for two-tailed tests.

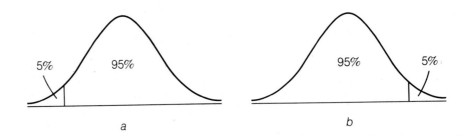

FIGURE C-1.6   Normal distributions showing areas of rejection for one-tailed tests.

When there is a good reason to use a one-tailed test, you are more likely to reject the null hypothesis simply because there is a wider range of values in 5% of one tail than in 2½% of both tails.

Read Exhibit C-1.1 for some alternative definitions of these statistical terms.

Median. That which signs on the highway tell you to keep off of the.

Formulas For The Mean. How-to-do-it-yourself books on vandalism, theft, and murder. Also, some segments of the Watergate hearings.

Mean Square. Central Park. Also, a member of the Establishment who refuses to contribute to the United Fund.

Mode. Meaning varies according to whether preceded by "a la" or "com."

Frequency polygon. Chart showing number of times the parrot has flown the coop.

Standard deviation. Relationship of one's wardrobe to current styles.

Normal curve. That physical attribute which develops with the typical female teenager.

Analysis of variance. Task of arbitration team working with school board and striking teacher's union.

Chi-square. Chinese trading center in which samples are dealt with.

One-tailed tests. Those which are as hard as the devil.

Two-tailed tests. Tests twice as hard as those cited above.

Sampling distribution. Technique of mailing new products to "occupants."

Distribution-free tests. Those which the publisher cannot sell. At the university level, a nonexistent item.

X̄ (X bar). Adult-only drinking establishment.

x (little x). Rating of film which is naughty, but not obscene.

U-shaped distribution. Has been said to some politicians regarding campaign contributions.

Sign tests. What some students have done to examinations sent home.

Unequal *n*'s. A football situation which will favor the team with the larger *n*'s.

Significance of difference. At exam time what there may be a great deal of between what the author of the stat book said and what I thought he said.

***N*.** What this is in relation to this official list.

***N*-1.** A means of improving this list.

EXHIBIT C-1.1 Alternative statistical definitions. From Rita S. Bryant, Statistics for the simple, *Phi Delta Kappa School Research Information Service Quarterly*, 1974, *7*, (3). Used by permission.

Section C-2: Correlation and Prediction

Correlation and prediction are two statistical concepts that are concerned with how variables are related to each other. The meaning of each of these concepts is described in the sections that follow. In addition, we also give some intuitive ideas about how to interpret correlation coefficients, followed by a brief description of several kinds of correlation coefficients.

CORRELATION

Many things in nature are related to each other. When the sun rises, there is usually a rise in the temperature outside. When the temperature changes over a period of months from warm to cool, leaves on deciduous trees change color and drop from branches and limbs. There are also other kinds of relationships, like the one between your waist size and the length of your belt or between your chest size and your coat size. Like these relationships in the physical world, there are also relationships between behavioral characteristics. For example, a person with a relatively large vocabulary can probably solve crossword puzzles, and an outgoing person probably has many friends. We often take these relationships for granted as commonplace, everyday happenings. But they also provide rough examples of what we mean by correlation.

In educational research correlation is typically concerned with relationships between behaviors demonstrated by students, teachers, counselors, administrators, and others. Educational researchers may wonder whether there is a relationship between reading comprehension and spelling ability, between interest in social studies and achievement in that subject, or between scores on a test and scores on the same test given three weeks later. Each of these questions lends itself to analysis of the relevant data using correlation techniques.

Suppose a researcher measured the amount of time that students spent during class doing activities that were prescribed—on task behavior—and also found out what grades the students earned following these activities. Here is a partial set of results:

Student	Time-on-task (minutes)	Grade (percent correct)
Fred	18	80
John	15	75
Lorraine	10	60
Wally	7	50

As you read the data, did you notice that Fred, who spent the most time, also made the highest grade, and that Wally, who spent the least amount of time, made the lowest grade? As a matter of fact there is a one-to-one correspondence between time-on-task and grades:

Student	Time-on-task (rank)	Grade (rank)
Fred	1—longest	1—highest
John	2	2
Lorraine	3	3
Wally	4—shortest	4—lowest

This comparison by ranks shows a perfect relationship between the rankings on these variables.

Spotting relationships is not always so easy, particularly when you use actual measurements rather than ranks. One way to get an idea of how much of a relationship exists between two variables is to make a picture of the data. On the accompanying diagram, for example, we have plotted Fred's time-on-task (18 minutes) on the horizontal axis and his grade (80%) on the vertical axis.

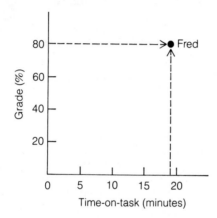

Now we add information about John, Lorraine, and Wally to the same plot.

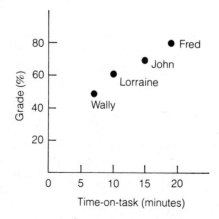

Let's really complicate the diagram and put in data for other members of the class. We now have a picture of how a larger group of students performed. You'll notice that some students who spent less time than others made higher grades—for example, Lucy and Don. There were also students who spent more time than others but made lower grades—for example, Bruce and Jean. Despite these exceptions, as you look at the complete picture, do you notice that there seems to be a trend that grades increase as more time is spent on task?

Next we'll draw a straight line through the points to show this trend. The line represents the best-fitting line that could be drawn through the points. Because the plots cluster closely around this line, we can say that there is a linear relationship between these variables. This is also an example of a positive relationship between two variables, because as one variable increases, the second variable also increases.

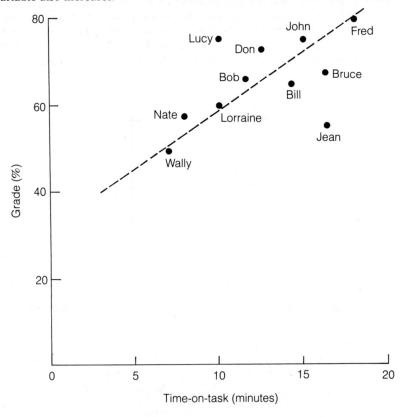

Not all relationships are positive, however, nor are they all linear. Suppose a researcher investigated the relationship between different lengths of time for typing a set number of words and typing accuracy. The results might be as shown in the accompanying diagram. The predominant trend in the plots suggests that as the amount of time increases, the number of errors decreases. This relationship indicates a negative correlation, which is every bit as informative as a positive correlation. The difference from the previous example is that the direction of the correlation is reversed.

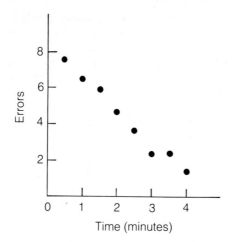

It's unlikely that you'll find diagrams like these in research reports because correlation is figured much more quickly using mathematical formulas. The results of these calculations give correlation coefficients, which are usually labeled as r values between $+1.00$ and -1.00. **Correlation coefficients** are index numbers that give you an idea of the strength (from 0 to 1) and the direction (positive or negative) of the relationship between variables.

The decimal number in a correlation coefficient is not like a regular number or percentage. A correlation coefficient is not interpreted by its absolute value nor as a percentage. The correlation coefficient of .54 is *not* twice as much as an r value of .27. Neither does an r of .54 mean 54%. What r does tell is how much variation is shared by the two variables used in its calculation. Suppose that creativity and intelligence scores are put through a correlation formula with the result $r = .54$. Squaring this r value (.54 $\times$ .54) gives .29. This squared correlation coefficient (r^2) means that variation in creativity can be related to variations in intelligence to this extent. Since this is a relatively small percentage of *covariation* (variance common to both), you can see that a lot of variation in intelligence and creativity is not accounted for by their association.

Sometimes researchers who are involved in association studies plot their data to get an idea of the relationship between the variables before they go through the calculations. Here are some diagrams that show other kinds of relationships. In each instance you are to imagine that scores on one of the variables are plotted on the horizontal axis, while the corresponding scores on the other variable are plotted on the vertical axis.

This diagram shows a very high positive correlation. Notice that the plots are clustered around an imaginary line drawn from the low to the high values.

A distinctly negative correlation is shown in this diagram. The plots are not so closely clustered around a line, but their general trend seems to be from the high value on the vertical axis to the high value on the horizontal axis.

Most researchers do not look forward to seeing this kind of plot. Since there seems to be no discernible pattern, we can say there is little or no correlation.

The pattern formed by the plots in this diagram seems to indicate that this is a nonlinear relationship—also known as a curvilinear relationship. When the plots take on this kind of pattern, special mathematical formulas have to be used to calculate the correlation coefficient.

We have referred to r several times in this section. This symbol stands for the Pearson product-moment coefficient. Several other coefficients are used, depending on the nature of the data. When variables are at the interval level, the Pearson product-moment formula is used. Ordinal level measurements call for either Spearman's rank order correlation or Kendall's tau. On some occasions data from instruments are transformed from a higher to a lower level of measurement which requires still other correlation techniques. For example, interval data may be transformed to either ordinal or nominal data, and ordinal data to nominal data, depending on the particular problem. When data from one variable of the pair under study are transformed to the nominal level, a biserial correlation coefficient can be computed. If both sets of data are changed to nominal, a tetrachoric correlation coefficient can be calculated.

Table C-2.1 lists most of the commonly used correlation coefficients, their symbols, and the levels of measurement of the variables. You may also want to consult one or more of the recommended references at the end of Chapter 6.

PREDICTION

One of the chief uses of correlation is in prediction studies. Once a researcher has established that there is a moderate amount of covariation between two or more variables, he or she may be able to predict one variable for members of the population if the second variable is known. To understand this idea, we need to explain the meaning of regression toward the mean.

Regression, which is what r stands for in correlation, is as old as Sir Francis Galton. In doing studies on the heights of many parents and children, he found that the children of taller parents, while still tall, tended not to be so tall as their parents. Children of shorter parents, on the other hand, tended to be short but not so short as their parents. In effect he noted that extremes tended to move toward the middle, an occurrence known as regression toward the mean.

Table C-2.1
CORRELATION TECHNIQUES FOR TWO-VARIABLE STUDIES

Technique	Symbol	Level of measurement	
		Variable 1	Variable 2
Pearson product moment	r	Interval	Interval
Spearman rank	rho or r_s	Ordinal	Ordinal
Kendall's tau	τ	Ordinal	Ordinal
Point-biserial	r_{pbis}	Interval	Nominal
Biserial	r_{bis}	Interval	Nominal*
Tetrachoric	r^t	Nominal*	Nominal*
Contingency	C	Nominal	Nominal
Phi	ϕ	Nominal	Nominal

* Data have been transformed from a higher level of measurement to a lower level. For information about this process, see section C-1.

This same phenomenon is noted when a large group of students takes one test and a little while later takes an equivalent form of the test. Students who score high on the first test tend to score not quite so high on the second test, while those who score low on the first test tend to score not quite so low on the second exam. Obviously, the scores on the two forms of the test are correlated. However, the second set is closer to the average of the group (not so spread out) than is the first set of scores. This is another illustration of regression toward the mean.

In the previous section on correlation, we described a relationship between time-on-task and grades. Let's put the regression idea into that illustration. If a second or third series of measures were taken on these students, it's likely that Fred would continue to spend a good part of his time on task and make good grades. It's also likely that Wally will not bloom into a student who spends a lot of time on task or makes really good grades. However, Fred could move down in ranking among the students and Wally could move up depending on which day the measures were taken. Their overall rankings are likely to stay about the same, however. This could also be said for other students at the extremes of the distribution.

Here is the same diagram you saw previously. As we said before, the line represents the best-fitting one for the points. Suppose also that there are other students in this class whose times and grades were not available for this plot. Using the line as a very rough guide, we could *estimate* their grades if we knew how long each person spent in time-on-task. If Jeff spends 12 minutes, would you estimate that his grade would be between 50% and 70%? If Merry spends only about 7 minutes, would you expect her to do much better than 40% to 50%? You can read these grades off the diagram. It's also possible to estimate the amount of time a student in this group spends on task activities if the grade is known—simply by reversing the process. Note that we are talking about predictions for other students in this same class. We could not use this information in any other classroom, because the observed relationship may not hold.

We hope you noticed the emphasis on *estimation* because that is what we have. We cannot know for sure how well any student will perform until he or she is asked to do so. The estimate is rough and cannot predict exactly what the

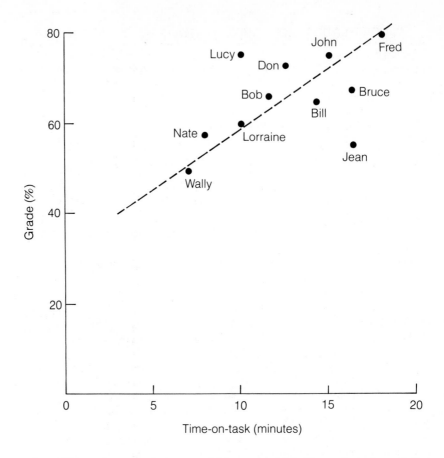

grade will be or how much time would be spent. This illustration of prediction has been kept simple deliberately to help you understand the concept.

Prediction studies in research projects typically use many more subjects than we've mentioned in the illustration. Sometimes samples have hundreds or thousands of people representing still larger populations. Regardless of size, however, the idea is the same that the correlation of variables within the sample is probably true for the population. Therefore the more nearly the sample represents the population, the more accurate the prediction can be.

Prediction is also affected by the strength of the correlation and the standard deviation of the criterion variable. Strength of the correlation, as explained in the previous section, is shown by the magnitude of r. An r value of .80 shows more strength, hence more variation in common than an r of .50. Unless variables share some covariation, it is not very helpful to use one to predict the other. The standard deviation of the criterion variable is used to calculate the estimated error of prediction. A relatively small standard deviation plugged into the formula for estimated error gives a relatively small estimated error. This in turn produces a better prediction.

For additional information about prediction, see the recommended references at the end of Chapter 6. Exhibit C-2.1 presents additional definitions.

Biserial—punch line on kids' TV cartoons.

Point-biserial correlation—relationship observed by cereal sales people: If kids point, mamas buy cereal.

Spearman's rho—term used to designate work responsibility, such as, "I ain't gonna pick dat cotton, Dat's Spearman's Rho."

Product moment—according to P. T. Barnum, your exact time of birth. (A sucker is born every moment.)

Regression on the line—football term indicating a loss of yardage.

Multiple regression—number of workshop participants backing up when volunteers are asked to step forward.

Regression analysis—figuring out why a 50-year-old woman dresses like a teenager.

Curvilinear regression—backing down a mountain road.

Contingency coefficient—amount of "mad money" a nice young woman takes on a blind date.

Kendall's coefficient—Kendall's mad money.

Null hypothesis—That if you assume there is no significant difference between these definitions and the ones in the statistics texts, you will have made a type II error (and flunked your stat test).

EXHIBIT C-2.1 More alternate statistical definitions. The first five items are from Rita S. Bryant, Statistics for the simple, *Phi Delta Kappa School Research Information Service Quarterly*, 1974, *7* (3). Used by permission. The remaining items are from Rita S. Bryant, W. G. Gephart, and J. Wilson, More statistics for the simple, *Phi Delta Kappa Center on Evaluation, Development, and Research Quarterly*, 1978, *11* (2), 22. Used by permission.

Section C-3:
Analysis of Variance and Related Procedures

This section describes the rationale underlying analysis of variance, one of the most frequently used inferential tests. Before we begin the rationale, however, here is a brief review of some definitions that are necessary for an understanding of this important test.

Variance was generally defined in Chapter 1 as any aspect of the research setting that produces change in variables, and was defined statistically in Appendix C-1 as the square of the standard deviation. The total amount of variance in a study can be labeled according to its source, as *systematic* or *error*.

Systematic variance is variation in the data caused by the experimental conditions, from either known or unknown influences. Researchers hope to put systematic variance into an experiment by manipulating independent variables and controlling extraneous variables that could influence the dependent variable. Systematic variance can also be introduced into the design without the researcher's intention. If, for example, the subjects developed very negative attitudes toward one of the persons administering the treatment, the results would probably be contaminated because of the variance introduced into their responses. This is systematic variance, but it is not wanted. A carefully designed study will minimize undesirable systematic variance so the effect of the intentional systematic variance can be assessed.

Error variance is the name given to all the variance in a situation after the systematic sources of variance have been accounted for. Usually we refer to this variance as that which happens because of chance, or normal variation in the population of subjects. The error variance found in the sample depends on the amount of variance in the population. Samples that have high error variance are more likely to result when the population varies greatly than when the population shows less total variance. Error variance is also introduced in the process of subject selection. Even with scientific methods of sampling, there will be fluctuations in the sample that make it less than a perfect replica of the population.

What analysis of variance (ANOVA) does is to identify the variance that comes from these two sources of variation, and test them for statistical significance. In the simplest form of ANOVA, total variance is separated into the two major sources: systematic variance, labeled **between-groups variance** and error variance, derived from **within-groups variance**. The variance due to variations that occur *between* the different groups is brought about by manipulation of the independent variable, or treatment. The remaining variance is error variance, and is obtained by subtracting the systematic variance from the total variance. Error variance is found *within* all subjects in all the groups, as a result of general variance in the population from which the sample was taken. Variance cannot be measured exactly, but it can be estimated through a mathematical procedure. The best estimate of systematic variance is a measure of the variation of each group's mean from the total mean of all measures. Error variance is estimated by a measure of variation of all scores from the total mean. These measures are calculated from sums of squared deviations converted to mean squares that are estimations of variance in the population. After the mean squares are known, they are put in ratio form for the F-test.

233
STATISTICS
SECTION C-3:
ANALYSIS OF
VARIANCE AND
RELATED
PROCEDURES

$$F = \frac{\text{mean square between groups}}{\text{mean square within groups}} = \frac{\text{systematic variance estimate}}{\text{error variance estimate}}$$

Although the numerator and denominator of the F-ratio are not always calculated the way this simple ANOVA was done, their meaning remains the same. The numerator represents variance thought to be due to the systematic relationship between the independent and dependent variables in the population. The denominator represents variance in the sample due to chance variations in the population. Unless the systematic variance is greater than the variance that shows up by chance, the F-ratio is *not* statistically significant.

How different do the systematic and error variance estimates have to be for statistical significance? This depends on the size of the sample and the variance of the population. Large samples require less systematic variance than do smaller samples in order to get statistically significant results. Furthermore, if a population is rather homogeneous, it will produce samples with lower error variances on the average than samples drawn from highly varied populations.

When a complete table of results from an analysis of variance is presented, it's possible to determine how much of the total variance is due to systematic influences. For example, Table C-3.1 presents the results of ANOVA from a study by Edwards and Surma (1980). The total variance is represented by the total sum of squares, 15,796.96. Systematic variance is the between-groups sum of squares, 12,106.80. To find the proportion of the total variance accounted for by systematic variation, form a ratio of these two numbers.

$$\frac{\text{sum of equal squares between groups}}{\text{sum of squares total}} = \frac{12,106.80}{15,796.96} = .77$$

The systematic variance in this case is responsible for 77% of the total variability in the data. This .77 is actually a squared correlation coefficient, R^2. When

Table C-3.1
ANALYSIS OF VARIANCE FOR REINFORCEMENT TREATMENTS

Source of variation	Sum of squares	Degrees of freedom	Mean squares	F
Between groups	12,106.80	3	4,035.60	25.15[*]
Within groups	3,690.16	20	160.44	
Total	15,796.96	23		

[*] $p < .001$

From C. H. Edwards & M. Surma, The relationship between type of teacher reinforcement and student inquiry behavior in science, *Journal of Research in Science Teaching*, 1980, *17*(4), 341. Copyright © 1980 by John Wiley & Sons. Reprinted by permission of John Wiley & Sons, Inc.

you are able to do so, figuring out R^2 from an ANOVA is a very good way to judge the strength of the systematic or treatment effects. Suppose you read two reports of research done with approximately the same population and sample sizes, both with statistically significant results. By finding the R^2 (proportion of the total variance explained by the independent variable) for each study, you could tell which treatment was more powerful. If the two studies had $R^2 = .34$ and $R^2 = .65$, respectively, you would conclude that more variance (65% as opposed to 34%) was explained by the treatment in the second research effort.

You may more commonly think of R^2 in conjunction with multiple regression. In fact, analysis of variance is actually a special form of multiple regression. In some cases, it is better to do a regression analysis instead of ANOVA in difference studies. This is particularly true in situations where there are unequal numbers of subjects in the groups. ANOVA can be difficult in such cases, but regression analysis is not. The outcome of multiple regression can be expressed as an F-ratio identical with that from ANOVA, and the R^2 values for the systematic sources of variance are also provided (Hays, 1981).

Analyses of variance are also frequently used in factorial designs. In these situations there are two or more independent variables or factors that affect the dependent variable either singly or in interaction. To handle this situation, the systematic variance is subdivided into variance due to each independent variable and variance due to the interaction of the independent variables. A separate F-ratio is computed for each independent variable and for their interaction. The order in which the F values in a factorial ANOVA are calculated is determined by the nature of the independent variable.

ANOVA serves as a model for understanding other inferential tests, such as t, χ^2, and many others. The common pattern is this—researchers look at their data, which are presumed to reflect the hypothesized relationship between the variables. They compare what they got with what they could expect to get due to the general characteristics of the population. Unless the results exceed what could be expected by chance, they are not statistically significant.

Section C-4: Tables of Critical Values

TABLE C-4.1
CRITICAL VALUES OF *F*

Degrees of freedom in error term	*p*	Degrees of freedom in systematic term									
		1	2	3	4	5	6	8	12	24	∞
6	.10	3.78	3.46	3.29	3.18	3.11	3.05	2.98	2.90	2.82	2.72
	.05	5.99	5.14	4.76	4.53	4.39	4.28	4.15	4.00	3.84	3.67
	.01	13.74	10.92	9.78	9.15	8.75	8.47	8.10	7.72	7.31	6.88
	.001	35.51	27.00	23.70	21.90	20.81	20.03	19.03	17.99	16.89	15.75
7	.10	3.59	3.26	3.07	2.96	2.88	2.83	2.75	2.67	2.58	2.47
	.05	5.59	4.74	4.35	4.12	3.97	3.87	3.73	3.57	3.41	3.23
	.01	12.25	9.55	8.45	7.85	7.46	7.19	6.84	6.47	6.07	5.65
	.001	29.22	21.69	18.77	17.19	16.21	15.52	14.63	13.71	12.73	11.69
8	.10	3.46	3.11	2.92	2.81	2.73	2.67	2.59	2.50	2.40	2.29
	.05	5.32	4.46	4.07	3.84	3.69	3.58	3.44	3.28	3.12	2.93
	.01	11.26	8.65	7.59	7.01	6.63	6.37	6.03	5.67	5.28	4.86
	.001	25.42	18.49	15.83	14.39	13.49	12.86	12.04	11.19	10.30	9.34
9	.10	3.36	3.01	2.81	2.69	2.61	2.55	2.47	2.38	2.28	2.16
	.05	5.12	4.26	3.86	3.63	3.48	3.37	3.23	3.07	2.90	2.71
	.01	10.56	8.02	6.99	6.42	6.06	5.80	5.47	5.11	4.73	4.31
	.001	22.86	16.39	13.90	12.56	11.71	11.13	10.37	9.57	8.72	7.81
10	.10	3.28	2.92	2.73	2.61	2.52	2.46	2.38	2.28	2.18	2.06
	.05	4.96	4.10	3.71	3.48	3.33	3.22	3.07	2.91	2.74	2.54
	.01	10.04	7.56	6.55	5.99	5.64	5.39	5.06	4.71	4.33	3.91
	.001	21.04	14.91	12.55	11.28	10.48	9.92	9.20	8.45	7.64	6.76
11	.10	3.23	2.86	2.66	2.54	2.45	2.39	2.30	2.21	2.10	1.97
	.05	4.84	3.98	3.59	3.36	3.20	3.09	2.95	2.79	2.61	2.40
	.01	9.65	7.20	6.22	5.67	5.32	5.07	4.74	4.40	4.02	3.60
	.001	19.69	13.81	11.56	10.35	9.58	9.05	8.35	7.63	6.85	6.00
12	.10	3.18	2.81	2.61	2.48	2.39	2.33	2.24	2.15	2.04	1.90
	.05	4.75	3.88	3.49	3.26	3.11	3.00	2.85	2.69	2.50	2.30
	.01	9.33	6.93	5.95	5.41	5.06	4.82	4.50	4.16	3.78	3.36
	.001	18.64	12.97	10.80	9.63	8.89	8.38	7.71	7.00	6.25	5.42

TABLE C-4.1
CRITICAL VALUES OF F (Continued)

Degrees of freedom in error term	p	\multicolumn{10}{c}{Degrees of freedom in systematic term}
		1	2	3	4	5	6	8	12	24	∞
13	.10	3.14	2.76	2.56	2.43	2.35	2.28	2.20	2.10	1.98	1.85
	.05	4.67	3.80	3.41	3.18	3.02	2.92	2.77	2.60	2.42	2.21
	.01	9.07	6.70	5.74	5.20	4.86	4.62	4.30	3.96	3.59	3.16
	.001	17.81	12.31	10.21	9.07	8.35	7.86	7.21	6.52	5.78	4.97
14	.10	3.10	2.73	2.52	2.39	2.31	2.24	2.15	2.05	1.94	1.80
	.05	4.60	3.74	3.34	3.11	2.96	2.85	2.70	2.53	2.35	2.13
	.01	8.86	6.51	5.56	5.03	4.69	4.46	4.14	3.80	3.43	3.00
	.001	17.14	11.78	9.73	8.62	7.92	7.43	6.80	6.13	5.41	4.60
15	.10	3.07	2.70	2.49	2.36	2.27	2.21	2.12	2.02	1.90	1.76
	.05	4.54	3.68	3.29	3.06	2.90	2.79	2.64	2.48	2.29	2.07
	.01	8.68	6.36	5.42	4.89	4.56	4.32	4.00	3.67	3.29	2.87
	.001	16.59	11.34	9.34	8.25	7.57	7.09	6.47	5.81	5.10	4.31
16	.10	3.05	2.67	2.46	2.33	2.24	2.18	2.09	1.99	1.87	1.72
	.05	4.49	3.63	3.24	3.01	2.85	2.74	2.59	2.42	2.24	2.01
	.01	8.53	6.23	5.29	4.77	4.44	4.20	3.89	3.85	3.18	2.75
	.001	16.12	10.97	9.00	7.94	7.27	6.81	6.19	5.55	4.85	4.06
17	.10	3.03	2.64	2.44	2.31	2.22	2.15	2.06	1.96	1.84	1.69
	.05	4.45	3.59	3.20	2.96	2.81	2.70	2.55	2.38	2.19	1.96
	.01	8.40	6.11	5.18	4.67	4.34	4.10	3.79	3.45	3.08	2.65
	.001	15.72	10.66	8.73	7.68	7.02	6.56	5.96	5.32	4.63	3.85
18	.10	3.01	2.62	2.42	2.29	2.20	2.13	2.04	1.93	1.81	1.66
	.05	4.41	3.55	3.16	2.93	2.77	2.66	2.51	2.34	2.15	1.92
	.01	8.28	6.01	5.09	4.58	4.25	4.01	3.71	3.37	3.00	2.57
	.001	15.38	10.39	8.49	7.46	6.81	6.35	5.76	5.13	4.45	3.67
19	.10	2.99	2.61	2.40	2.27	2.18	2.11	2.02	1.91	1.79	1.63
	.05	4.38	3.52	3.13	2.90	2.74	2.63	2.48	2.31	2.11	1.88
	.01	8.18	5.93	5.01	4.50	4.17	3.94	3.63	3.30	2.92	2.49
	.001	15.08	10.16	8.28	7.26	6.61	6.18	5.59	4.97	4.29	3.52
20	.10	2.97	2.59	2.38	2.25	2.16	2.09	2.00	1.89	1.77	1.61
	.05	4.35	3.49	3.10	2.87	2.71	2.60	2.45	2.28	2.08	1.84
	.01	8.10	5.85	4.94	4.43	4.10	3.87	3.56	3.23	2.86	2.42
	.001	14.82	9.95	8.10	7.10	6.46	6.02	5.44	4.82	4.15	3.38
22	.10	2.95	2.56	2.35	2.22	2.13	2.06	1.97	1.86	1.73	1.57
	.05	4.30	3.44	3.05	2.82	2.66	2.55	2.40	2.23	2.03	1.78
	.01	7.94	5.72	4.82	4.31	3.99	3.76	3.45	3.12	2.75	2.31
	.001	14.38	9.61	7.80	6.81	6.19	5.76	5.19	4.58	3.92	3.15

TABLE C-4.1
CRITICAL VALUES OF *F* (Continued)

237
STATISTICS
SECTION C-4:
TABLES OF
CRITICAL VALUES

Degrees of freedom in error term	p	\multicolumn{10}{c}{Degrees of freedom in systematic term}
		1	2	3	4	5	6	8	12	24	∞
24	.10	2.93	2.54	2.33	2.19	2.10	2.04	1.94	1.83	1.70	1.53
	.05	4.26	3.40	3.01	2.78	2.62	2.51	2.36	2.18	1.98	1.73
	.01	7.82	5.61	4.72	4.22	3.90	3.67	3.36	3.03	2.66	2.21
	.001	14.03	9.34	7.55	6.59	5.98	5.55	4.99	4.39	3.74	2.97
26	.10	2.91	2.52	2.31	2.17	2.08	2.01	1.92	1.81	1.68	1.50
	.05	4.22	3.37	2.98	2.74	2.59	2.47	2.32	2.15	1.95	1.69
	.01	7.72	5.53	4.64	4.14	3.82	3.59	3.29	2.96	2.58	2.13
	.001	13.74	9.12	7.36	6.41	5.80	5.38	4.83	4.24	3.59	2.82
28	.10	2.89	2.50	2.29	2.16	2.06	2.00	1.90	1.79	1.66	1.48
	.05	4.20	3.34	2.95	2.71	2.56	2.44	2.29	2.12	1.91	1.65
	.01	7.64	5.45	4.57	4.07	3.75	3.53	3.23	2.90	2.52	2.06
	.001	13.50	8.93	7.19	6.25	5.66	5.24	4.69	4.11	3.46	2.70
30	.10	2.88	2.49	2.28	2.14	2.05	1.98	1.88	1.77	1.64	1.46
	.05	4.17	3.32	2.92	2.69	2.53	2.42	2.27	2.09	1.89	1.62
	.01	7.56	5.39	4.51	4.02	3.70	3.47	3.17	2.84	2.47	2.01
	.001	13.29	8.77	7.05	6.12	5.53	5.12	4.58	4.00	3.36	2.59
40	.10	2.84	2.44	2.23	2.09	2.00	1.93	1.83	1.71	1.57	1.38
	.05	4.08	3.23	2.84	2.61	2.45	2.34	2.18	2.00	1.79	1.51
	.01	7.31	5.18	4.31	3.83	3.51	3.29	2.99	2.66	2.29	1.80
	.001	12.61	8.25	6.60	5.70	5.13	4.73	4.21	3.64	3.01	2.23
60	.10	2.79	2.39	2.18	2.04	1.95	1.87	1.77	1.66	1.51	1.29
	.05	4.00	3.15	2.76	2.52	2.37	2.25	2.10	1.92	1.70	1.39
	.01	7.08	4.98	4.13	3.65	3.34	3.12	2.82	2.50	2.12	1.60
	.001	11.97	7.76	6.17	5.31	4.76	4.37	3.87	3.31	2.69	1.90
120	.10	2.75	2.35	2.13	1.99	1.90	1.82	1.72	1.60	1.45	1.19
	.05	3.92	3.07	2.68	2.45	2.29	2.17	2.02	1.83	1.61	1.25
	.01	6.85	4.79	3.95	3.48	3.17	2.96	2.66	2.34	1.95	1.38
	.001	11.38	7.31	5.79	4.95	4.42	4.04	3.55	3.02	2.40	1.54
∞	.10	2.71	2.30	2.08	1.94	1.85	1.77	1.67	1.55	1.38	1.00
	.05	3.84	2.99	2.60	2.37	2.21	2.09	1.94	1.75	1.52	1.00
	.01	6.64	4.60	3.78	3.32	3.02	2.80	2.51	2.18	1.79	1.00
	.001	10.83	6.91	5.42	4.62	4.10	3.74	3.27	2.74	2.13	1.00

Taken from Table V of R. A. Fisher and F. Yates, *Statistical tables for biological, agricultural and medical research*, published by Longman Group Ltd., London (previously published by Oliver and Boyd, Edinburgh). Used by permission of the authors and publishers.

TABLE C-4.2
CRITICAL VALUES OF *t*
(TWO-TAILED)

df	.10	.05	.01	.001
			p	
6	1.94	2.45	3.71	5.96
7	1.90	2.37	3.50	5.41
8	1.86	2.31	3.36	5.04
9	1.83	2.26	3.25	4.78
10	1.81	2.23	3.17	4.59
11	1.80	2.20	3.11	4.44
12	1.78	2.18	3.06	4.32
13	1.77	2.16	3.01	4.22
14	1.76	2.14	2.98	4.14
15	1.75	2.13	2.95	4.07
16	1.75	2.12	2.92	4.02
17	1.74	2.11	2.90	3.97
18	1.73	2.10	2.88	3.92
19	1.73	2.09	2.86	3.88
20	1.72	2.09	2.84	3.85
21	1.72	2.08	2.83	3.82
22	1.72	2.07	2.82	3.79
23	1.71	2.07	2.81	3.77
24	1.71	2.06	2.80	3.75
25	1.71	2.06	2.79	3.73
30	1.70	2.04	2.75	3.65
40	1.68	2.02	2.70	3.55
60	1.67	2.00	2.66	3.46
120	1.66	1.98	2.62	3.37
∞	1.64	1.96	2.58	3.29

Taken from Table III of R. A. Fisher and F. Yates, *Statistical tables for biological, agricultural and medical research,* published by Longman Group Ltd., London (previously published by Oliver and Boyd, Edinburgh). Used by permission of the authors and publishers.

TABLE C-4.3
CRITICAL VALUES OF *r*

df	p			
	.10	.05	.01	.001
6	.622	.707	.834	.925
7	.582	.666	.798	.898
8	.549	.632	.765	.872
9	.521	.602	.735	.847
10	.497	.576	.708	.823
11	.476	.553	.684	.801
12	.458	.532	.661	.780
13	.441	.514	.641	.760
14	.426	.497	.623	.742
15	.412	.482	.606	.725
16	.400	.468	.590	.708
17	.389	.456	.575	.693
18	.378	.444	.561	.679
19	.369	.433	.549	.665
20	.360	.423	.537	.652
25	.323	.381	.487	.597
30	.296	.349	.449	.554
35	.275	.325	.418	.519
40	.257	.304	.393	.490
45	.243	.288	.372	.465
50	.231	.273	.354	.443
60	.211	.250	.325	.408
70	.195	.232	.302	.380
80	.183	.217	.283	.357
90	.173	.205	.267	.338
100	.164	.195	.254	.321

Taken from Table VII of R. A. Fisher and F. Yates, *Statistical tables for biological, agricultural and medical research,* published by Longman Group Ltd., London (previously published by Oliver and Boyd, Edinburgh). Used by permission of the authors and publishers.

TABLE C-4.4
CRITICAL VALUES OF χ^2

df	p			
	.10	.05	.01	.001
1	2.7	3.8	6.6	10.8
2	4.6	6.0	9.2	13.8
3	6.3	7.8	11.3	16.3
4	7.8	9.5	13.3	18.5
5	9.2	11.1	15.1	20.5
6	10.6	12.6	16.8	22.5
7	12.0	14.1	18.5	24.3
8	13.4	15.5	20.1	26.1
9	14.7	16.9	21.7	27.9
10	16.0	18.3	23.2	29.6
11	17.3	19.7	24.7	31.3
12	18.5	21.0	26.2	32.9
13	19.8	22.4	27.7	34.5
14	21.1	23.7	29.1	36.1
15	22.3	25.0	30.6	37.7
16	23.5	26.3	32.0	39.3
17	24.8	27.6	33.4	40.8
18	26.0	28.9	34.8	42.3
19	27.2	30.1	36.2	43.8
20	28.4	31.4	37.6	45.3
21	29.6	32.7	38.9	46.8
22	30.8	33.9	40.3	48.3
23	32.0	35.2	41.6	49.7
24	33.2	36.4	43.0	51.2
25	34.4	37.7	44.3	52.6
26	35.6	38.9	45.6	54.0
27	36.7	40.1	47.0	55.5
28	37.9	41.3	48.3	56.9
29	39.1	42.6	49.6	58.3
30	40.3	43.8	50.9	59.7

Taken from Table IV of R. A. Fisher and F. Yates, *Statistical tables for biological, agricultural and medical research*, published by Longman Group Ltd., London (previously published by Oliver and Boyd, Edinburgh). Used by permission of the authors and publishers.

Appendix D

Using Educational Resources

This appendix will describe procedures for locating research and authoritative opinion materials for your own professional reading or for reviews of literature. Ways of using indexes and abstracts will be described in some detail. At the end of the appendix are lists of journals and ERIC clearinghouses that may assist your search.

CARD CATALOG

The card catalog is your best source for finding books in a particular library.* Each book in the library is listed by title, author, and subject in card files. Cards for authors and titles are arranged alphabetically by the first letter of the author's last name or the first letter of the title, exclusive of articles "the," "a," and "an." If there is more than one author, there are usually author cards for each person. Subject heading cards are usually arranged in files separate from the author-title file.

In the upper left-hand corner of each card is a call number, which will allow you to locate books on the shelves or call for them at the circulation desk. See the sample title card in Figure D.1. There is also complete information about the title, author's name, birth date, city of publication, publisher's name, and year.

Near the bottom of the card is a section called tracings. Subject headings numbered with Arabic numerals are included here. There are also added entries for titles, alternative titles, series, and names of corporate bodies (e.g., Rutgers University), which are not actually the subject of the book. Added entries in the tracings are preceded by Roman numerals and filed in the author-title catalog rather than in the subject catalog. By using the tracings, you can often find related subject headings that may relate to your topic precisely.

You may find that title or author cards are easier to use than subject cards. Subject headings may be difficult to use at times, but the Library of Congress Subject Headings List, which is usually kept near the catalog, can simplify the process. This reference lists all possible subject headings for topics, exclusive of proper names, with subdivisions and cross-references.

The card catalog can help you find out whether the book is important for your purpose. For one thing, the date may be very important. If you are looking for recent materials, a book published in the 1960s may not be worth checking out. If you are working on the history of a topic, however, you may find that dates are very helpful in getting the chronology of events.

Sometimes the edition of the book may help substantiate that what the author said was well accepted, by *buyers* anyway. Publishers seldom have authors revise

* Some libraries may have microfiche or computerized catalogs instead.

books that don't sell well. So if you're looking at a card for a book in a revised edition, that book may be a better source than some others you could read.

Finally, you should note whether the book has a bibliography. If it does, you may want to look at it to get additional sources of information.

EDUCATION INDEX

Published monthly and cumulated annually, *Education Index* lists entries from a wide range of periodicals, yearbooks, bulletins, and U.S. government publications. Each entry is indexed both by subject and by author's last name. Since this index uses the same system as the *Reader's Guide to Periodical Literature*, you may find it very easy to use depending on your past experience.

To use *Education Index* you need to know the subject heading or the author's name. Subject headings in this index, though not so broad as those in the card catalog, cover much information. This may make it difficult to locate a narrow topic. Also, it can be difficult to figure out the subject heading that covers a particular topic. For example, suppose you began a search to find examples of reports on "learning styles." That subject heading is not listed separately. However, papers on the topic are listed under the broader heading "Learning, Psychology of" and the major subdivisions of this heading. Topics under the heading "See also" suggest other possible sources of information.

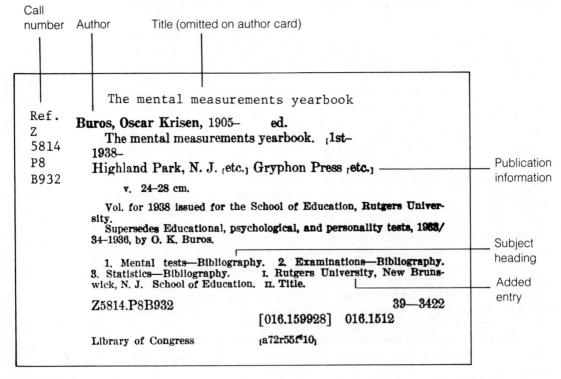

FIGURE D.1   Title card.

Figure D.2 shows a portion of the entries under "Learning, Psychology of." The two entries indicated seem to be closely related to the topic of learning style. For each entry there is a title, author's name, publication name, and exact source within the publication. The title of the first marked report is "Cognitive style: The individual difference variable that doesn't make a difference." Its author is J. K. Bengston, who has included a bibliography in the report. The paper was published in *Viewpoints on Teaching and Learning*, volume 55,

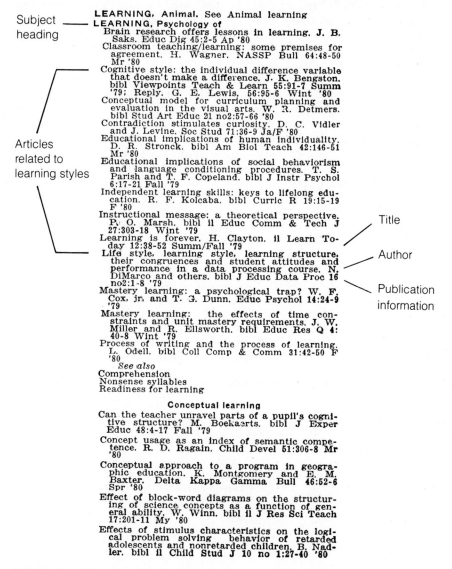

FIGURE D.2 Entries from *Education Index*. Copyright © 1980 by The H. W. Wilson Company. Reproduced by permission of the publisher.

pages 91–97, summer 1979. Since the names of periodicals are abbreviated, you should check listings in the front of *Education Index* to find the exact name of the periodical. Your next step is to see whether your library has that particular publication.

The major advantage in using *Education Index* is that you can usually locate current information about most educational topics. The chief disadvantage is that you must have a good idea of the subject heading or the author's name in order to find the literature. Subject headings used in card catalogs do not necessarily correspond to those used in this index. Another disadvantage shared by most indexes is that you can locate only published materials.

ERIC MATERIALS

Educational Resources Information Center (ERIC) provides access to almost all educational materials in print through the *Current Index to Journals in Education* (*CIJE*) and *Resources in Education* (*RIE*). Generally *CIJE* indexes journals and *RIE* indexes other printed materials, including books, guides, historical materials, information analyses, legal materials, nonprint media, numerical/quantitative data, opinion papers, reference materials (bibliographies, directories, catalogs, and vocabularies), reports (research, evaluative, general, and descriptive), speeches and meeting papers, tests, and questionnaires. Although many of the topics in *Education Index* are also included in *CIJE*, the advantage in the ERIC listing is that many new and less well-known topics are also included.

To use either *CIJE* or *RIE* you need to know the ERIC descriptors for your subject headings. The *Thesaurus of ERIC Descriptors* provides this information. To illustrate how the *Thesaurus* works, we'll again use the topic "learning styles." The listing for this term tells us to use "cognitive style" instead. Figure D.3 shows all the information under this entry. The date, October 1976, indicates that the descriptor for cognitive style has been used only since that time. The scope note (SN) defines the term as ERIC uses it. The listing also indicates that "cognitive style" is used for (UF) the term "learning style." Other descriptors are noted as narrower terms (NT), broader terms (BT), and related terms (RT). These descrip-

```
COGNITIVE STYLE            Oct. 1976
     CIJE: 281        RIE: 282
SN   Information processing habits which
     represent the learner's typical modes
     of perceiving, thinking, remembering,
     and problem solving
UF   Learning Style
     Perceptual Style
NT   Conceptual Tempo
BT   Psychological Characteristics
RT   Aptitude Treatment Interaction
     Cognitive Development
     Cognitive Measurement
     Cognitive Processes
     Cognitive Tests
     Learning Modalities
     Personality Traits
```

FIGURE D.3 Entry from *Thesaurus of ERIC Descriptors*, 1980. Reprinted by permission.

tors may be used as guides to additional information, which, though not so directly related to learning style, may be of value.

The next step is using either *CIJE* or *RIE* is usually to look up the descriptor(s) in the subject index. Looking up "cognitive style" in the subject index of one monthly collection showed 13 entries in *CIJE* for this topic. Each entry bears a title, a source, and an EJ (educational journal) number (see Figure D.4). Sometimes titles will tell you whether that listing is important for your purpose. At other times you will need to read the abstract, which is in the same volume under the Main Entry heading. The EJ number tells you where to look in the Main Entry section.

Using *Resources in Education* involves similar processes. By looking for your topic in a subject index, you are directed to main entries through an educational document (ED) number. At the beginning of the main entry, there's quite a bit of information that is helpful if you decide you should read the complete report. For example, authors' names are given immediately below the ED number, followed by the title and publication information. A note is commonly placed in this section giving particular information about the report concerning its completeness, the reproducibility of various parts, or its availability in paper form. The type of publication is next, followed by ordering information for microfiche or paper copies of the report (see Figure D.5). Sometimes there is a notation "not available from EDRS." Often these documents are copyrighted published books

Cognitive Style

Effect of Classroom Reading Approach on Learning Style of Fourth and Fifth Graders. *Reading Improvement;* v17 n1 p80-84 Spr 1980   EJ 217 588

Socialization, Culture and Ecology in the Development of Group and Sex Differences in Cognitive Style. *Human Development;* v22 n5 p358-72 1979   EJ 218 076

Encoding of Personal Information: Self-Other Differences. *Journal of Personality and Social Psychology;* v37 n4 p499-514 Apr 1979   EJ 218 187

Theory and Measurement of Androgyny: A reply to the Pedhazur-Tetenbaum and Locksley-Colten Critiques. *Journal of Personality and Social Psychology;* v37 n6 p1047-54 Jun 1979   EJ 218 201

Use of Strategies and Individual Differences in Children's Memory. *Developmental Psychology;* v15 n3 p251-55 May 1979   EJ 218 237

Developmental Changes in Dichotic Listening with Categorized Word Lists. *Developmental Psychology;* v15 n3 p280-87 May 1979   EJ 218 241

Development of Three Strategies of Attention in Dichotic Monitoring. *Developmental Psychology;* v15 n3 p299-310 May 1979   EJ 218 243

Bilingualism and Cognition: Some Recent Findings. *NABE: The Journal for the National Association for Bilingual Education;* v4 n1 p15-50 Fall 1979   EJ 218 345

Relationships among Level of Intellectual Development, Cognitive Style, and Grades in a College Biology Course. *Science Education;* v64 n1 p95-102 Jan 1980   EJ 218 381

Interactions of Field Independence and General Reasoning with Inductive Instruction in Mathematics. *Journal for Research in Mathematics Education;* v11 n2 p94-103 Mar 1980   EJ 218 493

Effect of Cognitive Style and Learning Passage Organization on Study Technique Effectiveness. *Journal of Educational Psychology;* v71 n5 p620-26 Oct 1979   EJ 218 627

Individual Characteristics and Children's Learning in Large-Group and Small-Group Approaches. *Journal of Educational Psychology;* v71 n5 p677-87 Oct 1979 EJ 218 633

FIGURE D.4 Entries from the subject index of *CIJE*, 1980. Reprinted by permission.

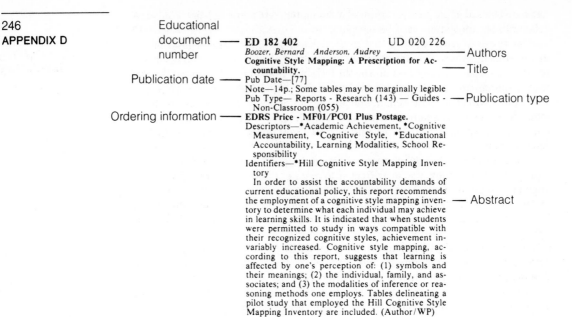

Educational document number ⸺ ED 182 402   UD 020 226 ⸺ Authors

Boozer, Bernard   Anderson, Audrey
Cognitive Style Mapping: A Prescription for Accountability. ⸺ Title

Publication date ⸺ Pub Date—[77]

Note—14p.; Some tables may be marginally legible

Pub Type— Reports - Research (143) — Guides - ⸺ Publication type
Non-Classroom (055)

Ordering information ⸺ **EDRS Price - MF01/PC01 Plus Postage.**

Descriptors—*Academic Achievement, *Cognitive Measurement, *Cognitive Style, *Educational Accountability, Learning Modalities, School Responsibility

Identifiers—*Hill Cognitive Style Mapping Inventory

In order to assist the accountability demands of current educational policy, this report recommends the employment of a cognitive style mapping inventory to determine what each individual may achieve in learning skills. It is indicated that when students were permitted to study in ways compatible with their recognized cognitive styles, achievement invariably increased. Cognitive style mapping, according to this report, suggests that learning is affected by one's perception of: (1) symbols and their meanings; (2) the individual, family, and associates; and (3) the modalities of inference or reasoning methods one employs. Tables delineating a pilot study that employed the Hill Cognitive Style Mapping Inventory are included. (Author/WP) ⸺ Abstract

FIGURE D.5   Entry from the main entry section of *RIE*, 1980. Reprinted by permission.

and may be located in the card catalog. Just before the abstract is a section that contains descriptors and identifiers.

In searching you will find the ED number, and then check the title to be sure you have the entry you want. You may also read the abstract. Only if the information is pertinent to your purpose are you likely to read all the initial information. If you want to read the entire report, you may find it on microfiche in libraries that have major collections in education. If the report is not available there, you can order it through interlibrary loan or from ERIC at some expense.

The subject index is just one of four ways to find materials through ERIC. If you know about persons who are working on a particular topic, you can check the author index for listings of their publications and trace them through the main entry sections to their original sources. You can also look up work done at particular institutions in another index. If you have either an ED or an EJ number, you can locate the source, too.

SPECIALIZED ABSTRACTS

Several additional sources are in the form of specialized abstracts. These include *Dissertation Abstracts International, Child Development Abstracts, Psychological Abstracts,* and *Sociological Abstracts.* Each of these sources serves a particular audience but may overlap with other audiences, too.

Dissertation Abstracts International (DAI) is published monthly and the index is cumulated annually. *DAI* is separated into part A, which includes the humanities and social sciences, and part B, which has science and engineering. Education is included in part A. Each volume contains a subject index similar to *Education Index*, which enables you to use the key-word system for searching. For each dissertation, there is a 600-word abstract, which was written by the doctoral candidate who wrote the dissertation. The abstract may provide enough information for your purpose. Or, if you wish to read the complete study, you may order it from University Microfilms, the publisher, either in photocopy or on microfilm. Ordering information is at the front of each volume, and the order number is given with each abstract.

Child Development Abstracts is published three times a year, with two numbers in each issue. It contains abstracts from professional publications as well as book reviews related to childhood growth and development. Abstracts are listed under one of six categories: (1) biology, health, and medicine; (2) cognition, learning, and perception; (3) social, psychological, cultural, and personality studies; (4) educational processes; (5) psychiatry and clinical psychology; and (6) history, theory, and methodology. This is a good source to consult if you are interested in topics related to childhood.

Psychological Abstracts provide indexes and summaries of reports in psychology. Although many reports were published in education journals, abstracts are included from more than 500 journals published worldwide. Originals of the reports, therefore, are not always in English. If your topic is in any way related to psychology, you should consult this source. (See Figure D.6.)

Sociological Abstracts serves essentially the same purpose for studies in sociology.

Abstract number — Author — Author's institutional affiliation

11671. **Atohama, Kyoko.** (Hiroshima U, Japan) **[The effect of nursery school children's reliance on a model and of their cognition of the model's nursing attitude upon their imitative behavior.]** (Japn) *Japanese Journal of Psychology,* 1978(Dec), Vol 49(5), 241–248. —Ss were 48 5-yr-old children, classified into 4 experimental groups according to tests of their reliance upon and cognition of the attitude of their nurses. A control group consisted of 32 same age Ss. In each group, each S was asked twice to choose one alternative out of 10 pairs of pictures and then to arrange the pictures into a story. After the 1st trial, the Ss nurse served as a model and displayed a series of choices opposite to those made by the S. Shifts of choice made by the child on the 2nd trial were recorded as a measure of imitation. All the experimental groups except the low reliance–low attitude made significantly more shifts than the control group. The high reliance–high attitude Ss, who were highly reliant on their models and had a highly satisfactory relationship with their nurses, showed significantly more shifts than the other experimental groups. Results support the hypothesis that, depending on the child's reliance on the model itself, the child's cognition of the model affects imitative behavior. (6 ref) —*English abstract.*

Title — Publication name — Publication information — Abstract (original article in Japanese)

FIGURE D.6   Entry in *Psychological Abstracts*. Copyright 1980 by the American Psychological Association. Reprinted by permission.

SUMMARY

Eight tools for locating research reports and other information in libraries have been described in this appendix. To enable you to make comparisons among these tools, the contents, methods of indexing, and some advantages and disadvantages of each index or set of abstracts are summarized in Table D.1.

Table D.1
COMPARISONS OF WAYS TO LOCATE INFORMATION

Title	Contents	Methods of indexing	Advantages/disadvantages
Card catalog	Books (usually)	Title, author, subject	Only way to know which books your library has/Not many ways to evaluate listings; subject headings may be difficult to use
Education Index	Periodicals, yearbooks, government publications	Subject, author	Most current periodicals are listed; easy to use/Subject headings may be difficult to figure out; narrow topics may be hard to find
CIJE	Periodicals	Subject, author, institution, accession number	Almost all current periodicals are listed; several ways of indexing/Descriptors must be known (use *Thesaurus*)
RIE	Unpublished papers, some books, other documents	Same as *CIJE*	Can get to little-known sources; current listings/Descriptors must be known; can be a delay in using sources unless library owns them
DAI	Dissertation abstracts	Subject, author	Can get to little-known sources of research; current listings/ Can be a delay in using dissertations
Psychological Abstracts	Reports of psychological research and other psychological literature	Subject, author	Almost all psychological literature is included
Child Development Abstracts	Reports of psychological research	Subject, author	Specialized source of information related to children
Sociological Abstracts	Reports of sociological research and other sociological literature	Subject, author	Almost all sociological literature is included

JOURNALS

The following journals contain research reports, reviews, or other material that may be useful in a review of literature. This is only a partial list of journals.

American Educational Research Journal. Washington, D.C.: American Educational Research Association, 1964–

Child Development. Chicago: University of Chicago Press for the Society for Research in Child Development, 1930–

Educational Administration Quarterly. Columbus, Oh.: University Council for Educational Administration, 1965–

Educational and Psychological Measurement. Durham, N.C.: Educational and Psychological Measurement, 1941–

Elementary School Journal. Chicago: Department of Education, University of Chicago Press, 1900–

Harvard Educational Review. Cambridge, Mass.: Harvard University Graduate School of Education, 1931–

Interchange. Toronto, Canada: Ontario Institute for Studies in Education, 1970–

Journal of Applied Psychology. Washington, D.C.: American Psychological Association, 1917–

Journal of Educational Measurement. East Lansing, Mich.: National Council of Measurement in Education, 1964–

Journal of Educational Psychology. Washington, D.C.: American Psychological Association, 1910–

Journal of Educational Research. Washington, D.C.: HELDREF Publications, 1920–

Journal of Experimental Education. Washington, D.C.: HELDREF Publications, 1932–

Journal of Psychology. Provincetown, Mass.: Journal Press, 1935–

Journal of Research and Development in Education. Athens: College of Education, University of Georgia, 1967–

Journal of Research in Mathematics Education. Reston, Va.: National Council of Teachers of Mathematics, 1970–

Journal of Research in Music Education. Vienna, Va.: Music Educators National Conference, 1953–

Journal of Research in Science Teaching. New York: Wiley, 1962–

Journal of School Psychology. New York: Behavioral Publications, 1962–

Journal of Special Education. New York: Grune & Stratton, 1967–

Journal of Social Psychology. Provincetown, Mass.: Journal Press, 1930–

Psychological Bulletin. Washington, D.C.: American Psychological Association, 1904–

Psychological Review. Washington, D.C.: American Psychological Association, 1894–

Psychology in the Schools. Brandon, Vt.: Clinical Psychology Publishing Company, 1964–

Reading Research Quarterly. Newark, Del.: International Reading Association, 1965–

Research in the Teaching of English. Urbana, Ill.: National Council of Teachers of English, 1967–

Research Quarterly for Exercise and Sport. Washington, D.C.: American Alliance for Health, Physical Education and Recreation, 1930–

Review of Educational Research. Washington, D.C.: American Educational Research Association, 1930–

Sociology and Social Research. Los Angeles: University of Southern California, 1916–

Sociology of Education. Albany, N.Y.: American Sociological Association, 1927–

ERIC CLEARINGHOUSES

Educational Resources Information Center (ERIC) contains 16 clearinghouses, each representing a nationwide network. Each clearinghouse searches out current research findings, project and technical reports, speeches and unpublished manuscripts, books, and professional journal articles. These materials are prepared for use by the educational community by the staff of ERIC. If you are interested in material from a particular clearinghouse, you may request that your name be placed on the mailing list to receive announcements of new information. These are the names and addresses:

Adult, Career, and Vocational Education
Center for Vocational Education
Ohio State University
1960 Kenny Road
Columbus, OH 43210

Counseling and Personnel Services
University of Michigan
School of Education Building, Room 2108
East University and South University Streets
Ann Arbor, MI 48104

Early Childhood Education
University of Illinois
805 W. Pennsylvania Avenue
Urbana, IL 61801

Educational Management
University of Oregon
Eugene, OR 97403

Handicapped and Gifted Children
Council for Exceptional Children
1920 Association Drive
Reston, VA 22091

Higher Education
George Washington University
One Dupont Circle, NW, Suite 630
Washington, DC 20036

Information Resources
Area Instructional Technology
Syracuse University, School of Education
Syracuse, NY 13210

Junior Colleges
University of California at Los Angeles
Powell Library, Room 96
405 Hilgard Avenue
Los Angeles, CA 90024

Languages and Linguistics
Center for Applied Linguistics
1611 North Kent Street
Arlington, VA 22209

Reading and Communication Skills
National Council of Teachers of English
1111 Kenyon Road
Urbana, IL 61801

Rural Education and Small Schools
New Mexico State University
Box 3 AP
Las Cruces, NM 88003

Science, Mathematics, and Environmental Education
Ohio State University
1200 Chambers Road, Third Floor
Columbus, OH 43212

Social Studies/Social Science Education
Social Science Education Consortium, Inc.
855 Broadway
Boulder, CO 80302

Teacher Education
American Association of Colleges for Teacher Education
One Dupont Circle, NW, Suite 616
Washington, DC 20036

Tests, Measurement and Evaluation
Educational Testing Service
Princeton, NJ 08540

Urban Education
Teachers College Columbia University
Box 40
New York, NY 10027

Appendix E

Historical Research

Whenever educational questions are raised that focus on past events, a line of inquiry is called for that cannot use the descriptive and experimental methodologies of scientific research. In these situations, *historical* research and its methods are appropriate. The goal of historical research is the description, explanation, and interpretation of past events through a careful analysis and evaluation of the sources of historical evidence. Certainly educational research as we define it has its historical context. It is important for researchers to know what historical efforts and forces bear on current research, so that the proper interpretations and conclusions can be drawn from research results.

Historical research can coincide with the scientific goal of explanation if researchers are trying to explain relationships that existed among variables observed in the past. However, because the past occurrence of variables is not observable or measurable by the researchers, it is not possible to test hypothesized relationships between variables directly. Some historical inquiry is not concerned so much with the investigation of hypotheses as with the reconstruction or reinterpretation of historical events.

In all cases historical researchers are very concerned with the quality of the evidence or data they find. The validity of such data directly affects the interpretations and descriptions that can be made. Therefore, much of the work of historical researchers is to analyze and evaluate their sources of information. Generally, historical evidence is divided into two types: primary sources and secondary sources. A *primary source* contains evidence recorded by an eyewitness to a historical event, or some original record of historical information. A *secondary source* contains historical evidence that is less direct, such as a report summarizing what eyewitnesses said about some event.

Historians prefer to use primary sources whenever they are available since they are closer to the actual phenomenon; however, frequently they must rely on secondary sources. This makes the careful evaluation of sources a necessity. Researchers seek to confirm the accuracy of evidence by examining the consistency of information from different sources and determining the authenticity of the documents. Even authentic, well-supported information must be carefully examined in the light of biases and deficiencies in knowledge that were operating at the time the source was created. After careful evaluation of the evidence, interpretations are made.

Because historical research is concerned with past events, the subject matter of such inquiry can be much more difficult to investigate than scientifically researchable problems. It is often hard to collect and analyze data. Interpretations of historical findings are particularly likely to be colored by present-day circumstances. Therefore, we suggest that a person who is seriously interested in a historical problem become a student of *historiography*, the study of methods of historical inquiry, before proceeding further. Although some of the general principles of scientific research can be applied to historical questions, the limitations on direct observation make other methods more appropriate.

Glossary

abstract. An abbreviated version of a research report, consisting of a statement of the problem along with a brief statement of procedures, results, and implications.

analysis of covariance. A test of significance in which groups are made equivalent by statistically removing the initial differences between the groups that are due to a variable (called the covariate) that is thought to be correlated with the dependent variable.

analysis of variance. A test of statistical significance used to assess differences between means or variances; abbreviated ANOVA. The result of this test is an F-ratio, which expresses the ratio of variations caused by the treatment to variations caused by error.

association study. Project in which the investigator wants to determine the strength and direction of the relationship between two or more variables. Both correlation and prediction studies are classified as association studies.

between-groups variance. The variation between the measures of one treatment group and other groups, usually expressed as the difference between or among the group means. This variance is presumed to reflect differences caused by the treatment conditions.

cluster sampling. A variation of random sampling in which the unit selected is a group rather than individual persons. Each group has an equal chance of being selected from a population of groups.

conclusions. A researcher's generalized statement about the results of a research investigation.

context. A review of related literature, including a justification for the research problem.

control. The goal of science that reveals cause-and-effect relationships. In a general sense, control is the power to influence or direct events.

convenience sampling. A nonscientific process used to select subjects from a population. Persons are selected on the basis of availability. Subjects may or may not be representative of the population.

correlation coefficient. A numerical index expressing the strength and direction of a relationship between variables. It is usually written as a decimal number ranging from -1.00 to $+1.00$.

correlation study. Project whose main purpose is to determine the strength and direction of an association between two or more variables; no cause-and-effect relationship is implied.

counterbalanced design. A kind of repeated measures design in which the effects of the order of treatments on the dependent variable are controlled by determining the order at random for each group or subject, or by using all possible orders of treatments for every group.

criterion level. A quantitative value of a dependent variable chosen before the treatment as a way to evaluate the educational significance of the results. The researcher considers the results to be educationally significant only if the appropriate measure of the dependent variable meets or exceeds the criterion level.

data analysis. The procedures of sorting, summarizing, analyzing, and interpreting the observations that are made on subjects in a research study. They may range from simple classification by hand to complex mathematical calculations on a computer.

dependent variable. The variable that is changed by or responds to the independent variable.

descriptive methodology. Methods used in research studies that seek explanation and prediction as their goals. Researchers may use existing situations for data collection. No manipulation of variables is involved.

descriptive statistics. Procedures for collecting and summarizing data to make their communication and interpretation easier.

difference study. Project in which the investigator wants to find out whether differences introduced in one variable result in changes in a second, responding variable. Cause-and-effect relationships between variables are studied.

educational research. The product of applying the scientific method to the study of problems in education; also the process by which these problems are studied.

educational significance. A judgment about the worth of the results of a research study based on the educational value and implications of the project.

effect size. An index of the degree of departure from the null hypothesis. It indicates the degree to which a phenomenon exists in a population. Effect size is usually stated in terms of a correlation coefficient or a standard scoring unit such as a standard deviation or z-score.

error variance. Variability in data that is not due to the influence of the independent variable. It occurs by chance and is minimized by the researcher's attempts to control variance.

experimental methodology. The methods used in research studies that seek control as their goal. They require deliberate effort on the part of researchers to structure situations in which variables can be controlled and investigated. Studies involve cause-and-effect relationships.

explanation. The goal of science that makes the underlying relationships between variables understandable.

ex post facto. A type of descriptive research in which the independent variable is selected rather than manipulated. *Ex post facto* research provides less control than true experimental research and therefore produces no definitive conclusions about causality.

external validity. The degree to which the results of research can be generalized to situations beyond the subjects of the study.

factorial design. A plan for research that allows the investigation of levels of independent variables in combination with other independent variables. Such a plan provides results for the effects of each separate independent variable as well as the interactions of these variables on the dependent variable.

frequency distribution. The result of a procedure in which a group of observations is arranged to show how many observations fall within specified intervals on the measurement scale.

generalizability. The extent to which research results can be considered truthful for persons who were not subjects in the research project. When subjects have been selected at random from a population, the results obtained in the study can be inferred to exist in the population from which the subjects were drawn.

hypothesis, null. A statement that any association between variables or differences between experimental conditions or treatments is due solely to chance variation within the population studied. Also called a statistical hypothesis, the null hypothesis is used to assess the statistical significance of the results of a research study.

hypothesis, research. A statement of the tentative answer to a research problem.

independent variable. The variable that is manipulated in experimental studies to see if there is an effect on another responding variable. The term also refers to variables in *ex post facto* designs and in some types of factorial designs that are selected rather than manipulated by the researcher.

inferential statistics. Procedures for organizing and analyzing data from a sample that permit investigators to draw conclusions about a population.

instrumentation. All tests, scales, interview schedules, rating scales, and other devices used to collect data in a research project.

interaction. The effect of the joint action of two or more independent variables on a dependent variable. This effect is different from the separate or main effects of each independent variable. Interaction is studied in factorial designs.

internal validity. The degree to which the observed results of an experimental study can be attributed to the manipulation of the independent variable rather than to uncontrolled variance.

interpretation. Explanation of the results of a research effort with reference to the body of related research and theory as well as to the circumstances of the study.

interval data. A level of measurement in which there are equal intervals between units on the scale. The data in this level are expressed as numbers, thus permitting a full range of mathematical operations.

justification for the study. A section of a proposal or a research report in which the researcher outlines reasons for doing the study. It often cites literature as support.

level of significance. The probability of rejecting a null hypothesis when it is true, also known as the alpha level.

levels of measurement. A hierarchy of four kinds of measurement scales that control the assignment of quantitative values to data according to the rules of each level. The levels of measurement are nominal, ordinal, interval, and ratio.

mean. A measure of central tendency, also called the arithmetic mean or average. It is obtained by summing a set of measures and dividing the sum by the number of measures.

median. A measure of central tendency that represents the midpoint of a distribution of measures.

mode. A measure of central tendency that is the score that occurs most frequently in a set of measures.

multivariate analysis. Statistical analysis of data in which multiple dependent variables are represented.

nominal data. The lowest level of measurement. Data are classified into categories that are mutually exclusive and exhaustive. Each piece of data can be assigned to one and only one category.

nonparametric test. A statistical test of significance used to analyze nominal or ordinal data and higher levels of data that are not normally distributed.

normal distribution. A symmetrical frequency distribution in which most of the measures fall near the mean and fewer scores are found near the extremes of the distribution. The normal distribution forms a bell-shaped curve, with the mean, median, and mode at the same point on the curve.

one-tailed test. A label applied to any test of statistical significance used when the research hypothesis predicts a direction for the hypothetical relationship under investigation. In a one-tailed test the area of possible values leading to rejection of the null hypothesis includes only one end of the sampling distribution of the test statistic.

operational definition. A definition of a variable that assigns meaning to it by setting out the observable behaviors or operations that will represent the variable.

ordinal data. A level of measurement in which data are assigned to ordered categories. Each piece of data so assigned has a particular rank with respect to data at other points on the scale, although there is no fixed value between ranks.

parametric test. A statistical test in which inferences are made about the significance of results for a population based on conclusions derived from sample data. Parametric tests assume that data are interval or ratio level, and that one or more of the variables is normally distributed.

population. Any collection of people defined as a group by one or more characteristics of the group.

prediction. The goal of science that predicts relationships between variables based on known relationships between similar variables.

prediction study. A project whose main purpose is to find out whether a known correlation between variables in one situation holds true in a similar but separate situation. Data on one of the variables are used to estimate the values of a second variable.

preexperimental design. A plan for research that uses a manipulated variable and sometimes a control group, but has no other features of a true experiment.

quartile deviation. A measure of dispersion, also called the semi-interquartile range. It is obtained by subtracting the value of the first quartile (Q_1) from that of the third quartile (Q_3) and dividing by 2.

quasi-experimental design. A plan for research that has some but not all the features of a true experiment.

random assignment. Procedures for placing subjects in groups so all subjects have an equal chance of being assigned to any of the groups. The term also applies when groups have an equal chance of being assigned to any treatment conditions.

randomization. Procedures used by researchers to control extraneous variables that could influence the outcome of a project. Selecting subjects by random methods and assigning subjects and treatments to groups at random are included in these processes.

range. The simplest measure of dispersion, and can be used with ordinal data. It is obtained by finding the difference between the highest and lowest measures in a set.

ratio data. A level of measurement that has equal intervals between units on the scale and has a true zero point. Data in this level are expressed as numbers, permitting the full range of mathematical operations.

recommendations. Statements made by a researcher concerning possible uses of information obtained in research. Recommendations may be made to other

researchers for additional studies in the same area or to practitioners for application in educational settings.

regression. The prediction of the value of one variable given the value of another variable and an association of known strength and direction between the variables.

reliability. The degree to which a measuring instrument is consistent or dependable.

repeated measures design. A plan for research in which subjects serve as their own control group. Frequently in this design a pretest is given to subjects, a treatment administered, and the same subjects are posttested, followed by repetitions of the cycle.

replication. Repetition of a research project, often involving subjects from a different population than the original. Most of the procedures are the same as those used in the original study. Data from replication studies are used to support research hypotheses.

research. The product of applying the scientific method to the investigation of problems; also the process by which problems are studied.

research design. The generalized plan by which a research study is done. The major purposes of the plan are to control variance and outline procedures for executing the research project.

research problem. Contains a description of the question or topic that the researcher plans to study. The concern of the problem is to determine what kind of relationship exists between two or more variables. "Problem" is used interchangeably with "purpose of the study."

sample. A subgroup drawn from a population by a specified procedure. These procedures include simple random, stratified random, cluster, and systematic sampling.

sampling. Procedures for selecting subjects from a population. They may be either scientific or nonscientific.

sampling distribution. A frequency distribution that is made of the means obtained from repeated sampling. Samples of a fixed size are selected from a population, the mean is calculated and recorded, and the sample is replaced before the next sample is drawn.

sampling error. The difference between a sample statistic such as the mean and the corresponding parameter of the population from which the sample was drawn.

significance. A judgment of the importance or worth of the results of a research study. The term can refer to statistical significance or educational significance or both.

simple random sampling. A scientific procedure used to select subjects from a population. In its simple form each person in the population has an equal chance of being selected.

standard deviation. A measure of the dispersion of a set of measures around the mean of the set. It is obtained by summing the squared deviations from the mean, dividing this sum of squares by the number of scores, and taking the square root of the quotient.

standard score. A score in which the value of each measure in a set of measures is expressed in terms of standard deviation units from the mean.

statistical power analysis. A mathematical procedure for determining sample size, effect size, power of a statistical test, and level of significance. In the procedure when three of these are known, the fourth can be obtained by using appropriate tables.

statistical significance. A judgment about the worth of the results of a research study based on the probability that they would happen by chance. Results are statistically significant if there is a low probability of their chance occurrence when the null hypothesis is true.

statistical test. A procedure for analyzing research data to determine whether the results are statistically significant.

stratified random sampling. A variation of random sampling in which persons in the population are subdivided into strata by specified characteristics prior to sampling. A prescribed number of subjects per strata

are then selected by random methods to ensure adequate representation of each strata in the population.

subjects. People who participate in a research study. They may be chosen from a larger group by either scientific or nonscientific methods.

systematic sampling. A scientific procedure used to select subjects at equal intervals throughout a population. Each person in the population is identified in some unbiased way, and subjects are selected according to a predetermined interval, such as every seventh or tenth identification number.

systematic variance. Variability in a set of data that is due to the influence of the independent variable or other experimental conditions.

time series design. A research plan in which data are collected on the dependent variable from a single group of subjects at periodic intervals, with treatment occurring between two consecutive intervals.

treatment. Procedures administered to subjects in an experiment to see whether a noticeable effect is produced in some preselected variables. Sometimes the manipulated or independent variable is called the treatment.

true experimental design. A plan for research that uses a manipulated variable, random assignment of subjects, and random assignment of treatment. This is the classic design in research.

two-tailed test. Any test of statistical significance used when the research hypothesis does not predict a direction for the hypothetical relationship under investigation. In a two-tailed test the area of possible values leading to rejection of the null hypothesis includes both ends of the sampling distribution of the test statistic.

validity. The degree to which a procedure or device fulfills the function it is intended to carry out. Validity can refer to how well a research design provides answers to the problems of a research study. It can also refer to how well an instrument measures what it is supposed to measure.

variable. A characteristic, condition, or quantity that can have different values.

variance. A measure of variability that takes into account the size and location of each individual score in terms of the mean score. It is obtained by summing the squared deviations from the mean and dividing this sum of squares by the number of scores. In a more general sense, variance can refer to all the variation in a research study.

within-groups variance. The variation of scores from all groups in a study around the mean of the scores. This variance is presumed to reflect variation within the larger population from which the subjects were drawn or variation due to sampling error, also called chance variation.

References Cited

Alexander, L., Frankiewicz, R. G., & Williams, R. E. Facilitation of learning and retention of oral instruction using advance and post organizers. *Journal of Educational Psychology*, 1979, *71*, 701-07.

American Psychological Association. *Standards for educational and psychological tests*. Washington, D.C.: APA, 1974.

Babbit, C. E., & Burbach, H. J. Perceptions of social control among black college students. *Journal of Negro Education*, 1979, *48*(1), 37-42.

Baird, L. L. Prediction of accomplishments in college: A study of achievement. *Journal of Counseling Psychology*, 1970, *16*, 246-53.

Bell, M. Needed r & d on hand-held calculators. *Educational Researcher*, 1977, *6*(5), 7-13.

Bracht, G. H., & Glass, G.V. The external validity of experiments. *American Educational Research Journal*, 1968, *5*, 437-74.

Bryant, R. S. Statistics for the simple. *Phi Delta Kappa School Research Information Service Quarterly*, 1974, *7*(3), back cover.

Bryant, R. S., Gephart, W. G., & Wilson, J. More statistics for the simple. *Phi Delta Kappa Center on Evaluation, Development and Research Quarterly*, 1978, *11*(2), 22.

Buros, O. K. (Ed.). *Mental measurements yearbooks* (Vols. 1-8). Highland Parks, N.J.: Gryphon Press, 1938-78.

Buros, O. K. (Ed.). *Personality tests and reviews*. Highland Parks, N.J.: Gryphon Press, 1970.

Campbell, D. T., & Stanley, J. C. Experimental and quasi-experimental designs for research. In N. L. Gage (Ed.), *Handbook of research on teaching*. Chicago: Rand McNally, 1963.

Cartwright, C. A., & Cartwright, G. P. *Developing observational skills*. New York: McGraw Hill, 1974.

Cohen, J. *Statistical power analysis for the behavioral sciences* (Rev. ed.). New York: Academic Press, 1977.

Committee on Scientific and Professional Ethics and Conduct. Ethical standards of psychologists. *APA Monitor*, 1977, *8*(3), 22-23.

Cook, T. D., & Campbell, D. T. *Quasi-experimentation: Design and analysis issues for field settings*. Chicago: Rand McNally, 1979.

Dailey, R. C. Relationship between locus of control, perceived group cohesiveness, and satisfaction with coworkers. *Psychological Reports*, 1978, *42*, 311-16.

Daniels, B., & Hewitt, J. Anxiety and classroom examination performance. *Journal of Clinical Psychology*, 1978, *34*, 340-45.

Dutton, W. H. Attitudes of junior high school pupils toward arithmetic. *School Review*, 1956, *64*(1), 18-22.

Edwards, C. H., & Surma, M. The relationship between type of teacher rein-forcement and student inquiry behavior in science. *Journal of Research in Science Teaching*, 1980, *17*(4), 337–41.

Ennis, R. H. Operational definitions. *American Educational Research Journal*, 1964, *1*, 183–201.

Fredrick, W. C., Walberg, H. J., & Rasher, S. P. Time, teacher comments, and achievement in urban high schools. *Journal of Educational Research*, 1979, *73*, 63–65.

Frick, T., & Semmel, M. I. Observer agreement and reliabilities of classroom observational measures. *Review of Educational Research*, 1978, *48*, 157–84.

Gronlund, N. E. *Sociometry in the classroom*. New York: Harper & Row, 1959.

Gronlund, N. E. *Measurement and evaluation in teaching* (4th ed.). New York: Macmillan, 1981.

Grover, B. L., & Charlton, K. How hypotheses are unstated in research reports. *Phi Delta Kappa Center on Evaluation, Development and Research Quarterly*, 1979, *12*(3), 6–9.

Hilgard, E. R. A perspective on the relationship between learning theory and educational practices. In E. R. Hilgard (Ed.), *Theories of learning and instruction*. The Sixty-third Yearbook of the National Society for the Study of Education, Part I. Chicago: NSSE, 1964.

Huesmann, L. R. (Ed.). Special issue: Learned helplessness as a model of depression. *Journal of Abnormal Psychology*, 1978, *87*, 1–197.

Jurs, S. G., & Glass, G. V. The effects of experimental mortality on the internal and external validity of the randomized comparative experiment. *Journal of Experimental Education*, 1971, *40*, 62–66.

Kerlinger, F. N. *Foundations of behavioral research* (2nd ed.). New York: Holt, Rinehart and Winston, 1973.

Lawton, J. T., & Fowell, N. Effects of advance organizers on preschool children's learning of math concepts. *Journal of Experimental Education*, 1978, *47*, 76–81.

Mangieri, J. N., & Baldwin, R. S. Meaning as a factor in predicting spelling difficulty. *Journal of Educational Research*, 1979, *72*, 285–87.

Meissner, J. A. Judgment of clue adequacy by kindergarten and second-grade children. *Developmental Psychology*, 1978, *14*, 18–23.

Messé, L. A., Crano, W. D., Messé, S. R. & Rice, W. Evaluation of the predictive validity of tests of mental ability for classroom performance in elementary grades. *Journal of Educational Psychology*, 1979, *71*, 233–41.

Osgood, C., Suci, J., & Tannebaum, P. *The measurement of meaning*. Urbana: University of Illinois Press, 1975.

Rosenshine, B., & Furst, N. The use of direct observation to study teaching. In R.M.W. Travers (Ed.). *Second handbook of research on teaching*. Chicago: Rand McNally, 1973.

Rothney, J.W.M. Review of Ohio Vocational Interest Survey. In O. K. Buros (Ed.), *Seventh mental measurements yearbook* (Vol. II). Highland Parks, N.J.: Gryphon Press, 1972.

Sax, G. *Principles of educational and psychological measurement and evaluation* (2nd ed.). Belmont, Calif.: Wadsworth, 1980.

Seligman, M.E.P., & Maier, S. F. Failure to escape traumatic shock. *Journal of Experimental Psychology*, 1967, *74*, 1–4.

Sepie, A. C., & Keeling, B. The relationship between types of anxiety and under-achievement in mathematics. *Journal of Educational Research*, 1978, *72*, 15–19.

Serbin, L. A., Connor, J. M., Burchardt, C. J., & Citron, C. C. Effects of peer presence on sex-typing of children's play behavior. *Journal of Experimental Child Psychology*, 1979, *27*, 303–09.

Siegel, S. *Nonparametric statistics for the behavioral sciences.* New York: McGraw-Hill, 1956.

Solomon, R. L. An extension of control group design. *Psychological Bulletin*, 1949, *46*, 137–40.

Spiegel, M. R., & Bryant, N. D. Is speed of processing information related to intelligence and achievement? *Journal of Educational Psychology*, 1978, *70*, 904–10.

Tuckman, B. W. *Measuring educational outcomes: Fundamentals of testing.* New York: Harcourt Brace Jovanovich, 1975.

Tyler, R. W. What is statistical significance? *Educational Research Bulletin*, 1931, *10*, 115–18.

Westervelt, V. D., & McKinney, J. D. Effects of a film on nonhandicapped children's attitudes toward handicapped children. *Exceptional Children*, 1980, *46*, 294–96.

Author Index

Subject Index